OXFORD READINGS IN POLITICS AND GOVERNMENT

LEGISLATURES

OXFORD READINGS IN POLITICS AND GOVERNMENT

General Editors: Vernon Bogdanor and Geoffrey Marshall

The readings in this series are chosen from a variety of journals and other sources to cover major areas or issues in the study of politics, government, and political theory. Each volume contains an introductory essay by the editor and a select guide to further reading.

LEGISLATURES

EDITED BY
PHILIP NORTON

OXFORD UNIVERSITY PRESS
1990

Oxford University Press, Walton Street, Oxford OX2 6DP
Oxford New York Toronto
Delhi Bombay Calcutta Madras Karachi
Petaling Jaya Singapore Hong Kong Tokyo
Nairobi Dar es Salaam Cape Town
Melbourne Auckland
and associated companies in
Berlin Ibadan

Oxford is a trade mark of Oxford University Press

Published in the United States
by Oxford University Press, New York

British Library Cataloguing in Publication Data
Legislatures.—(Oxford readings in politics and government)
I. Norton, Philip
328'.3
ISBN 0–19–827582–X
ISBN 0–19–827581–1 (pbk.)

Library of Congress Cataloging in Publication Data
Legislatures/edited by Philip Norton.
(Oxford readings in politics and government)
Includes bibliographical references.
1. Legislative bodies. I. Norton, Philip. II. Series.
JF511.L37 1990 328.3—dc20 89–22989
ISBN 0–19–827582–X
ISBN 0–19–827581–1 (pbk.)

Typeset by Cambrian Typesetters, Frimley, Surrey
Printed in Great Britain by
Biddles Ltd.
Guildford and King's Lynn

To the memory of my father

CONTENTS

PART III
NEW DIMENSIONS: CLASSIFYING LEGISLATURES

PART IV
EXECUTIVE–LEGISLATIVE RELATIONS

PART V
LEGISLATURES AND THE QUESTION OF REFORM

GENERAL INTRODUCTION

PHILIP NORTON

The word 'legislature' constitutes a generic term for an institution that goes by many different names: among those in common usage are congress, parliament, and national assembly; country-specific names include Supreme Soviet (USSR), Cortes (Spain), Sejm (Poland), Oireachtas (Republic of Ireland), Folketing (Denmark), and Storting (Norway). Definitions of the term are almost as numerous as the specific names employed.

Yet what such bodies have in common is that they are constitutionally designated institutions for giving assent to binding measures of public policy, that assent being given on behalf of a political community that extends beyond the government élite responsible for formulating those measures.

This provides an encompassing definition, avoiding the pitfalls of those definitions that exclude, for example and most notably, the British House of Lords and the Canadian Senate. Both fall foul of definitions that stipulate the requirement of election. Legislatures may be, and usually are, elected but that is not a defining characteristic. If we are to understand those institutions which go by the name of legislatures there seems little purpose in stipulating a definition that excludes a number of them.

Defining a legislature is a necessary starting-point but it is not sufficient for understanding 'legislatures'. They are functionally adaptable bodies, the tasks ascribed to them varying over time and between countries. Some legislatures are essentially little more than mono-functional bodies, meeting on occasion to give formal assent to measures placed before them. Others are multi-functional, fulfilling tasks other than that which is common to, and defines, all. Before giving assent, some (nowadays, very few) legislatures share with the executive body the task of drawing up measures of public policy. Some (the categories are not mutually exclusive) undertake the task of administrative oversight. Some, indeed most, will discuss measures before giving assent to them. Such additional functions do not define legislatures but they are functions that derive essentially from the fact that they are legislatures.

Legislatures are distinctive also by their prevalence. Every country in Europe has one. (The last European country to spend some time without one was Greece). They are to be found in small mountain kingdoms, such as Bhutan. They are to be found in Communist states, including Albania. They are to be found in small islands, such as Western Samoa. Indeed, they are to be found in most countries on the globe. Of 138 states that were members of the United Nations in 1971, 108 had legislatures.[1] And, as Jean Blondel has noted, of those 138 only five—all in the Middle East—have never had one.[2] Of the states currently without a legislature, the majority are grouped in the Middle East and Africa south of the Sahara.

Given the number that exist, and their constitutional significance, it is not surprising that the literature on legislatures is substantial. Most of it is country-specific. Studies of particular legislatures—and some cross-national compilations—regularly come off the printing presses, or from the pens of Ph.D. candidates.[3] Material on the US Congress and West European legislatures is especially dense. Every so often, review articles and some edited volumes are published which draw together the strands of these studies and assess the current state of legislative studies (Mezey 1978).[4] Yet, for reasons to be discussed, material on legislatures as a particular genus of institution is sparse.

Only infrequently have writings appeared which have

[1] D. Olson, *Legislative Process: A Comparative Approach* (New York, 1980), 5.

[2] J. Blondel, *Comparative Legislatures* (Englewood Cliffs, NJ, 1973), 7.

[3] The bibliography in M. Mezey, *Comparative Legislatures* (Durham, NC, 1979), 285–300, provides some fine examples of these studies.

[4] See e.g. N. Meller, 'Legislative Behavior Research', *Western Political Quarterly*, 13 (1960), 131–53; id., ' "Legislative Behavior Research" Revisited: A Review of Five Years' Publications', *Western Political Quarterly*, 18 (1965), 776–93; S. C. Patterson, 'Comparative Legislative Behavior: A Review Essay', *Midwest Journal of Political Science*, 12 (1968), 599–616; G. Loewenberg, S. C. Patterson, and M. E. Jewell, *Handbook of Legislative Research* (Cambridge, Mass., 1985).

affected perceptions of and added significantly to our understanding of legislatures, as opposed to a particular legislature; some publications have had an impact upon legislative development. Individually and collectively, recent seminal works have not been sufficient to raise the study of legislatures to a new paradigm. But they have moved forward significantly the frontiers of analysis and research.

THE PROBLEM OF LEGISLATIVE ANALYSIS

The significance of the writings chosen for inclusion in this volume is best explained within the context of the principal problems faced by students of legislatures. The problems can be subsumed under two broad headings: historical and methodological.

The historical problem derives from early assumptions as to what legislatures should do and the extent to which they have done what is expected of them. Since at least the seventeenth century, political and constitutional theorists have advanced two propositions that have formed the basis of much constitution-writing as well as most of the scholarly literature on legislatures.

The first is that the principal task of legislatures is that of law-making. Hence the very name. *Legis* is the genitive of *lex*, meaning law; *lator* means carrier or proposer. A *legislator* was thus one who carried law. The identification of a law-making body, the legislature, distinct from the body for executing the laws made (the executive) was central to the works of both Locke and Montesquieu. 'The legislative', declared Locke, 'is no otherwise legislative of the society but by the right it has to make laws for all the parts and for every member of society, prescribing rules to their actions, and giving power of execution where they are transgressed'.[5] Montesquieu, drawing on a crucial misperception of British experience, provided the fundamental distinction between legislature, executive, and judiciary that was to find expression in the US Constitution and later constitutions. His definition of the

[5] J. Locke, *Of Civil Government: Second Treatise* (1689; Chi., Ill., 1955), ch. 13, p. 125.

legislative power was as succinct as that of Locke: that of enacting temporary or perpetual laws and the amending or abrogating of those already made.[6] Law was thus 'made', 'enacted', by legislatures. It was the very task that gave them their name and justified their very existence.

The second proposition concerns the nature of the legislature best suited to law-making. From the time that legislatures were identified as such, writers have variously asserted the desirability of laws being enacted by men of independence, both in thought and means, free of vested interests and the base desires of an uninformed majority. Liberal writers of the nineteenth century were particularly active in defending this proposition. For Bagehot, a 'good' Parliament could be chosen only by an informed or a deferential electorate. The century witnessed a significant increase in the number of legislatures and this, coupled with the maintenance of a restricted franchise, allowed a picture of a 'golden age' of parliaments to emerge. Yet no sooner had this desirable state of affairs been discerned than fears were expressed as to its future. Bagehot was not alone in decrying the likely effects of mass suffrage—the 'ultra-democratic theory'. Bagehot's fears were to be realized towards the end of the century, with a new, mass franchise and the growth of organized political parties, writers such as Ostrogorski and Lowell identifying and bewailing the consequential effects of party caucuses and discipline in parliamentary parties. The most influential analysis was that provided by Bryce in 1921. Noting the effects of party and the growth of group influence, he concluded that 'the dignity and moral influence of representative legislatures have been declining'.[7] Though recording that legislatures remained an indispensable part of the machinery of government in large democracies, his work was to be remembered principally for the title he gave to chapter 58: 'The Decline of Legislatures'.

Twentieth-century study of legislatures has thus taken place within the inheritance of three basic and related axioms:

[6] Baron de Montesquieu, *The Spirit of the Laws*, intro. F. Neumann (1748; New York, 1949), bk. xi, ch. 6.

[7] Lord Bryce, *Modern Democracies* (London, 1921), ii. 391.

that the fundamental task of legislatures is the making of laws; that legislatures in and since the nineteenth century have 'declined'; that the explanation for such decline lies in the growth of party, a growth that in the context of legislatures has been cancerous.

The second principal problem, the methodological, encompasses not only the limited means and data available for political scientists to undertake a comparative study of legislatures but also the nature of political science itself.

Political science in the United States has been at the forefront of advances within the discipline. Yet, as Somit and Tanenhaus have shown, descriptive study was a feature of both the formative and the emergent years of American political science.[8] The middle years (1921–45) saw not only an attachment to practical involvement in public affairs but also an attempt at more scientific study. Bryce's work was an early attempt at a scientific, comparative analysis and, once published, his identification of the 'decline' of legislatures constituted an accepted dictum that encouraged political scientists to shift their focus of enquiry to more significant institutions. Bureaucracy and, more especially, the executive overshadowed legislatures as magnets for investigation by political scientists.

With the behavioural revolution in the years after 1945 the focus shifted decisively away from institutions. The emphasis was on people and empiricism. However, recognition that legislatures comprised collections of individuals led in time to a growth—building on earlier individual and eclectic studies[9]—in the analysis of legislative behaviour. Improved quantitative techniques and their application to roll-call votes added impetus to this development. By the mid 1960s, literature on legislative behaviour was extensive and, compared with what had gone before, added an element of distinctiveness to the behavioural study of the legislative process.[10] The studies, observed Meller, displayed greater rigour in theory and

[8] A. Somit and J. Tanenhaus, *Development of Political Science: From Burgess to Behavioralism* (Boston, Mass., 1967).

[9] Meller, 'Legislative Behavior Research', pp. 134–8.

[10] Meller, ' "Legislative Behavior Research" Revisited', p. 776.

methodology. As he also noted,[11] they were diverse. Furthermore, advances in, and concentration upon, the study of legislative *behaviour* constituted but a partial contribution to the understanding of legislatures.

Advances in the study of legislatures, and more especially of legislative behaviour, thus took place *within* the United States. Such advanced study was also largely focused *upon* the United States. Scholars in the United States were able to deploy their knowledge and quantitative skills in analysing the US Congress. There was an existing literature to build on. Hard data in the form of roll-call votes were available. Members of Congress could be observed and interviewed. Congress provided a natural focus for behavioural analysis. And given the recognition that the same or similar attributes of accessible data applied to the legislatures of the individual states, state legislatures also came to provide a valuable focus for political science inquiry.[12]

Knowledge and understanding of American legislatures thus came to outstrip knowledge and understanding of legislatures elsewhere. Even without rigorous comparative analysis, it was apparent that the US Congress was sufficiently atypical not to allow generalizations to be drawn about legislatures from studies of that particular body. To generalize about legislatures, rather than a legislature, comparative analysis was necessary. But how to achieve such analysis?

Attempts to achieve a useful analysis of legislatures, allowing of generalization, model building, and even the generation of theories, has been limited by difficulties of conceptualizing and ensuring comparability of data derived from different social and political environments. The problem has been compounded outside the United States by the disparate state of legislative studies. In some countries, political science has yet to emerge as a recognizable discipline in its own right, rather than as a sub-discipline of law or history. In other countries, development of the discipline has followed a path very different to that of the United States,

[11] Meller, ' "Legislative Behavior Research" Revisited', p. 792.

[12] M. E. Jewell and S. C. Patterson, *Legislative Process in the United States* (2nd edn., New York, 1973).

avoiding the paradigmatic shifts from one era to another and/or avoiding the hegemony achieved by one particular approach within the discipline. In Britain, for example, both traits have been missing.[13] For legislative scholars keen to advance their studies beyond the shores of the United States, problems of logistics and limited resources have precluded them from making an extensive analysis of other countries, certainly on a personal basis. Hence they have been dependent upon the work undertaken by scholars in other parts of the globe. Given the disparate nature of the discipline, it is hardly surprising that such work has been disparate.

The problem has been a quantitative as well as a qualitative one. In a footnote in *Comparative Legislatures* Michael Mezey wrote: 'The absence of a particular country from the table [classifying legislatures] means that I haven't the faintest idea where it should go and that I am not including the country in the analysis.'[14] Such a statement casts no reflection upon Mezey's scholarship. It rather reflects the fact that for some countries material is so sparse, out of date, or non-existent that no reliable use can be made of it for comparative purposes. Of the 108 nations with legislatures in 1971, only a little over half of them are listed in Mezey's table.

Of the material that does exist, there is a clear imbalance in country focus. There is a mass of literature on the US Congress. There is a substantial amount of material on West European legislatures, especially the British Parliament; Goehlert and Martin,[15] for example, identify in excess of 2,500 published and unpublished sources dealing wholly or in part with Parliament. There is less but still a fair amount of literature on the older Commonwealth countries, especially India and Canada. There is much less—in some cases, very little indeed—on legislatures in Third World and Communist countries. There is now much more than before—legislatures in developing countries have attracted greater interest from scholars; on Communist legislatures see especially the volume

[13] J. E. S. Hayward and P. Norton (edd.), *Political Science of British Politics* (Brighton, 1986), 202–18.

[14] Mezey, *Comparative Legislatures*, p. 44 n. 5.

[15] R. Goehlert and F. Martin, *Parliament of Great Britain: A Bibliography*, (Lexington, Mass., 1983).

by Nelson and White[16]—but the disparity remains marked. Even within these groupings, there are wide variations.

Where material does exist, quantity on occasion exceeds quality. This criticism has been notable of the British study of Parliament. In a review in 1973 of seventeen books—'a rather formidable assortment'—on the House of Commons published between the mid-1960s and 1972, Samuel Patterson concluded that the study of Parliament in Britain was notable for its lack or inadequacy of research, theory, description, comparison, and methodology. Too much reliance, he argued, was placed on anecdote and a 'kind of petty inside-dopesterism'[17] in an environment that was notable for its insularity: 'the British work constitutes a kind of enclave in the more general, worldwide field of legislative research, an enclave which goes on in its own way pretty much without learning anything from the outside'.[18] Few of the British studies could be used alongside those of legislatures elsewhere as contributions to the formulation of comparative analytic theory about legislative institutions and behaviour.

The insularity—less marked now but still a feature of parliamentary studies in Britain[19]—has not been peculiar to the United Kingdom. Similar insularity and neglect have been exhibited by legislative scholars in other countries. The point was well made by Mogens Pedersen in his review of thirteen books written about seven European legislatures. 'The books that have been discussed here almost entirely fail to apply a comparative perspective. Notwithstanding some exceptions . . . all these authors are content to describe and analyze parliamentary phenomena within one country only—just as their American counterparts are'.[20] The effects of this insularity are exacerbated by the different approaches adopted,

[16] D. Nelson and S. White (edd.), *Communist Legislatures in Comparative Perspective* (London, 1982).

[17] S. C. Patterson, 'Review Article: The British House of Commons as a Focus for Political Research', *British Journal of Political Science*, 3 (1973), 376.

[18] Ibid. 376.

[19] P. Norton, 'Parliament Redivivus?' in Hayward and Norton (edd.), *Political Science of British Politics*, pp. 120–36.

[20] M. Pedersen, 'Research on European Parliaments: A Review Article on Scholarly and Institutional Variety', *Legislative Studies Quarterly*, 9 (1984), 527.

from the smaller European countries which have been influenced by the behavioural approach and research methods of American political science to Britain and Sweden, which have largely resisted such influences. 'The European parliaments tend to look like very dissimilar institutions in these books . . . it is evident that several of these differences are generated by differences in scholarly outlooks and perspective.'[21] There is a tendency for scholars to view their particular legislature as *sui generis*; they write accordingly. Consequently, we know much about a great many legislatures; we know very little about legislatures as a particular species of institution.

THE PRINCIPAL LITERATURE

It is, then, in the context of these two principal problems—the historical and the methodological—that the contributions selected for this volume have to be viewed. The model of legislatures advanced by pre-twentieth-century writers, and the dictum of 'decline' established by Bryce early in this century, have provided the basic paradigm for legislative studies. Advances beyond that, seeking to achieve a new paradigm, have been limited by the disparate and not infrequently immature state of legislative studies. But advances there have been, nudging students of legislatures to a new level of understanding, not least through the generation of more sophisticated concepts and, in some cases, identifying the means by which those concepts may be operationalized. Other works, not necessarily from scholars, have had an impact upon the development of legislatures (usually particular legislatures). Such advances have themselves been disparate, emanating from a variety of sources. But, collectively and individually, they have moved the study of legislatures, if not to a new paradigm, at least to a somewhat higher plane.

This volume brings together the principal writings which have, first, established the paradigm for legislative studies; second, advanced significantly the level of analysis and understanding of legislatures in the twentieth century; and,

[21] Ibid. 528.

third, had a practical impact upon legislative developments. Thanks to Montesquieu, the categories are not mutually exclusive.

Establishing the paradigm. The essential paradigm for legislative studies in the twentieth century was established particularly though not exclusively by three writers. Other scholars have variously contributed to the development of legislative studies, but without the seminal contributions of Montesquieu, Bagehot, and Bryce, it is unlikely that a basic model for legislative study would have existed and certainly not that which has pertained for most of this century.

The contribution of Montesquieu in *The Spirit of the Laws* (1748) is of especial significance. He both distinguished and defined legislatures. His delineation of a separation—or division—of powers between legislature, executive, and judiciary was original and was to provide a basic—and continuing—framework for written constitutions, as much utilized in the twentieth century as in the eighteenth. With other writers, he established various constitutional axioms, most notably for our purposes that legislation meant the enactment of fixed, abstract, general rules and that legislation was the monopoly of the legislature. Legislatures alone could legislate: that was their principal, defining function. *The Spirit of the Laws* is thus an appropriate, and necessary, point of departure.

In *The English Constitution* (1867), Bagehot offered what was to become a much-cited—and -criticized—analysis of the British polity as it then was. The criticisms were directed at both the descriptive and normative aspects of this work. However, the book was to have a strong influence on students not just of the British Parliament but of the US Congress and Commonwealth legislatures. Bagehot's delineation of Parliament's functions, in particular, was to be widely utilized and constitutes his most distinctive contribution to comparative legislative study. The delineation was not unique—John Stuart Mill[22] offered a similar one—but it was particularly influential.

The significance of Bryce's *Modern Democracies* (1921) we have

[22] J. S. Mill, *Considerations on Representative Government* (1861; London, 1910), 239.

identified already. His empirical study, applied to a liberal interpretation of legislatures, produced a (qualified) perception of the 'decline' of legislatures. Power was passing to executives and to electorates; political parties were the conduit for this shift of power. 'Writing just after the First World War, Bryce at once summarized the view of an entire generation of observers of representative institutions and provided a dogma for a new generation of disillusioned democrats. To this day, it is part of the conventional wisdom about parliaments to regard the influence of parties as pernicious.'[23] It remains common for works on British politics and Parliament to identify or to proceed on the basis of a 'decline' of Parliament since the nineteenth century.

Recent advances. The twentieth century, and the period since 1970 in particular, has witnessed a number of major contributions to the literature. These contributions have been diverse. They have not been integrated to generate a new model of or framework for legislative studies. Individually and collectively, they do not serve to negate the work of Montesquieu, Bagehot, and Bryce. Rather, they constitute advances on their work, offering greater depth and sophistication. Among the writers are to be found modern-day Bagehots and Bryces.

The literature that falls within this category is grouped under three heads. First, there are those essays which have, in the manner of Bagehot, extended understanding of the functions of legislatures beyond that of policy-making (or policy-influencing) on behalf of the political community. Beer (1966), Packenham (1970), Wahlke (1971) have focused attention not on the relationship of legislature to the executive but on the relationship of the legislature to the political community.[24] Packenham's work has been especially valuable

[23] G. Loewenberg (ed.), *Modern Parliaments: Change or Decline?* (Chi. Ill., 1971), 7.

[24] S. H. Beer, 'British Legislature and the Problem of Mobilizing Consent' in E. Frank (ed.), *Lawmakers in a Changing World* (Englewood Cliffs, NJ, 1966), 30–48; R. Packenham, 'Legislatures and Political Development', in A. Kornberg and L. D. Musolf (edd.), *Legislatures in Developmental Perspective* Durham, NC, 1970), 521–82; J. Wahlke, 'Policy Demands and System Support: The Role of the Represented', *British Journal of Political Science*, II (1971), 271–90.

for identifying the multi-functional role of legislatures. Drawing on an analysis of the Brazilian legislature, he identitifes (under three umbrella categories) eleven functions, including the 'safety valve', or 'tension release', function. Beer, focusing on the British Parliament, identifies the significance of mobilizing consent. If government is to govern without recourse to force, 'it must continuously mobilise consent and win acceptance for its policies. The legislature is one of the agencies that helps perform this task.'[25] It is, Beer argues, a function not well performed by Parliament in Britain. Wahlke shifts the focus to more diffuse support, legislatures fulfilling a significant role as agents of regime support. The significance of legislatures is thus greater than suggested by analyses that focus simply on observable policy-making. Merely by meeting regularly and uninterruptedly, a legislature can fulfil—in Pakenham's terminology—an important function of latent legitimization. They are thus more complex—and politically significant—institutions than traditional literature suggests.

Second, the realization that legislatures are multi-functional bodies, and that those functions and the capacity to fulfil them vary from country to country and over time, has meant that it has been possible to think not in terms of *a* legislature but in terms of different types of legislatures. Various taxonomies have been provided, the two more significant coming from the pens of two distinguished American political scientists—Nelson Polsby and Michael Mezey.[26] Polsby provides a spectrum, ranging from arena to transformative legislatures, Mezey a six-box classification based on the support accruing to a legislature and its role in policy-making. This writer[27] has sought to refine Mezey's categorization as it affects legislatures in policy-making and this modest contribution is also included.

Third, though advances in the literature have extended the focus of legislative studies beyond executive–legislative relations, that is not to say that such relations are not important,

[25] Beer, 'British Legislature', p. 30.

[26] N. W. Polsby, 'Legislatures', in F. I. Greenstein and N. W. Polsby, (edd.), *Handbook of Political Science*, v (Reading, Mass., 1975), 257–319; Mezey, *Comparative Legislatures*.

[27] P. Norton, 'Parliament and Policy in Britain: The House of Commons as a Policy Influencer', *Teaching Politics*, 13 (1984), 198–221.

nor that they have been neglected in the literature. Writings on executive–legislative relations have been extensive, though often implicitly or explicitly accepting—indeed, often seeking to prove—Bryce's dictum. There have none the less been some sophisticated attempts to extend understanding of executive–legislative relationships. Three of the most notable have been made by Blondel, King, and Shaw.[28] Focusing on law-making, Blondel made an ambitious attempt to generate criteria to assess the importance of legislation and the 'viscosity' which legislatures introduced in the legislative process. King, drawing on a study of the British, French, and West German legislatures, identified different patterns—or modes—of executive legislative relations. As he put it, 'we need . . . to "think behind" the Montesquieu formula'.[29] Shaw, in drawing together the results of an eight-country survey, fleshed out the significance of committees and the variables that determine committee strength in influencing public policy. All three writers have provided important conceptual tools for comparative analysis.

As a result of these various contributions to the literature, the field of legislative studies has been enriched, though far from satiated. Students of legislatures have much more to draw on—qualitatively as well as quantitatively—than twenty years ago. The major impact of the literature, though, has been within the intellectual discipline.

Practical impact. It is rare for scholars to have a practical impact on legislative development. Some clearly have: of those within this volume, Montesquieu is the most notable. Others have been influential, if not affecting directly legislative change at least affecting the perceptions—and discourse—of legislators. In terms of defending the position of the independent-minded (and independent-acting) MP, it is *de rigueur* in Britain to quote Edmund Burke. In terms of discussing the

[28] J. Blondel, 'Legislative Behaviour: Some Steps towards a Cross-National Measurement', *Government and Opposition*, 5 (1970), 67–85; A. King, 'Modes of Executive–Legislative Relations: Great Britain, France, and West Germany', *Legislative Studies Quarterly*, 1 (1976), 37–65; M. Shaw, 'Conclusions', in J. D. Lees and M. Shaw (edd.), *Committees in Legislatures* (Oxford, 1979).

[29] King, 'Executive–Legislative Relations', p. 11.

need for reform, it has been not quite *de rigueur*, but certainly fashionable to quote Bernard Crick.[30] *The Reform of Parliament*—the first subheading of chapter 1 being 'The Decline of Parliament'—was variously reprinted and highly influential in the debate on parliamentary reform in the 1960s. It has been drawn on by politicians and scholars alike, not only in Britain but also in other English-speaking countries.

The literature that has had the most practical impact, however, has been that which has emanated from official bodies, those usually established for the very purpose of considering reform. By their nature, such bodies have been confined to considering their respective legislatures. Many legislatures have committees vested with responsibility for considering procedure. Their work, though sometimes prolific, has usually been essentially insular and often focused on minor items (concerned, for example, with procedural adjustments rather than structural reform). The Procedure Committee of the House of Commons in Britain was, for the first half of the century, notable for its insularity in national perception—and, consequently, for complacency in its reports. More recently, it has been notable for its output: seventy-one reports in the period from 1958 to 1987. However, in recent years there appears to have been something of a tendency for legislatures to establish committees to consider major structural—indeed, constitutional—reform and for those committees to look beyond their own shores for inspiration.

Indeed, in some respects, legislative committees vested with the task of considering reform appear to have been ahead of the academic community in engaging in comparative analysis. 'How can British political scientists', asked Pedersen 'go on year after year discussing the possible effects of introducing specialised select committees without apparently noticing the fact that more or less similar reforms of the committee system took place in some of the Scandinavian countries during the early 1970s and that a considerable amount of inspiration and experience could be imported from that continent . . . ?'[31] A review of recent reports from committees of a number of

[30] B. Crick, *Reform of Parliament* (London, 1964).

[31] Pedersen, 'Research on European Parliaments', p. 528.

legislatures would point to the fact that legislatures, at least, have learned the need for comparative analysis and have been willing to consider experience in other continents in order to import appropriate 'inspiration and experience'.

I have in mind three particular cases, each drawn from a Commonwealth country. The Procedure Committee of the House of Commons in Britain drew on Canadian and Australian experience in its most significant enquiry of recent years, that of 1976–8, producing in its First Report of the 1977–8 Session the recommendations that were to result in the establishment of fourteen departmentally related Select Committees charged with the oversight of the expenditure, administration, and policy of government departments. The committees constituted the most significant reform witnessed in the House of Commons for over seventy years. They have also provided an important focus of enquiry for reform-minded legislators in other countries.

The Special Committee on Reform of the Canadian House of Commons, established in December 1984, travelled to the United States, West Germany, France, and Britain to consider procedures there—'the committee had an opportunity to compare procedures through discussions with legislators and staff in these countries'[32]—and in its Third Report, issued in June 1985, made recommendations which, in its own assessment, constituted 'the most ambitious attempt to pursue major and comprehensive reform in the more than one-hundred-year history of the Canadian House of Commons'.[33] It sought a shift in the relationship between Parliament and the executive, not only through changes in procedures and structures but also—drawing on British experience—through an attitudinal change on the part of MPs.

Most recently, and most extensive in remit, the New Zealand Royal Commission on the Electoral System explored a wide range of constitutional issues, including—in addition to the electoral system itself—the size of the country's unicameral legislature, the length of parliamentary terms, the

[32] *Third Report from the Special Committee on Reform of the Canadian House of Commons* (Ottawa, 1985), p. xi.

[33] Ibid.

use of referenda, and political finance. Members of the Commission visited West Germany, Ireland, Australia, Canada, and Britain in the course of their enquiry: 'Although for reasons of cost and time our overseas inquiries were very compressed, we found them to be exceptionally informative and valuable in clarifying our views'.[34] The Commission reported at the end of 1986. On 12 October 1987 the New Zealand Government announced a referendum to be held in November 1989 on a four-year parliamentary term, proportional representation, and possibly a Bill of Rights.

Were legislative scholars to emulate such committees in comparative analysis, the literature in the field would be more extensive and, indeed, stand a greater chance of influencing debate on legislative change.

In combination, then, the writings chosen for inclusion in this volume have, in their different ways, contributed to the field of legislative studies. Other candidates for inclusion were also considered. The dividing-line was a fine one and the final choice necessarily a personal one. Of those selected for inclusion, a number have—for reasons of space, clarity, and relevance—been abridged.[35] The intention throughout has been to place in the hands of the students the principal literature in the field in as concise a form as possible. If the collection serves also to stimulate further, truly comparative research it will have served an equally worthy purpose.

[34] New Zealand Royal Commission on the Electoral System, *Towards a Better Democracy: Report on the Electoral System* (Wellington, NZ, 1986), 2.

[35] In one or two cases footnotes in the original texts have been modernized.

PART I

THE HISTORICAL PARADIGM

CENTRALITY AND 'DECLINE'

INTRODUCTION

Two noblemen and a journalist, writing in three separate centuries, were instrumental in establishing the basic framework for legislative studies in the twentieth century. Though variously criticized, the writings of all three were essentially comparative and were to have an international impact.

The contribution of Baron de Montesquieu, as observed in the introduction, was of especial significance. In *The Spirit of the Laws*, drawing on a misreading of English experience, he delineated the separation, and overlap, of powers that was to form the basis for much constitution-writing since. His work provided the theoretical justification for what the framers of the US Constitution, assembled in Philadelphia in 1787, were looking to establish in practice. (Like Locke, Montesquieu did not instil novel thoughts in the minds of the Founding Fathers; rather, he served to justify what they were already thinking and inclined to do.) It was to have a direct effect also upon constitutionalism in Germany and an indirect effect elsewhere as other countries followed the example of the United States.[1] Indeed, it is now common to see in written constitutions the formal separation—and some overlap—of the executive, legislature, and judiciary, with the legislature being vested with the legislative, i.e. law-making (or now, as Olson has aptly termed it, 'law-effecting') power. Thus, to take Article 26 of Europe's most recent constitution, the 1975 Greek Constitution:

1. Legislative power shall be vested in Parliament and the President of the Republic.
2. Executive power shall be vested in the President of the Republic and the Government.
3. Judicial power shall be vested in the courts of law, the decisions of which shall be executed in the name of the Greek People.

[1] F. Neumann, 'Introduction' to Montesquieu, *Spirit of the Laws* (New York, 1949), p. lxiii.

The relevance of Montesquieu to legislatures has been profound. He was the first to distinguish the governmental trinity in this manner and, with other writers, helped establish the doctrine that law-making was the principal and defining function of a legislature.

The chapter in *The Spirit of the Laws* which was to be the basis of Montesquieu's impact was, in Neumann's words 'the most famous Book XI'.[2] It is that, in abridged form, which is reproduced in this section.

The influence of Walter Bagehot, an English journalist writing over a century later, was not as profound but nonetheless has been widespread and lasting. *The English Constitution* has been variously criticized, not least for conveying an idealistic and time-bound picture of the British House of Commons that was empirically invalid by the time the book was widely read, but a portrayal which has influenced—and constrained—subsequent generations of writers on Parliament. Indeed, responsibility for the descriptive and insular characteristics of the study of Parliament in Britain appears often to be laid at Bagehot's door. Bagehot, however, was more perceptive—and relevant—than critics allow. He recognized clearly that the 1867 Reform Act was likely to have important consequences but, in the second edition published in 1872, noted that it was 'too soon as yet to attempt to estimate the effect'.[3] More important for our purposes was the relevance of his work for comparative legislative study. As LeMay has observed, *The English Constitution* is essentially a comparative work,[4] Bagehot recognizing that there was an essential choice for advanced nations between 'the Presidential government and the Parliamentary'. 'And nothing therefore can be more important than to compare the two, and decide upon the testimony of experience, and by facts, which of them is the better.'[5] The book's main impact, though, in terms of legislative study, was in its delineation of the functions of Parliament. They were not confined to policy-making (the

[2] F. Neumann, 'Introduction' to Montesquieu, *Spirit of the Laws* (New York, 1949), p. lx.

[3] W. Bagehot, *English Constitution* (1867; London, 1963), 268.

[4] G. LeMay, *Victorian Constitution* (London, 1979), 4–5.

[5] Bagehot, *English Constitution*, p. 310.

function of legislation) but included broader system-maintenance functions (such as the teaching function) which today are reformulated in more sophisticated terminology, but rarely added to in any significant degree. They have been variously utilized, both in Britain and abroad, and are reproduced here. The rest of the chapter on the House of Commons, Bagehot gives over to attack the consequences of a mass suffrage, reflecting a pessimistic approach to mass electoral behaviour, in contrast to the more optimistic assumptions of John Stuart Mill in *Considerations of Representative Government* (1861). Bagehot's perception of a 'good'—that is, detached and independent—Parliament reflected the prevalent liberal view that was to find expression in subsequent works, including those of Bryce.

James (Lord) Bryce was a statesman and scholar, whose influence extended beyond the field of legislative studies. He was well travelled and, like a contemporary scholar–statesman in the United States, Woodrow Wilson, keen to learn from comparative experience. His comparative study was not confined to legislatures *qua* legislatures, but encompassed also second chambers. However, his relevance for this volume lies especially in his perception of the 'decline' of legislatures. 'It is sometimes assumed', Kenneth Wheare noted, 'by those whose readings may perhaps have gone no further than the chapter headings, that Bryce believed in a general decline of legislatures'.[6] He in fact produced a varied and qualified assessment. The chapter that gave rise to the widely accepted dictum of decline is reproduced here. It is one of two chapters in which Bryce treated the subject. In the other—chapter 59 on 'The Pathology of Legislatures'—he expanded upon five 'chronic ailments' that had undermined representative assemblies: parliamentary obstruction; the multiplication of parties; the political strength wielded by small organized groups (eliciting promises of particular action from candidates); the conflict for legislators in seeking to represent constituents, party, and nation; and the development of the parliamentary caucus. Party was the principal culprit for these developments, with public opinion being too absorbed with the economic and social aims to which legislation should be

[6] K. C. Wheare, *Legislatures* (1963; Oxford, 1968), 147.

directed 'to give due attention to legislative methods'.[7] He concluded none the less that

> though the dignity and moral influence of representative legislatures have been declining, they are still an indispensable part of the machinery of government in large democracies . . . Hence the quality of a legislature, the integrity and capacity of its members, the efficiency of the methods by which it passes law and supervises the conduct of the Executive, must continue to be of high significance to a nation's welfare.'[8]

Despite the qualifications injected by Bryce—and despite the fact that perceptions of legislatures not fulfilling the expectations of nineteenth-century liberal norms were not original to him (Lowell had identified the problem in Europe more than two decades earlier)[9]—the notion of 'the decline of legislatures' remains firmly associated with him. It is a notion that ever since has been central to the study of legislatures.

[7] Lord Bryce, *Modern Democracies* (London, 1921), ii. 390.
[8] Ibid. 391.
[9] A. L. Lowell, *Government and Parties in Continental Europe* (Cambridge, Mass., 1896).

I

OF THE LAWS WHICH ESTABLISH POLITICAL LIBERTY WITH REGARD TO THE CONSTITUTION

BARON DE MONTESQUIEU

DIFFERENT SIGNIFICATIONS OF THE WORD LIBERTY

There is no word that admits of more various significations, and has made more varied impressions on the human mind, than that of liberty. Some have taken it as a means of deposing a person on whom they had conferred a tyrannical authority; others for the power of choosing a superior whom they are obliged to obey; others for the right of bearing arms, and of being thereby enabled to use violence; others, in fine, for the privilege of being governed by a native of their own country, or by their own laws. A certain nation for a long time thought liberty consisted in the privilege of wearing a long beard. Some have annexed this name to one form of government exclusive of others: those who had a republican taste applied it to this species of polity; those who liked a monarchical state gave it to monarchy. Thus they have all applied the name of liberty to the government most suitable to their own customs and inclinations: and as in republics the people have not so constant and so present a view of the causes of their misery, and as the magistrates seem to act only in conformity to the laws, hence liberty is generally said to reside in republics, and to be banished from monarchies. In fine, as in democracies the people seem to act almost as they please, this sort of government has been deemed the most free, and the power of the people has been confounded with their liberty.

IN WHAT LIBERTY CONSISTS

It is true that in democracies the people seem to act as they please; but political liberty does not consist in an unlimited freedom. In governments, that is, in societies directed by laws, liberty can consist only in the power of doing what we ought to will, and in not being constrained to do what we ought not to will.

We must have continually present to our minds the difference between independence and liberty. Liberty is a right of doing whatever the laws permit, and if a citizen could do what they forbid he would be no longer possessed of liberty, because all his fellow citizens would have the same power.

Democratic and aristocratic states are not in their own nature free. Political liberty is to be found only in moderate governments; and even in these it is not always found. It is there only when there is no abuse of power. But constant experience shows us that every man invested with power is apt to abuse it, and to carry his authority as far as it will go. Is it not strange, though true, to say that virtue itself has need of limits? To prevent this abuse, it is necessary from the very nature of things that power should be a check to power. A government may be so constituted, as no man shall be compelled to do things to which the law does not oblige him, nor forced to abstain from things which the law permits.

OF THE END OR VIEW OF DIFFERENT GOVERNMENTS

Though all governments have the same general end, which is that of preservation, yet each has another particular object. Increase of domination was the object of Rome; war, that of Sparta; religion, that of the Jewish laws; commerce, that of Marseilles; public tranquillity, that of the laws of China; navigation, that of the laws of Rhodes; natural liberty, that of the policy of the Savages; in general, the pleasures of the prince, that of despotic states; that of monarchies, the prince's and the kingdom's glory; the independence of individuals is the end aimed at by the laws of Poland, thence results the oppression of the whole.

One nation there is also in the world that has for the direct end of its constitution political liberty. We shall presently examine the principles on which this liberty is founded; if they are sound, liberty will appear in its highest perfection.

To discover political liberty in a constitution, no great labour is requisite. If we are capable of seeing it where it exists, it is soon found, and we need not go far in search of it.

OF THE CONSTITUTION OF ENGLAND

In every government there are three sorts of power: the legislative; the executive in respect to things dependent on the law of nations; and the executive in regard to matters that depend on the civil law.

By virtue of the first, the prince or magistrate enacts temporary or perpetual laws, and amends or abrogates those that have been already enacted. By the second, he makes peace or war, sends or receives embassies, establishes the public security, and provides against invasions. By the third, he punishes criminals, or determines the disputes that arise between individuals. The latter we shall call the judiciary power, and the other simply the executive power of the state.

The political liberty of the subject is a tranquillity of mind arising from the opinion each person has of his safety. In order to have this liberty, it is requisite the government be so constituted as one man need not be afraid of another.

When the legislative and executive powers are united in the same person, or in the same body of magistrates, there can be no liberty; because apprehensions may arise, lest the same monarch or senate should enact tyrannical laws, to execute them in a tyrannical manner.

Again, there is no liberty, if the judiciary power be not separated from the legislative and executive. Were it joined with the legislative, the life and liberty of the subject would be exposed to arbitrary control; for the judge would be then the legislator. Were it joined to the executive power, the judge might behave with violence and oppression.

There would be an end of everything, were the same man or the same body, whether of the nobles or of the people, to exercise those three powers, that of enacting laws, that of executing the public resolutions, and of trying the causes of individuals.

Most kingdoms in Europe enjoy a moderate government because the prince who is invested with the two first powers leaves the third to his subjects. In Turkey, where these three powers are united in the Sultan's person, the subjects groan under the most dreadful oppression.

In the republics of Italy, where these three powers are united, there is less liberty than in our monarchies. Hence their government is obliged to have recourse to as violent methods for its support as even that of the Turks; witness the state inquisitors, and the lion's mouth into which every informer may at all hours throw his written accusations.

In what a situation must the poor subject be in those republics! The same body of magistrates are possessed, as executors of the laws, of the whole power they have given themselves in quality of legislators. They may plunder the state by their general determinations; and as they have likewise the judiciary power in their hands, every private citizen may be ruined by their particular decisions.

The whole power is here united in one body; and though there is no external pomp that indicates a despotic sway, yet the people feel the effects of it every moment.

Hence it is that many of the princes of Europe, whose aim has been levelled at arbitrary power, have constantly set out with uniting in their own persons all the branches of magistracy, and all the great offices of state.

I allow indeed that the mere hereditary aristocracy of the Italian republics does not exactly answer to the despotic power of the Eastern princes. The number of magistrates sometimes moderate the power of the magistracy; the whole body of the nobles do not always concur in the same design; and different tribunals are erected, that temper each other. Thus at Venice the legislative power is in the council, the executive in the *pregadi*, and the judiciary in the *quarantia*. But the mischief is that all these different tribunals are composed of magistrates all belonging to the same body; which constitutes almost one and the same power.

The judiciary power ought not to be given to a standing senate; it should be exercised by persons taken from the body of the people at certain times of the year, and consistently with a form and manner prescribed by law, in order to erect a tribunal that should last only so long as necessity requires.

By this method the judicial power, so terrible to mankind, not being annexed to any particular state or profession, becomes, as it were, invisible. People have not then the judges continually present to their view; they fear the office, but not the magistrate.

In accusations of a deep and criminal nature, it is proper the person accused should have the privilege of choosing, in some measures, his judges, in concurrence with the law; or at least he should have a right to except against so great a number that the remaining part may be deemed his own choice.

The other two powers may be given rather to magistrates or permanent bodies, because they are not exercised on any private subject; one being no more than the general will of the state, and the other the execution of that general will.

But though the tribunals ought not to be fixed, the judgments ought; and to such a degree as to be ever conformable to the letter of the law. Were they to be the private opinion of the judge, people would then live in society, without exactly knowing the nature of their obligations.

The judges ought likewise to be of the same rank as the accused, or, in other words, his peers; to the end that he may not imagine he is fallen into the hands of persons inclined to treat him with rigour.

If the legislature leaves the executive power in possession of a right to imprison those subjects who can give security for their good behaviour, there is an end of liberty; unless they are taken up, in order to answer without delay to a capital crime, in which case they are really free, being subject only to the power of the law.

But should the legislature think itself in danger by some secret conspiracy against the state, or by a correspondence with a foreign enemy, it might authorize the executive power, for a short and limited time, to imprison suspected persons, who in that case would lose their liberty only for a while, to preserve it forever.

And this is the only reasonable method that can be substituted to the tyrannical magistracy of the Ephori, and to the state inquisitors of Venice, who are also despotic.

As in a country of liberty, every man who is supposed a free agent ought to be his own governor; the legislative power should reside in the whole body of the people. But since this is impossible in large states, and in small ones is subject to many inconveniences, it is fit the people should transact by their representatives what they cannot transact by themselves.

The inhabitants of a particular town are much better acquainted with its wants and interests than with those of other places; and are better judges of the capacity of their neighbours than of that of the rest of their countrymen. The members, therefore, of the legislature should not be chosen from the general body of the nation; but it is proper that in every considerable place a representative should be elected by the inhabitants.[1]

The great advantage of representatives is, their capacity of discussing public affairs. For this the people collectively are extremely unfit, which is one of the chief inconveniences of a democracy.

It is not at all necessary that the representatives who have received a general instruction from their constituents should wait to be directed on each particular affair, as is practised in the diets of Germany. True it is that by this way of proceeding the speeches of the deputies might with greater propriety be called the voice of the nation; but, on the other hand, this would occasion infinite delays; would give each deputy a power of controlling the assembly; and, on the most urgent and pressing occasions, the wheels of government might be stopped by the caprice of a single person.

When the deputies, as Mr Sidney well observes, represent a body of people, as in Holland, they ought to be accountable to their constituents; but it is a different thing in England, where they are deputed by boroughs.

[1] See Aristotle, *Politics*, bk. III, ch. 7.

All the inhabitants of the several districts ought to have a right of voting at the election of a representative, except such as are in so mean a situation as to be deemed to have no will of their own.

One great fault there was in most of the ancient republics, that the people had a right to active resolutions, such as require some execution, a thing of which they are absolutely incapable. They ought to have no share in the government but for the choosing of representatives, which is within their reach. For though few can tell the exact degree of men's capacities, yet there are none but are capable of knowing in general whether the person they choose is better qualified than most of his neighbours.

Neither ought the representative body to be chosen for the executive part of government, for which it is not so fit; but for the enacting of laws, or to see whether the laws in being are duly executed, a thing suited to their abilities, and which none indeed but themselves can properly perform.

In such a state there are always persons distinguished by their birth, riches, or honours: but were they to be confounded with the common people, and to have only the weight of a single vote like the rest, the common liberty would be their slavery, and they would have no interest in supporting it, as most of the popular resolutions would be against them. The share they have, therefore, in the legislature ought to be proportioned to their other advantages in the state; which happens only when they form a body that has a right to check the licentiousness of the people, as the people have a right to oppose any encroachment of theirs.

The legislative power is therefore committed to the body of the nobles, and to that which represents the people, each having their assemblies and deliberations apart, each their separate views and interests.

Of the three powers above mentioned, the judiciary is in some measure next to nothing: there remains, therefore, only two; and as these have need of a regulating power to moderate them, the part of the legislative body composed of the nobility is extremely proper for this purpose.

The body of the nobility ought to be hereditary. In the first place it is so in its own nature; and in the next there must be a considerable interest to preserve its privileges—privileges that in themselves are obnoxious to popular envy, and of course in a free state are always in danger.

But as a hereditary power might be tempted to pursue its own particular interests, and forget those of the people, it is proper that where a singular advantage may be gained by corrupting the nobility, as in the laws relating to the supplies, they should have no other share in the legislation than the power of rejecting, and not that of resolving.

By the power of resolving I mean the right of ordaining by their own authority, or of amending what has been ordained by others. By the power of rejecting I would be understood to mean the right of annulling a resolution taken by another; which was the power of the tribunes at Rome. And though the person possessed of the privilege of rejecting may likewise have the right of approving, yet this approbation passes for no more than a declaration, that he intends to make no use of his privilege of rejecting, and is derived from that very privilege.

The executive power ought to be in the hands of a monarch, because this branch of government, having need of despatch, is better administered by one than by many: on the other hand, whatever depends on the legislative power is oftentimes better regulated by many than by a single person.

But if there were no monarch, and the executive power should be committed to a certain number of persons selected from the legislative body, there would be an end then of liberty; by reason the two powers would be united, as the same persons would sometimes possess, and would be always able to possess, a share in both.

Were the legislative body to be a considerable time without meeting, this would likewise put an end to liberty. For of two things one would naturally follow: either that there would be no longer any legislative resolutions, and then the state would fall into anarchy; or that these resolutions would be taken by the executive power, which would render it absolute.

It would be needless for the legislative body to continue always assembled. This would be troublesome to the representatives, and, moreover, would cut out too much work for the executive power, so as to take off its attention to its office, and oblige it to think only of defending its own prerogatives, and the right it has to execute.

Again, were the legislative body to be always assembled, it might happen to be kept up only by filling the places of the deceased members with new representatives; and in that case, if the legislative body were once corrupted, the evil would be past all remedy. When different legislative bodies succeed one another, the people who have a bad opinion of that which is actually sitting may reasonably entertain some hopes of the next: but were it to be always the same body, the people upon seeing it once corrupted would no longer expect any good from its laws; and of course they would either become desperate or fall into a state of indolence.

The legislative body should not meet of itself. For a body is supposed to have no will but when it is met; and besides, were it not to meet unanimously, it would be impossible to determine which was really the legislative body; the part assembled, or the other. And if it had a right to prorogue itself, it might happen never to be prorogued; which would be extremely dangerous, in case it should ever attempt to encroach on the executive power. Besides, there are seasons, some more proper than others, for assembling the legislative body: it is fit, therefore, that the executive power should regulate the time of meeting, as well as the duration of those assemblies, according to the circumstances and exigencies of a state known to itself.

Were the executive power not to have a right of restraining the encroachments of the legislative body, the latter would become despotic; for as it might arrogate to itself what authority it pleased, it would soon destroy all the other powers.

But it is not proper, on the other hand, that the legislative power should have a right to stay the executive. For as the execution has its natural limits, it is useless to confine it; besides, the executive power is generally employed in momentary operations. The power, therefore, of the Roman tribunes was faulty, as it put a stop not only to the legislation, but likewise to the executive part of government; which was attended with infinite mischief.

But if the legislative power in a free state has no right to stay the executive, it has a right and ought to have the means of examining in what manner its laws have been executed; an advantage which this government has over that of Crete and Sparta, where the Cosmi and the Ephori gave no account of their administration.

But whatever may be the issue of that examination, the legislative body ought not to have a power of arraigning the person, nor, of course, the conduct, of him who is intrusted with the executive power. His person should be sacred, because as it is necessary for the good of the state to prevent the legislative body from rendering themselves arbitrary, the moment he is accused or tried there is an end of liberty.

In this case the state would be no longer a monarchy, but a kind of republic, though not a free government. But as the person intrusted with the executive power cannot abuse it without bad counsellors, and such as have the laws as ministers, though the laws protect them as subjects, these men may be examined and punished—an advantage which this government has over that of Gnidus, where the law allowed of no such thing as calling the Amymones[2] to an account, even after their administration, and therefore the people could never obtain any satisfaction for the injuries done them.

Though, in general, the judiciary power ought not to be united with any part of the legislative, yet this is liable to three exceptions, founded on the particular interest of the party accused.

The great are always obnoxious to popular envy; and were they to be judged by the people, they might be in danger from their judges, and would, moreover, be deprived of the privilege which the meanest subject is possessed of in a free state, of being tried by his peers. The nobility, for this reason, ought not to be cited before the ordinary courts of judicature, but before that part of the legislature which is composed of their own body.

It is possible that the law, which is clear-sighted in one sense, and blind in another, might, in some cases, be too severe. But as we have already observed, the national judges are no more than the mouth that pronounces the words of the

[2] There were magistrates chosen annually by the people. See Stephen of Byzantium.

law, mere passive beings, incapable of moderating either its force or rigour. That part, therefore, of the legislative body, which we have just now observed to be a necessary tribunal on another occasion, also is a necessary tribunal in this; it belongs to its supreme authority to moderate the law in favour of the law itself, by mitigating the sentence.

It might also happen that a subject intrusted with the administration of public affairs may infringe the rights of the people, and be guilty of crimes which the ordinary magistrates either could not or would not punish. But, in general, the legislative power cannot try causes: and much less can it try this particular case, where it represents the party aggrieved, which is the people. It can only, therefore, impeach. But before what court shall it bring its impeachment? Must it go and demean itself before the ordinary tribunals, which are its inferiors, and, being composed, moreover, of men who are chosen from the people as well as itself, will naturally be swayed by the authority of so powerful an accuser? No: in order to preserve the dignity of the people and the security of the subject, the legislative part which represents the people must bring in its charge before the legislative part which represents the nobility, who have neither the same interests nor the same passions.

Here is an advantage which the government has over most of the ancient republics, where this abuse prevailed, that the people were at the same time both judge and accuser.

The executive power, pursuant of what has been already said, ought to have a share in the legislature by the power of rejecting; otherwise it would soon be stripped of its prerogative. But should the legislative power usurp a share of the executive, the latter would be equally undone.

If the prince were to have a part in the legislature by the power of resolving, liberty would be lost. But as it is necessary he should have a share in the legislature for the support of his own prerogative, this share must consist in the power of rejecting.

The change of government at Rome was owing to this, that neither the senate, who had one part of the executive power, nor the magistrates, who were intrusted with the other, had the right of rejecting, which was entirely lodged in the people.

Here, then, is the fundamental constitution of the government we are treating of. The legislative body being composed of two parts, they check one another by the mutual privilege of rejecting. They are both restrained by the executive power, as the executive is by the legislative.

These three powers should naturally form a state of repose or inaction. But as there is a necessity for movement in the course of human affairs, they are forced to move, but still in concert.

As the executive power has no other part in the legislative than the privilege of rejecting, it can have no share in the public debates. It is not even necessary that it should propose, because as it may always disapprove of the resolutions that shall be taken, it may likewise reject the decisions on those proposals which were made against its will.

In some ancient commonwealths, where public debates were carried on by the people in a body, it was natural for the executive power to propose and debate in conjunction with the people, otherwise their resolutions must have been attended with a strange confusion.

Were the executive power to determine the raising of public money, otherwise than by giving its consent, liberty would be at an end; because it would become legislative in the most important point of legislation.

If the legislative power was to settle the subsidies, not from year to year, but forever, it would run the risk of losing its liberty, because the executive power would be no longer dependent; and when once it was possessed of such a perpetual right, it would be a matter of indifference whether it held it of itself or of another. The same may be said if it should come to a resolution of intrusting, not an annual, but a perpetual command of the fleets and armies to the executive power.

To prevent the executive power from being able to oppress, it is requisite that the armies with which it is intrusted should consist of the people, and have the same spirit as the people, as was the case at Rome till the time of Marius. To obtain this end, there are only two ways, either that the persons employed in the army should have sufficient property to answer for their conduct to their fellow subjects, and be enlisted only for a year, as was customary at Rome; or if there should be a standing army, composed chiefly of the most despicable part of the nation, the legislative power should have a right to disband them as soon as it pleased; the soldiers should live in common with the rest of the people; and no separate camp, barracks, or fortress should be suffered.

When once an army is established, it ought not to depend immediately on the legislative, but on the executive power; and this from the very nature of the thing, its business consisting more in action than in deliberation.

It is natural for mankind to set a higher value upon courage than timidity, on activity than prudence, on strength than counsel. Hence the army will ever despise a senate, and respect their own officers. They will naturally slight the orders sent them by a body of men whom they look upon as cowards, and therefore unworthy to command them. So that as soon as the troops depend entirely on the legislative body, it becomes a military government; and if the contrary has ever happened, it has been owing to some extraordinary circumstances. It is because the army was always kept divided; it is because it was composed of several bodies that depended each on a particular province: it is because the capital towns were strong places, defended by their natural situation, and not garrisoned with regular troops. Holland, for instance, is still safer than Venice; she might drown or starve the revolted troops; for as they are not quartered in towns capable of furnishing them with necessary subsistence, this subsistence is of course precarious.

In perusing the admirable treatise of Tacitus 'On the Manners of the Germans', we find it is from that nation the English have borrowed the idea of their political government. This beautiful system was invented first in the woods.

As all human things have an end, the state we are speaking of will lose its liberty, will perish. Have not Rome, Sparta, and Carthage perished? It will perish when the legislative power shall be more corrupt than the executive.

It is not my business to examine whether the English actually enjoy this liberty or not. Sufficient it is for my purpose to observe that it is established by their laws; and I inquire no further . . .

2

THE HOUSE OF COMMONS

WALTER BAGEHOT

The dignified aspect of the House of Commons is altogether secondary to its efficient use. It *is* dignified: in a government in which the most prominent parts are good because they are very stately, any prominent part, to be good at all, must be somewhat stately. The human imagination exacts keeping in government as much as in art; it will not be at all influenced by institutions which do not match with those by which it is principally influenced. The House of Commons needs to be impressive, and impressive it is: but its use resides not in its appearance, but in its reality. Its office is not to win power by awing mankind, but to use power in governing mankind.

The main function of the House of Commons is one which we know quite well, though our common constitutional speech does not recognize it. The House of Commons is an electoral chamber; it is the assembly which chooses our president. Washington and his fellow politicians contrived an electoral college, to be composed (as was hoped) of the wisest people in the nation, which, after due deliberation, was to choose for president the wisest man in the nation. But that college is a sham; it has no independence and no life. No one knows, or cares to know, who its members are. They never discuss, and never deliberate. They were chosen to vote that Mr Lincoln be president, or that Mr Breckenridge be president; they do so vote, and they go home. But our House of Commons is a real choosing body; it elects the people it likes. And it dismisses whom it likes too. No matter that a few months since it was chosen to support Lord Aberdeen or Lord Palmerston; upon a sudden occasion it ousts the statesman to whom it at first adhered, and selects an opposite statesman whom it at first rejected. Doubtless in such cases there is a tacit reference to probable public opinion; but certainly also there is much free will in the judgement of the Commons. The House only goes where it thinks in the end the nation will follow; but it takes its chance of the nation following or not following; it assumes the initiative, and acts upon its discretion or its caprice.

When the American nation has chosen its president, its virtue goes out of it, and out of the Transmissive College through which it chooses. But because the House of Commons has the power of dismissal in addition to the power of election, its relations to the premier are incessant. They guide him and he leads them. He is to them what they are to the nation. He only goes where he believes they will go after him. But he has to take the lead; he must choose his direction, and begin the journey. Nor must he flinch. A good horse likes to feel the rider's bit; and a great deliberative assembly likes to feel that it is under worthy guidance. A minister who succumbs to the House—who ostentatiously seeks its pleasure, who does not try to regulate it, who will not boldly point out plain errors to it—seldom thrives. The great leaders of Parliament have varied much, but they have all had a certain firmness. A great assembly is as soon spoiled by over-indulgence as a little child. The whole life of English politics is the action and reaction between the ministry and the Parliament. The appointees strive to guide, and the appointers surge under the guidance.

The elective is now the most important function of the House of Commons. It is most desirable to insist, and be tedious, on this, because our tradition ignores it. At the end of half the sessions of Parliament, you will read in the newspapers, and you will hear even from those who have looked close at the matter and should know better, 'Parliament has done nothing this session. Some things were promised in the Queen's speech, but they were only little things; and most of them have not passed.' Lord Lyndhurst used for years to recount the small outcomings of legislative achievement; and yet those were the days of the first Whig Governments, who had more to do in legislation, and did more, than any government. The true answer to such harangues as Lord Lyndhurst's by a minister should have been in the first person. He should have said firmly, 'Parliament has maintained ME, and that was its greatest duty; Parliament has carried on what, in the language of traditional respect, we call the Queen's Government; it has maintained what wisely or unwisely it deemed the best executive of the English nation.'

The second function of the House of Commons is what I may call an expressive function. It is its office to express the mind of the English people on all matters which come before it . . .

The third function of Parliament is what I may call—preserving a sort of technicality even in familiar matters for the sake of distinctness—the teaching function. A great and open council of considerable men cannot be placed in the middle of a society without altering that society. It ought to alter it for the better. It ought to teach the nation what it does not know. How far the House of Commons can so teach, and how far it does so teach, are matters for subsequent discussion.

Fourthly, the House of Commons has what may be called an informing function—a function which though in its present form quite modern is singularly analogous to a medieval function. In old times one office of the House of Commons was to inform the sovereign what was wrong. It laid before the Crown the grievances and complaints of particular interests. Since the publication of the parliamentary debates a corresponding office of Parliament is to lay these same grievances, these same complaints, before the nation, which is the present sovereign. The nation needs it quite as much as the king ever needed it. A free people is indeed mostly fair, liberty practises men in a give and take, which is the rough essence of justice. The English people, possibly even above other free nations, is fair. But a free nation rarely can be—and the English nation is not—quick of apprehension. It only comprehends what is familiar to it—what comes into its own experience, what squares with its own thoughts. 'I never heard of such a thing in my life,' the middle-class Englishman says, and he thinks he so refutes an argument. The common disputant cannot say in reply that his experience is but limited, and that the assertion may be true, though he had never met with anything at all like it. But a great debate in Parliament *does* bring home something of this feeling. Any notion, any creed, any feeling, any grievance which can get a decent number of English members to stand up for it, is felt by almost all Englishmen to be perhaps a false and pernicious opinion, but at any rate possible—an opinion within the intellectual sphere, an opinion to be reckoned with. And it is an immense achievement. Practical diplomatists say that a free government is harder to deal with than a despotic government; you may be able to get the despot to hear the other side; his ministers, men of trained intelligence, will be sure to know what makes against them; and they *may* tell him. But a free nation never hears any side save its own. The newspapers only repeat the side their purchasers like: the favourable arguments are set out, elaborated, illustrated, the adverse arguments maimed, misstated, confused. The worst judge, they say, is a deaf judge; the most dull government is a free government on matters its ruling classes will not hear. I am disposed to reckon it as the second function of Parliament in point of importance, that to some extent it makes us hear what otherwise we should not.

Lastly, there is the function of legislation, of which of course it would be preposterous to deny the great importance, and which I only deny to be *as* important as the executive management of the whole State, or the political education given by Parliament to the whole nation. There are, I allow, seasons when legislation is more important than either of these. The nation may be misfitted with its laws, and need to change them: some particular corn law may hurt all industry, and it may be worth a thousand administrative blunders to get rid of it. But generally the laws of a nation suit its life; special adaptations of them are but subordinate; the administration and conduct of that life is the matter which presses most. Nevertheless, the statute-book of every great nation yearly contains many important new laws, and the English statute-book does so above any. Any immense mass, indeed, of the legislation is not, in the proper language of jurisprudence, legislation at all. A law is a general command applicable to many cases. The 'special acts' which crowd the statute-book and weary parliamentary committees are applicable to one case only. They do not lay down rules according to which railways shall be made, they enact that such a railway shall be made from this place to that place, and they have no bearing upon any other transaction. But after every deduction and abatement, the annual legislation of Parliament is a result of singular importance; were it not so, it could not be, as it often is considered, the sole result of its annual assembling.

Some persons will perhaps think that I ought to enumerate a sixth function of the House of Commons—a financial function. But I do not consider that, upon broad principle, and omitting legal technicalities, the House of Commons has any special function with regard to financial different from its functions with respect to other legislation. It is to rule in both, and to rule in both through the cabinet. Financial legislation is of necessity a yearly recurring legislation; but frequency of occurrence does not indicate a diversity of nature or compel an antagonism of treatment.

In truth, the principal peculiarity of the House of Commons in financial affairs is nowadays not a special privilege, but an exceptional disability. On common subjects any member can propose anything, but not on money—the minister only can propose to tax the people. This principle is commonly involved in medieval metaphysics as to the prerogative of the Crown, but it is as useful in the nineteenth century as in the fourteenth, and rests on as sure a principle. The House of Commons—now that it is the true sovereign, and appoints the real executive—has long ceased to be the checking, sparing, economical body it once was. It now is more apt to spend money than the minister of the day. I have heard a very experienced financier say, 'If you want to raise a certain cheer in the House of Commons make a general panegyric on economy; if you want to invite a sure defeat, propose a particular saving.' The process is simple. Every expenditure of public money has some apparent public object; those who wish to spend the money expatiate on that object; they say, 'What is £50,000 to this great country? Is this a time for cheeseparing objection? Our industry was never so productive; our resources never so immense. What is £50,000 in comparison with this great national interest?' The members who are for the expenditure always come down; perhaps a constituent or a friend who will profit by the outlay, or is keen on the object, has asked them to attend; and any rate, there is a popular vote to be given, on which the newspapers—always philanthropic, and sometimes talked over—will be sure to make encomiums. The members against the expenditure rarely come down of themselves; why should they become unpopular without reason? The object seems decent; many of its advocates are certainly sincere: a hostile vote will make enemies, and be censured by the journals. If there were not some check, the 'people's House' would soon outrun the people's money.

That check is the responsibility of the cabinet for the national finance. If any one could propose a tax, they might let the House spend it as it would, and wash their hands of the matter; but now, for whatever expenditure is sanctioned—even when it is sanctioned against the ministry's wish—the ministry must find the money. Accordingly, they have the strongest motive to oppose extra outlay. They will have to pay the bill for it; they will have to impose taxation, which is always disagreeable, or suggest loans, which, under ordinary circumstances, are shameful. The ministry is (so to speak) the bread-winner of the political family, and has to meet the cost of philanthropy and glory, just as the head of a family has to pay for the charities of his wife and the *toilette* of his daughters.

In truth, when a cabinet is made the sole executive, it follows it must have the sole financial charge, for all action costs money, all policy depends on money, and it is in adjusting the relative goodness of action and policies that the executive is employed.

From a consideration of these functions, it follows that we are ruled by the House of Commons; we are, indeed, so used to be so ruled, that it does not seem to be at all strange. But of all odd forms of government, the oddest really is government by a '*public meeting*'. Here are 658 persons, collected from all parts of England, different in nature, different in interests, different in look, and language. If we think what an empire the English is, how various are its components, how incessant its concerns, how immersed in history its policy; if we think what a vast information, what a nice discretion, what a consistent will ought to mark the rulers of that empire, we shall be surprised when we see them. We see a changing body of miscellaneous persons, sometimes few, sometimes never, never the same for an hour; sometimes excited, but mostly dull and half weary—impatient of eloquence, catching at any joke as an alleviation. These are the persons who rule the

British Empire—who rule England, who rule Scotland, who rule Ireland, who rule a great deal of Asia, who rule a great deal of Polynesia, who rule a great deal of America, and scattered fragments everywhere.

Paley said many shrewd things, but he never said a better thing than that it was much harder to make men see a difficulty than comprehend the explanation of it. The key to the difficulties of most discussed and unsettled questions is commonly in their undiscussed parts: they are like the background of a picture, which looks obvious, easy, just what any one might have painted, but which, in fact, set the figures in their right position, chastens them, and makes them what they are. Nobody will understand parliament government who fancies it an easy thing, a natural thing, a thing not needing explanation. You have not a perception of the first elements in this matter till you know that government by a *club* is a standing wonder.

There has been a capital illustration lately how helpless many English gentlemen are when called together on a sudden. The Government, rightly or wrongly, thought fit to entrust the quarter-sessions of each county with the duty of combating its cattle-plague; but the scene in most 'shire halls' was unsatisfactory. There was the greatest difficulty in getting, not only a right decision, but *any* decision. I saw one myself which went thus. The chairman proposed a very complex resolution, in which there was much which every one liked, and much which every one disliked, though, of course, the favourite parts of some were the objectionable parts to others. This resolution got, so to say, wedged in the meeting; everybody suggested amendments; one amendment was carried which none were satisfied with, and so the matter stood over. It is a saying in England, 'a big meeting never does anything'; and yet we are governed by the House of Commons—by 'a big meeting'.

It may be said that the House of Commons does not rule, it only elects the rulers. But there must be something special about it to enable it to do that. Suppose the cabinet were elected by a London club, what confusion there would be, what writing and answering! 'Will you speak to So-and-So, and ask him to vote for my man?' would be heard on every side. How the wife of A and the wife of B would plot to confound the wife of C. Whether the club elected under the dignified shadow of a queen, or without the shadow, would hardly matter at all; if the substantial choice was in them, the confusion and intrigue would be there too. I propose to begin this paper by asking, not why the House of Commons governs well, but the fundamental—almost unasked question—how the House of Commons comes to be able to govern at all.

The House of Commons can do work which the quarter-sessions or clubs cannot do, because it is an organized body, while quarter-sessions and clubs are unorganized. Two of the greatest orators in England—Lord Brougham and Lord Bolingbroke—spent much eloquence in attacking party government. Bolingbroke probably knew what he was doing; he was a consistent opponent of the power of the Commons; he wished to attack them in a vital part. But Lord Brougham does not know; he proposes to amend parliamentary government by striking out the very elements which make parliamentary government possible. At present the majority of Parliament obey certain leaders; what those leaders propose they support, what those leaders reject they reject. An old Secretary of the Treasury used to say, 'This is a bad case, an indefensible case. We must apply our *majority* to this question.' That secretary lived fifty years ago, before the Reform Bill, when majorities were very blind, and very 'applicable'. Nowadays, the power of leaders over their followers is strictly and wisely limited: they can take their followers but a little way, and that only in certain directions. Yet still there are leaders and followers. On the Conservative side of the House there are vestiges of the despotic leadership even now. A cynical politician is said to have watched the long row of county members, so fresh and respectable-looking, and muttered, 'By Jove, they are the finest brute votes in Europe!' But all satire apart, the principle of Parliament is obedience to leaders. Change your leader if you will, take another if you will, but obey No. 1 while you serve No. 1, and obey No. 2 when you have gone over to No. 2. The penalty of not doing so, is the penalty of impotence. It is not that you will not be able to do any good, but you will not be able to do anything at all. If everybody does what he thinks right, there will be 657 amendments to every motion, and none of them will be carried or the motion either.

The moment, indeed, that we distinctly conceive that the House of Commons is mainly and above all things an elective assembly, we at once perceive that party is of its essence. There never was an election without a party. You cannot get a child into an asylum without a combination. At such places you may see 'Vote for orphan A' upon a placard, and 'Vote for orphan B (also an idiot!!!)' upon a banner, and the party of each is busy about its placard and banner. What is true at such minor and momentary elections must be much more true in a great and constant election of rulers. The House of Commons lives in a state of perpetual choice; at any moment it can choose a ruler and dismiss a ruler. And therefore party is inherent in it, is bone of its bone, and breath of its breath.

Secondly, though the leaders of party no longer have the vast patronage of the last century with which to bribe, they can coerce by a threat far more potent than any allurement—they can dissolve. This is the secret which keeps parties together. Mr Cobden most justly said: 'He has never been able to discover what was the proper moment, according to members of Parliament, for a dissolution. He had heard them say they were ready to vote for everything else, but he had never heard them say they were ready to vote for that.' Efficiency in an assembly requires a solid mass of steady votes; and these are *collected* by a deferential attachment to particular men, or by a belief in the principles those men represent, and they are *maintained* by fear of those men—by the fear that if you vote against them, you may yourself soon not have a vote at all.

Thirdly, it may seem odd to say so, just after inculcating that party organization is the vital principle of representative government, but that organization is permanently efficient, because it is not composed of warm partisans. The body is eager, but the atoms are cool. If it were otherwise, parliamentary government would become the worst of governments—a sectarian government. The party in power would go all the lengths their orators proposed—all that their formulas enjoined, as far as they had ever said they would go. But the partisans of the English Parliament are not of such a temper.

They are Whigs, or Radicals, or Tories, but they are much else too. They are common Englishmen, and, as Father Newman complains, 'hard to be worked up to the dogmatic level'. They are not eager to press the tenets of their party to impossible conclusions. On the contrary, the way to lead them—the best and acknowledged way—is to affect a studied and illogical moderation. You may hear men say, 'Without committing myself to the tenet that three plus two makes five, though I am free to admit that the honourable member for Bradford has advanced very grave arguments in behalf of it, I think I may, with permission of the committee, assume that two plus three do not make four, which will be a sufficient basis on the present occasion.' This language is very suitable to the greater part of the House of Commons. Most men of business love a sort of twilight. They have lived all their lives in an atmosphere of probabilities and of doubt, where nothing is very clear, where there are some chances for many events, where there is much to be said for several courses, where nevertheless one course must be determinedly chosen and fixedly adhered to. They like to hear arguments suited to this intellectual haze. So far from caution or hestitation in the statement of the argument striking them as an indication of imbecility, it seems to them a sign of practicality. They got rich themselves by transactions of which they could not have stated the argumentative ground—and all they ask for is a distinct though moderate conclusion, that they can repeat when asked; something which they feel *not* to be abstract argument, but abstract argument diluted and dissolved in real life. 'There seems to me,' an impatient young man once said, 'to be no stay in Peel's arguments.' And that was why Sir Robert Peel was the best leader of the Commons in our time; we like to have the rigidity taken out of an argument, and the substance left.

Nor indeed, under our system of government, are the leaders themselves of the House of Commons, for the most part, eager to carry party conclusions too far. They are in contact with reality. An opposition, on coming into power, is often like a speculative merchant whose bills become due. Ministers have to make good their promises, and they find a difficulty in so doing. They have said the state of things is so and so, and if you give us the power we will do thus and thus. But when they come to handle the official documents, to converse with the permanent under-secretary—familiar with disagreeable facts, and though in manner most respectful, yet most imperturbable in opinion—very soon doubts intervene. Of course, something must be done; the speculative merchant cannot forget his bills; the late opposition cannot, in office, forget those sentences which terrible admirers in the country still quote. But just as the merchant asks his debtor, 'Could you not take a bill at four months?' so the new minister says to the permanent under-secretary, 'Could you not suggest a middle course? I am of course not bound by mere sentences used in debate; I have never been accused of letting a false ambition of consistency warp my conduct; but,' etc. And the end always is that a middle course is devised which *looks* as much as possible like what was suggested in opposition, but which *is* as much as possible what patent facts—facts which seem to live in the office, so teasing and unceasing are they—prove ought to be done.

Of all modes of enforcing moderation on a party, the best is to contrive that the members of that party shall be intrinsically moderate, careful, and almost shrinking men; and the next best to contrive that the leaders of the party, who have protested most in its behalf, shall be placed in the closest contact with the actual world. Our English system contains both contrivances; it makes party government permanent and possible in the sole way in which it can be so, by making it mild . . .

3

THE DECLINE OF LEGISLATURES

LORD BRYCE

Every traveller who, curious in political affairs, enquires in the countries which he visits how their legislative bodies are working, receives from the elder men the same discouraging answer. They tell him, in terms much the same everywhere, that there is less brilliant speaking than in the days of their own youth, that the tone of manners has declined, that the best citizens are less disposed to enter the chamber, that its proceedings are less fully reported and excite less interest, that a seat in it confers less social status, and that, for one reason or another, the respect felt for it has waned. The wary traveller discounts these jeremiads, conscious of the tendency in himself, growing with his years, to dwell in memory chiefly upon the things he used to most enjoy in his boyhood—the long fine summers when one could swim daily in the river and apples were plentiful, the fine hard winters when the ice sheets on Windermere or Loch Lomond gathered crowds of skaters. Nevertheless this disparagement of the legislatures of our own day is too general, and appears in too many forms, to be passed by. There is evidence to indicate in nearly every country some decline from that admiration of and confidence in the system of representative government which in England possessed the generation who took their constitutional history from Hallam and Macaulay, and their political philosophy from John Stuart Mill and Walter Bagehot; and in the United States that earlier generation which between 1820 and 1850 looked on the federal system and the legislatures working under it in the nation and the States as the almost perfect model of what constitutional government ought to be. In the middle of last century most Liberal thinkers in France and Spain, in Italy and Germany expected a sort of millennium from the establishment in their midst of representative institutions like those of England, the greatest improvement, it was often said, that had ever been introduced into government, and one which, had the ancient world discovered it, might have saved the Greek republics from the Macedonian conqueror and Rome from the despotism of the Caesars. So the leaders of the revolutions which liberated Spanish America took as their pattern the American federal system which had made it possible for a central congress and legislative bodies in every state to give effect to the will of a free people scattered over a vast continent, holding them together in one great body while also enabling each division of the population to enact laws appropriate to their respective needs. By the representative system the executive would, they believed, be duly guided and controlled; by it the best wisdom of the country would be gathered into deliberative bodies whose debates would enlighten the people, and in which men fit for leadership could show their powers. Whoever now looks back to read the speeches and writings of statesmen and students between 1830 and 1870, comparing them with the complaints and criticisms directed against the legislatures of the twentieth century, will be struck by the contrast, noting how many of the defects now visible in representative government were then unforeseen.

These complaints and criticisms need to be stated and examined, if only in view of the efforts which peoples delivered from the sway of decadent monarchies are now making to establish constitutional governments in various parts of Central and Eastern Europe. . . .

. . . In the States of the American Union a sense of these failings has led to two significant changes. Many restrictions have been everywhere imposed by constitutional amendments on the powers of State legislatures; and more recently many States (nearly one-third of the whole number) have introduced the 'referendum' and the 'initiative', the former to review, the latter from time to time to supersede the action of those bodies. The virtue of members had so often succumbed to temptations proceeding from powerful incorporated companies, and the habit of effecting jobs for local interests was so common, that a general suspicion had attached itself to their action. Moreover, the so-called 'party machines', which have been wont to nominate candidates, and on whose pleasure depends the political future of a large proportion of the members, prevented the will of the people from prevailing, making many members feel themselves responsible rather to it than to their constituencies. Like faults have been sometimes charged against Congress, though conditions are better there than in most of the States, but the referendum and initiative are of course inapplicable to the national government since the federal constitution makes no provision for them.

In France, while Paris is enlivened, the nation has been for many years wearied by the incessant warfare of the Chamber, divided into many unstable groups, with frequent changes from one cabinet to another. The politicians have become discredited, partly by the accusations they bring against one another, partly by the brokerage of places to individuals and favours to localities in which deputies act as intermediates between ministers and local wire-pullers, while scandals occurring from time to time have, although few deputies have been tarnished, lowered the respect felt for the Chamber as a whole.

The same kind of brokerage is rife in Italy also. The deputy holds his place by getting grants or other advantages for his district, and is always busy in influencing patronage by intrigue.

In Great Britain these last-named evils have not appeared, partly because the Civil Service was taken entirely out of politics many years ago, partly because the passing of 'private bills' for local or personal purposes is surrounded by elaborate safeguards. Yet the House of Commons seems to hold a slightly lower place in the esteem of the people than it did in the days of Melbourne and Peel. Its intellectual quality has not risen. Its proceedings are less fully reported. The frequency of obstruction and of the use of the closure to overcome obstruction have reduced the value of the debates and affected the quality of legislation, while also lessening respect for a body which is thought—though this is inevitable under the party system—to waste time in unprofitable wrangling. The 'sterile hubbub of politics' was noted by a non-political critic even thirty years ago.[1] The independence of members has suffered by the more stringent party discipline. The results of these causes are seen in the diminished deference accorded to Parliament, perhaps also in its slightly diminished attractiveness for able and public-spirited men.

In the new overseas democracies—Canada, Australia, and New Zealand—we cannot, except perhaps in New Zealand, now talk of a falling off, for the level was never high. Corruption is rare, but the standard both of tone and manners and of intellectual attainment is not worthy of communities where everybody is well off and well educated, and where grave problems of legislation call for constructive ability.

Setting aside the special conditions of each particular country, because in each the presence or absence of certain institutions may give rise to special defects, let us seek for some general causes which in all the countries named, though in some more than others, have been tending to reduce the prestige and authority of legislative bodies.

The spirit of democratic equality has made the masses of the people less deferential to the class whence legislators used to be drawn, and the legislatures themselves are today filled from all classes except the very poorest. This is in some respects a gain, for it enables popular wishes to be better expressed, but it makes a difference to Parliamentary habits. In England, for example, the old 'country gentlemen', who used to form more than half the House of Commons and from whom many brilliant figures came, are now a small minority. Constituencies are everywhere larger than formerly, owing to the growth of population and to universal suffrage; while the personal qualities of a candidate do less to commend him to electors who are apt to vote at the bidding of party or because the candidate is lavish in his promises. Not only do the members of legislatures stand more than heretofore on the same intellectual level as their constituents, but their personal traits and habits and the way in which they do business are

[1] Matthew Arnold.

better known through the press. In some countries much of the space once allotted to the reports of debates is now given to familiar sketches, describing the appearance and personal traits of members, in which any eccentricity is 'stressed'. 'Scenes' are made the most of, and the disorders which mark them have left a painful impression. Legislators, no longer conventionally supposed to dwell in an Olympian dignity, set little store by the standards of decorum that prevailed when, as in France and England two generations ago, a large proportion of the chamber belonged to the same cultivated social circles, and recognized an etiquette which prescribed the maintenance of external forms of politeness. The defect perpetuates itself because men are apt to live up to no higher standard than that which they find. The less the country respects them, the less they respect themselves. If politicians are assumed to move on a low plane, on it they will continue to move till some great events recall the country and them to the ideals which inspired their predecessors.

The disappearance of this sense of social responsibility has affected the conduct of business. Every rule of procedure, every technicality is now insisted upon and 'worked for all it is worth'. This stiffening or hardening of the modes of doing business has made parliamentary deliberations seem more and more of a game, and less and less a consultation by the leaders of the nation on matters of public welfare.

A like tendency is seen in the stricter party discipline enforced in the British self-governing dominions. As party organizations are stronger, the discretion of representatives is narrowed: they must vote with their leaders. The member who speaks as he thinks is growing rare in English-speaking countries. Whips called him a self-seeker, or a crank, yet his criticisms had their value.

The payment of members has been supposed to lower the status and fetter the freedom of a representative. First introduced in the United States, where it was inevitable because in so large a country members had to leave their business and their often distant homes, to live in the national or in a State capital, it became inevitable in European countries also when the enfranchised wage earners desired to send members of their own class into Parliament. How far it has affected the character of the representatives is not yet clear, but it everywhere exposes the poorer members to the imputation of an undue anxiety to retain their seats as a means of livelihood.

Just as the increased volume of platform speaking by leading politicians has lessened the importance of the part which parliamentary debate used to play in forming public opinion, so has the growth of the newspaper press encroached on the province of the parliamentary orator. Only the very strongest statesmen can command an audience over the whole country, such as that which a widely read newspaper addresses every day. The average legislator fears the newspaper, but the newspaper does not fear the legislator, and the citizen who perceives this draws his own conclusions.

Other organizations occupying themselves with public questions and influencing large sections of opinion, have arisen to compete with legislatures for the attention of the nation. The conventions or conferences of the old and 'regular' parties, both in England and in America, have no great importance; for, being practically directed by the party leaders, they add little or nothing to the programmes whereto the party has been already committed. But the meetings of industrial sections and of the new class parties, such as the Trades Union Congress in England and the Congress of the Peasant Party in Switzerland, the Socialist Congresses in France, and the Labour Union Congresses or assemblies representing the farmers or miners in the United States, the gatherings of farmers in Canada, and the still more powerful meetings of Labour organizations in Australia—all these are important, for they represent a large potential vote, and their deliverances serve as a barometer showing the rise or fall of opinion on industrial issues. Those who lead them may win and wield a power equal to that of all but the most outstanding parliamentary chiefs.

Whether or not it be true, as is commonly stated, that in European countries the intellectual level of legislative assemblies has been sinking, it is clear that nowhere does enough of that which is best in the character and talent of the nation find its way into those assemblies. In this respect the anticipations of eighty years ago have not been realized. The entrance to political life is easier now than it was then, but the daily round of work less agreeable, while the number of alternative careers is larger.

These changes, taken all together, account for the disappointment felt by whoever compares the position held by legislatures now with the hopes once entertained of the services they were to render. Yet may we not ask whether there was ever solid ground for these hopes? Were they not largely due to the contrast which the earliest free assemblies offered to the arbitrary or obscurantist governments which had been ruling everywhere but in America, Britain, and Switzerland, and against which the noblest intellects in the oppressed countries were contending? It was natural to expect that when men of such a type came to fill the legislatures of France, Germany, Italy, and Spain, they would rival the assemblies of the countries that were already thriving on freedom. That expectation was largely fulfilled as regards the first free assemblies, for those who led them were exceptional men, produced or stimulated by the calls of their time. The next generation did not in days of peace rise to the standard set in the days of conflict.

The issues of policy which now occupy legislatures are more complex and difficult than those of half a century ago. The strife of classes and formation of class parties were not foreseen, nor the vast scale on which economic problems would present themselves, nor the constant additions to the functions of governments, nor that immense increase of wealth which has in some countries exposed legislators to temptations more severe than any that had assailed their predecessors. The work to be done then was largely a work of destruction. Old abuses had to be swept away, old shackles struck off, and for effecting this a few general principles were thought to suffice. The next generation was confronted by constructive work, a remodelling of old institutions in the effort to satisfy calls for social reorganization, a difficult task which needed more hard thinking and creative power than were forthcoming. Thus while the demands on representative assemblies were heavier the average standard of talent and character in their members did not rise. Never was it clearer than it is today that Nature shows no disposition to produce men with a greatness proportioned to the scale of the problems they have to solve.

Taking all these causes into account, whatever decline is visible in the quality and the influence of legislatures becomes explicable without the assumption that the character of free peoples has degenerated under democracy. It remains to enquire what have been the results of the reduced authority of representative assemblies. The power which has departed from them must have gone elsewhere. Whither has it gone?

In the several States of the American Union it has gone to the executive or to the people. The state governor has become a leading figure whenever he happens to be a strong man with some initiative, some force of will, some gift for inspiring that confidence which legislatures fail to command. Not often perhaps does such a man appear, but when he appears he counts for more than he would have done forty years ago. In an increasing number of States, the introduction of the initiative and referendum has narrowed the power of the representatives and transferred legislation to the citizens voting at the polls, while the recall has made members displaceable by a popular vote before their term comes to an end. All State legislatures have lost the function of choosing a US Senator, which has been now assigned to the popular vote, this being the only considerable change made in the federal system. Congress has fallen rather than risen, and the power of the President, when he knows how to use it, and happens to be a strong man who takes the fancy of the people, has been tending to grow.

The Constitutions of France and Great Britain have remained the same in form and on the whole in practice. But in France the recurring dissatisfaction with the frequent changes of ministry which intrigues in the Chamber bring about continues to evoke cries for a more stable executive. The discontent with 'parliamentarism' which nearly led to a *coup d'état* in 1888 may have serious consequences, especially if the steadying influence excited by the fear of external aggression should cease to operate. In Britain the House of Commons is still the centre of political life and the driving-wheel of government. But the power of the cabinet over the majority has grown as parties have stiffened their discipline, for majorities are strong in proportion to their docility. If that so-called 'control of the caucus' which British pessimists bewail really exists, it is not so much the tyranny of a party organization acting under the committees that manage it in the constituencies as an instrument in the hands of the party chiefs.

In Italy a somewhat different process seems to have made the Chamber more subservient than formerly to the ministry, for although the party system holds no great power, deputies are brought into line by the manipulation of patronage and benefits bestowed on powerful business interests or on localities. The Spanish Cortes, divided into a number of groups, each following its leader, are little regarded by the people, who have shown (except in Catalonia) scant interest in the exercise of their now widely extended suffrage.

In these European cases it is rather the moral ascendancy than the legal power of the legislature that has been affected. But when moral power droops legal power ceases to inspire affection or respect.

Can any useful conclusions, any lessons available for practice be drawn from these facts?

The mischiefs arising in the United States and (to a less extent) in Canada from the abuse, for electoral purposes, of legislative power in local and personal matters might be removed by stringent regulations, such as those which the British Parliament has imposed on the examination and enactment of private bills.

A scandal complained of in some countries might be reduced if a system of strict competitive examinations for posts in the civil service were to cut away the opportunities members have of misusing their position for the purposes of patronage, while the transfer to local self-governing bodies of the powers exercised in administrative areas by the central government, together with the discontinuance of grants from the national treasury for local purposes would, while saving public money, dry up a copious fountain of jobbery, for where the money to be spent comes from local taxes its expenditure is more likely to be carefully watched.[2] Anyhow the central legislature would be relieved from one form of temptation.

[2] Where, however, the undertaking extends over a wide area and has a national importance, national subventions may be unavoidable.

These are what may be called mechanical remedies for evils arising from defects in the mechanism of parliamentary institutions. With those causes of decline which are either independent of the legislatures themselves, or arise from the intensity of party spirit, or the indisposition of men qualified to serve their country to offer themselves as candidates—for these causes the remedies have to be sought elsewhere. Representative assemblies must remain the vital centre of the frame of government in every country not small enough to permit of the constant action of direct popular legislation; and even in such countries they cannot be altogether dispensed with. The utility which Mill and Bagehot saw in them remains, if perhaps reduced. The people as a whole cannot attend to details, still less exercise over the executive the watchful supervision needed to ensure honest and efficient administration.

PART II

NEW DIMENSIONS

MOVING BEYOND MONO-FUNCTIONALISM

INTRODUCTION

Studies of legislatures in the context of the wider political environment have focused usually on the relationship to government and the formulation of public policy. As the capacity to determine policy became centralized within the executive, and the capacity to choose the government passed elsewhere, so the perception of the decline of legislatures, voiced so notably by Bryce and a host of others since.

Recent work has served to look at legislatures in a different, broader, context: that is, in relation to citizens and the political system generally. What emerges is a much richer literature on the relevance of legislatures as instruments of regime support, having functions—defined, as by Packenham, as consequences for the political system—beyond that of 'law-making'.

Notable among such recent work are the three articles chosen for inclusion in this section. Samuel H. Beer identifies a paradox of British politics: a highly centralized capacity to make public policy but a weak capacity to implement it. In so far as Parliament can contribute to overcoming the problem of pluralist stagnation, it is through mobilizing consent for programmes of public policy, between as well as at general elections. Beer draws on US experience in order to identify the concept of consent mobilization. It is a concept that he does not develop in great detail, nor one which he seeks to discuss in a wider comparative context. None the less, it serves to move the focus of scholarly attention away from the narrow confines of the relationship of legislature to executive and has an important suggestive relevance for comparative legislative study.

While Beer identifies the function of consent mobilization, Robert Packenham—drawing on the experience of the Brazilian National Congress in the mid 1960s—identifies the multi-functional nature of legislatures. The eleven functions he pinpoints (under the three encompassing headings of legitimation; recruitment, socialization, and training; and political decision making or influence) are listed in order of their importance to the assembly he is studying. As he recognizes, the functions will vary in importance from legislature to legislature, that is, one legislature may have greater consequences for the political system in exerting influence (for example, the US Congress) than another, where legitimation may have the greatest impact (for example, the Brazilian National Congress). 'Specialists in legislative studies have not studied the functions of legislatures very much, but what knowledge we have suggests that the Brazilian case is much closer to the mode than the US Congress.' This is borne out by impressionistic evidence from developing countries (reproduced by Packenham, but not included here) which suggests 'even more strongly than I had originally anticipated, the hypothesis that legislatures do not usually allocate values but none the less perform other significant functions in the political system'. Packenham's taxonomy of functions provides a valuable framework for comparative legislative analysis, much richer than anything offered by earlier studies which focused on but one of the three main categories listed by Packenham.

While Beer has drawn attention to the significance of legislatures in mobilizing consent for particular programmes of public policy, and Packenham *inter alia* the importance of legislatures in generating consent for government (latent legitimation), John Wahlke has made a major contribution to the literature by drawing attention not to identifiable functions but rather to the concept of diffuse support, support for the political system being largely independent of specific demands channelled through legislatures and converted into policy preferences. Wahlke acknowledges that his work raises more questions than it answers: 'The question still is, how do representative bodies contribute to the generation and maintenance of support? In what respects and for what particular aspects of the task are they superior to non-representative institutions? These are questions to be answered by empirical research.'

In raising the questions, Wahlke points tentatively to

possible explanations. Diffuse support may derive not from specific decisions made but from the *way* in which they are made. Legislatures may thus justify attention not so much, or at least not solely, in terms of Lukes's first dimension of power (observable decision-making) but rather in terms of his third dimension (acceptance of the way the process works as a legitimate one).[1] From this perspective, legislatures are often powerful institutions. It is a perspective which also provides insights into the growth and continued prevalence of legislatures despite perceptions of their 'decline' in the making of public policy.

[1] S. Lukes, *Power: A Radical View* (London, 1974).

4

THE BRITISH LEGISLATURE AND THE PROBLEM OF MOBILIZING CONSENT

SAMUEL H. BEER

The tasks of legislatures change with the times. One of the newer and more important of these tasks, and one to which not nearly enough attention has been paid, is the function of mobilizing consent. Modern governments impose vast and increasing burdens on their citizens, not only in the form of deprivations in terms of money, time, effort, and so on—as in the payment of taxes or performance of military service—but, even more important in these days of the welfare state and managed economy, in the form of requirements of certain often intricate patterns of behaviour—such as conformity to wage and price 'guidelines'.

Yet the reasons for these impositions are usually technical, complex, and hard for the ordinary man to understand and make part of his personal motivation. If a government is to rule effectively, therefore, and since it cannot depend solely upon force, it must continuously mobilize consent and win acceptance for its policies. The legislature is one of the agencies that helps perform this task.

THE PARADOX OF POWER

This function of mobilizing consent, I wish to emphasize, is not one of the traditional functions of the legislature. It is certainly not the representative function by which in greater

Samuel H. Beer, 'The British Legislature and the Problem of Mobilizing Consent', in E. Frank (ed.), *Lawmakers in a Changing World* (Englewood Cliffs, NJ: Prentice-Hall, 1966), 30–48. Reprinted by permission of the author.

or lesser degree the legislature brings the grievances and wishes of the people to bear upon policy-making. It does not refer primarily to the kind of consent that is involved when the voters at an election give their approval to a certain body of men and/or to a certain programme of proposals. On the contrary, it is especially the consent that must be won in so far as the voters did not originate or mandate the policies being imposed upon them.

British experience in recent years illustrates vividly this new necessity of modern government. On the one hand, we find there a governmental system that might seem to satisfy all the conditions for decisional effectiveness. 'Of all governments of countries with free political institutions', Professor Bernard Crick has written, 'British government exhibits the greatest concentration of power and authority. Nowhere else is a Government normally as free to act decisively, so unfettered by formal restraints of Constitutional Law, by any Federal divisions of power, by any practice of strong and active local government, or by any likelihood of defeat in the Parliament.'[1]

Yet in recent years, according to many British critics, this powerful system has performed weakly. The burden of their complaint is not that it has been illiberal or undemocratic, but that it has been ineffective—in particular, ineffective in meeting the great but surely not unmanageable problems of the British economy. Here is a country that was once the workshop of the world. Yet year after year it has lagged behind the other economies of the free world. British government, it is alleged, must bear a large share of the responsibility.

It is this paradox that I wish first to develop. Why does a government so superbly equipped to govern not have a better record of achievement? Once the conditions of this paradox have been made clear, we can turn to the question of what role Parliament might have in overcoming it. This becomes precisely the question of how to enhance its role in mobilizing consent.

The decline of parliament. When we say that the British government is powerful we mean in the first place that it

[1] B. Crick, *Reform of Parliament* (London, 1964), 16.

concentrates great authority in the executive. The tradition and practice of a strong executive in Britain go back at least to Tudor times. Yet there have been ups and downs within that tradition and it will be useful to take a quick look back to the nineteenth century if we wish to understand the conditions which today support a balance of power weighted heavily in favour of the executive and against the legislature.

In this historical perspective by far the most important change in the position of Parliament has been the decline to the vanishing point of the probability that a cabinet will be defeated in the House of Commons . . . Today if a British government wins a party majority in the House of Commons at a general election, it can confidently count on that majority supporting it until the next general election. In Britain this is an age not of parliamentary government, but of cabinet government.

When one asks why this great shift in the balance of power between executive and legislature has taken place and what conditions maintain this powerful executive today, the principal clue may seem to be provided by the political party. Judged by modern standards, party discipline sat lightly on the shoulders of those mid-Victorian MPs and party cohesion was at a low ebb. Today an MP may still vote against his party on a rare occasion; rather more often he will express his dissidence by abstaining. But when one makes a statistical study of party voting, the figures are so monotonously 100 per cent or nearly 100 per cent that it is hardly worth making the count. If this is an age of cabinet government, the reason in the first instance is that it is an age of party government.

Yet even a superficial glance at other legislatures will force us to take our inquiry into causes a step or two farther, for the strengthening of the executive against the legislature has been a general development in the modern world and has taken place even where party government on the British model has not been present. The United States is the obvious illustration. In this century and especially since the New Deal our presidency has radically shifted the balance of power in its favour and against the Congress. Yet party cohesion is still low in comparison with British behaviour and has shown little significant increase in this century. Indeed, statistically speaking, party voting reached its peak not under Franklin Roosevelt or Lyndon Johnson, but under William McKinley.[2]

The conditions that have strengthened the executive may work through party, as in Britain, but they go beyond party. First among them, of course, has been the war. As has often been remarked, military operations are peculiarly the function of the executive. They take swiftness and secrecy in decision, for neither of which qualities legislatures are well known. They also require a kind of specific and *ad hoc* action which can hardly be derived from the application of general rules and which therefore comes more readily from the executive than the legislature. Parliamentary government, and legislatures generally, flourished during that great, abnormal century of peace that stretched from the Battle of Waterloo to the First Battle of the Marne. These present decades of war and cold war are inevitably an age of the executive.

Yet it is not only defence activities that have expanded the powers of the executive. Economic and social policy—the intervention of government in the management of the economy and the development of the welfare state—constantly make new calls upon executive action. The complexity and technicality of the issues put the administrator in a far better position than the legislator to make and adjust the rules for control of these growing sectors of government action. It is not, however, just technicality and complexity that are important, but rather what one may call *the increasing specificity of the essential governmental decision.*

The contrast I wish to draw is between government by specific decision and government by general rules. Any government, of course, involves decisions if there is to be action at all. But in the past it has been the expectation in Britain, as in the United States, that these decisions—by the policeman, the judge, the civil servant—could and would be largely controlled by laws cast in general form. Where, however, government gets as deeply engaged in the management of economic and social affairs as has British government, it must increasingly rely less upon general laws and more upon specific managerial decisions. . . .

[2] J. Turner, *Party and Constituency: Pressures on Congress* (Baltimore, 1951), 28; *Congressional Quarterly*, 23/45 (5 Nov. 1965), 2246.

Largely for these reasons, the practice of delegating legislative power to the executive has grown immensely in recent times. In making these delegations of power, Parliament contents itself with a broad authorization to the executive which then determines the more specific provisions. Law-making by the executive under such authorizations now greatly exceeds regular parliamentary legislation, at least in quantity, the 'statutory instruments' embodying such acts of executive law-making numbering between two and three thousand a year, some of very great length and complexity.[3]

My object here is not to praise or to lament these developments, but to show their connection with the present status of the legislature in Britain. First I want to point out how this new type of decision, the managerial decision, in economic and social affairs is remarkably similar to the traditional type of decision made by men in charge of military operations. In this respect, the managed economy and war have drawn power to the executive for essentially the same reason. Secondly, I hardly need stress the important fact that as general rules become less useful to the executive in its modern efforts to manage and control the economic and social environment, so also will that great, traditional source of general rules, the legislature, probably lose its central place in the governmental system. The decline of the legislature in Britain is deeply rooted in a new pattern of policy—the managed economy and the Welfare State—which in greater or lesser degree has forced itself forward in all self-governing countries.

The new group politics. So far, the sketch I have drawn of British government is very one-sided: a vast extension of power over society and a sharp centralization of power in the executive. But there is another side of this profile of power that makes the picture as a whole more complex and less one-dimensional. The key element is the pressure group.[4]

Pressure groups are nothing new in Britain. One can trace

[3] Erskine May, *Treatise on the Law, Privileges, Proceedings and Usage of Parliament*, ed. B. Cocks (17th edn., London, 1964), 610.

[4] In this discussion of group politics, I am for the most part summarizing from my book, *British Politics in the Collectivist Age* (New York, 1965), esp. ch. 12.

them back to the earliest days of representative government there. In the nineteenth century they were a major agent of political change, inspiring much of the legislation of that great age of reform. The typical pressure group of the period was a voluntary association of like-minded people who joined together to push their agitation, often for a single piece of legislation, and who might well disband once their aim had been achieved. One thinks of the Anti-Corn Law League, that model of successful middle-class reformist agitation.

The pressure groups of the present period of collective policy and politics are strikingly different. In Britain as in the United States, the centre of the stage is occupied by organized bodies of producers representing the main sectors of a highly industrialized economy. These are the big three of business, labour, and agriculture, along with the professions—doctors, teachers, civil servants, and others.

In social base, structure, purpose, political tactics, relations with government, and the foundations of their political power these bodies greatly differ from the transient, voluntary associations of like-minded reformers which sought to win Victorian Parliaments over to their schemes of reform. The primary base of their power is the vital productive function that their members perform in the economy. If government is to control or calculably influence the performance of this economic function, it must have their co-operation. It must have access to their advice—the information and expertise which is possessed only by those actually doing the work—and especially, it must enjoy a degree of acceptance of its policy that is more than a mere grudging consent to 'the law'. An obvious example: you cannot operate an effective nationalized health service if the doctors refuse to work for the service, or, indeed, even if they are seriously discontented with the way it is run.

For these reasons, the officials of these organizations have over the years been drawn into a vast, complex scheme of consultation with government departments. Officially in a series of advisory committees that runs into the hundreds and less formally in constant, daily contacts, the representatives of producer groups have been joined with departments of the executive in a system of functional representation that operates outside and alongside the established system of parliamentary representation. . . .

I call this arrangement of formal and informal contacts a system of representation because, in fact, the process of consultation is far from being a one-sided relation in which government merely listens to what the organized interests have to say and then decides its course regardless of their wishes. The very fact of government's large dependence on these bodies means that their wishes will have great weight. Looking at this new system of functional representation as a whole, one must recognize that it involves a process of bargaining as often as one of mere consultation. The *ad hoc* managerial decision is precisely the type of decision that one would expect to come from such a process of bargaining, and a large proportion of the business of economic management is performed in this network of functional representation.

I have stressed this system of functional representation, with its bargaining and its managerial decisions, because these are the most important and novel features of the new group politics in Britain. Yet the dramatis personae include not only producers, but also consumers. I am thinking here not of consumers in the technical economic sense, but of groups of people whose material well-being is affected in the same way by some measure of government action, actual or prospective. While the concerns of the producer groups are focused mainly on the programmes of the managed economy, the concerns of these consumer groups are directed toward the array of services provided by the Welfare State: social security, housing, education, and the like. These groups include old-age pensioners, health service patients, tenants of state housing, and similar beneficiaries of the social services. I do not mean, of course, to try to draw a physical line of distinction between producers and consumers, for obviously every person is normally both, and producers' organizations—trade unions for instance—will be concerned with welfare programmes as well as with government controls on their economic behaviour.

While the producers' interests are put forward mainly in relations with the executive, consumers' interests are especially the subject of party competition. For the past twenty years or so the two big parties in Britain have been fairly evenly matched in terms of popular support. As a result they have been forced into a sharp and continuous competition for the support of groups benefiting from the services of the Welfare State; competition bidding up promises of better pensions, housing, education, and the like has been a common feature of general elections. This use of terms from economics is appropriate. For if 'bargaining' is characteristic of the group politics of the new system of functional representation, 'bidding' is the word for the mode of competition in the parallel system of parliamentary and party representation.

In this complex manner, then, a new group politics has arisen simultaneously with, and yet as a counterbalance to, the extension and centralization of control over British society. We may breathe a sigh of relief for the liberties of the subject, for these processes of group representation are a formidable apparatus for protecting and forwarding the interests of certain minorities. Indeed, it takes no great imagination to see that the danger may be just the opposite from what a first glance at British government might suggest: that is, it is the danger not of oppressive efficiency, but rather of pluralistic stagnation. . . .

In crucial fields of policy one can convincingly establish a connection between the new group politics and tendencies to inaction and stagnation. Two critical failures of British economic policy will illustrate the point. Since the war the rate of economic growth of the British economy has consistently lagged behind that of the other principal countries of Western Europe. One major reason for this lag has been the relatively low proportion of national product used each year for net new investment in manufacturing. There is no simple explanation for this lag. Yet the situation has certainly not been helped by politics favouring expenditure on consumption. In so far as resources are diverted to satisfy immediate consumption needs—whether through individual purchase or provision by the welfare state—there will be that much less available for enlarging Britain's productive capital. I do not suggest that the choice is an easy one for a government to make—especially when its margin of favour with the electorate is constantly threatened by a competitor bidding for the votes of the same consumer groups in which the government itself has found crucial support.

A second and related problem has been inflation. With almost cyclical regularity the British economy has fallen into a crisis in its balance of payments with the rest of the world. Typically a cause of the trouble has been an inflationary rise of prices. While there has been no single cause of these price rises, very often the pushing up of wage costs by trade union pressure and by competition among employers for scarce labour, has been an important contributing factor. In order to meet this problem, governments—both Labour and Conservative—have attempted to establish what has come to be known as an 'incomes policy'. This means in simplest terms some form of restraint on wages and other income so that they rise no more than productivity.

One might well think that since inflation and payments crises are so obviously against the interests of all groups, it should not be too difficult for government to arrange a bargain with unions and managers that would result in the necessary restraint. And governments have devoted great efforts and much time to the bargaining process. Yet even when the official representatives of the groups have been able to agree, it has been difficult, if not impossible, to win acceptance of the policy of restraint among the rank and file and among leaders at lower levels. The failure of government policy in this crucial area of economic concern has been one of the most striking examples of how the new group politics has flourished undaunted by the imposing powers of modern British government.

The economic problems of which I have spoken are essentially political problems. I do not deny that there is a good deal more that economists would like to know about the causes of inflation and the conditions of economic growth. At the same time, modern economic analysis does give governments far greater understanding of these matters than was possessed by governments and their advisers in the 1920s and 1930s. The problem is therefore not so much to devise economic programmes, which, if they were carried out, would meet the problems. It is rather to win such understanding and acceptance of government programmes among the public, as individuals and as members of producer and consumer groups, that they will adjust their own behaviour to the requirements of these programmes. The central problem in short is to win consent—and winning consent is a political problem and a political process.

WHAT CAN PARLIAMENT DO?

My paradox is complete: a system which by the very extension and centralizing of power undertaken to deal with modern problems has set in train political consequences that make it exceedingly difficult to deal with those problems. The question now is: Has Parliament a role in helping Britain overcome these essentially political difficulties?

The functions of parliament traditionally and today. It may help us to see the possibilities if we briefly consider some of the conventional views of the functions of legislatures in general and of Parliament in particular. I will take these in the chronological order in which they have flourished, but I want to emphasize that in greater or lesser degree they still give us insight into what actually goes on today.

One of the oldest conceptions of the role of Parliament is that of controlling and restraining the executive. An acute Tory thinker of the last generation claimed that throughout British history, from the origins of the constitution in the Middle Ages, this had been the essential function of Parliament. In the view of L. S. Amery, there are and always have been two main elements in British government: one is the central, initiating, energizing element—formerly the monarchy, today the cabinet—while the other is the checking, criticizing, controlling element—the Parliament, and nowadays especially the opposition.[5] The task of the government is to govern; the task of Parliament is to criticize and control—that is, to present grievances and to let the ministers and bureaucrats know what the people will not stand. . . .

The opportunities for criticism are clear enough, but may one also speak of them as a means of control? To be sure, in

[5] L. S. Amery, *Thoughts on the Constitution* (2nd edn, London, 1953), ch. 1.

these days of monolithic majorities, such criticism is not expected to result in defeats for the government—not, at any rate, in defeats serious enough to cause a resignation or dissolution. Yet such criticism is not without influence. By building up points in these debates, the opposition may hope to sway voters when they next go to the polls. Moreover, one cannot neglect the real though immeasurable influence that criticism may have without reference to electoral consequences. The House itself is a community with its own standards of excellence in the light of which, quite apart from party considerations, reputations are made and lost. Furthermore, this community blends with a special public linked by communication centres such as the clubs of Pall Mall, university common rooms, and the editorial offices of the better daily newspapers and weekly political journals. No self-respecting minister or civil servant can enjoy having acts of injustice or stupidity for which he is responsible exposed to the scrutiny and comment of such circles in the House and adjacent to it. . . . To be sure, only the voters can ultimately withdraw or confer power. But not the least of the sweets of power is to use it in such a way as to earn the praise of a discriminating public. Otherwise, one may have power without glory.

This criticizing and controlling function of Parliament, although perhaps its most ancient task, is still important today. Another function, that first became prominent in a later historical period, however, gives the legislature a more positive role. In the light of this function, the essential task of the legislature is to legislate, to make laws—in a fundamental sense, to lay down the lines along which the country will be governed. Two major historical views that attribute this function to Parliament are the Liberal and the Radical.[6] The Liberal conceived of Parliament as performing this law-making function under the guidance of its own sense of what was right and prudent without regard to pressure from the outside. In short, he took Parliament to be a deliberative body, making its determinations in response to reasons and forces arising within it. According to the Radical democrat,

[6] I have discussed these attitudes and theories in *British Politics in the Collectivist Age*, ch. 2, 'Liberal and Radical Politics'.

Parliament was also to be the chief law-maker, but with the important proviso that it express the will of the people. In some versions, this relationship was to be secured by means of a party programme approved by the voters at a general election and conceived as giving the government a 'mandate' to carry out what was promised.

Today, of course, Parliament is not the chief law-maker, if by that we mean that it lays down a set of general rules which so far control the actions of administrators that they need merely apply them by deduction to particular cases. As we have previously observed, a continually larger proportion of government action consists of managerial decisions governed only broadly by statutory authority and formulated in many cases by the *ad hoc* bargaining of public and private bureaucrats. Moreover, even those broad statutory grants of power to the executive have not originated with the rank and file of the legislature. The initiative in legislation, as in other policy-making, is exercised almost exclusively by the executive. . . . Indeed, not only does the Government largely monopolize the initiative in drafting and proposing bills to Parliament, it also gets substantially all legislation for which it asks . . .

Yet, again speaking in terms of realities, we cannot neglect the influence of the legislature, in particular the parliamentary party upon which the government depends for its 'mechanical majorities'. When the governing party went to the country, it took a position on many public questions. It may have presented a detailed programme; at the least, it gave an impression of its broad approach to problems. This public stance in part reflects and in part creates a body of ideas and sentiments among the party's MPs which the government cannot easily disregard. 'Collectively and individually,' D. N. Chester has recently written, 'Ministers cannot get far out of line with the views of their supporters in the House. The electoral campaign and Party manifestoes, the basic attitudes of active Party members, are as much part of the heritage of the Government as of their supporters and almost as compulsive on their actions.'[7]

[7] D. N. Chester, 'British Parliament', paper presented at the Conference on the Future of the Legislative Power, Princeton University, 14–17 April 1966, p. 19.

An ancient task of the party whips is to keep leaders informed of feeling among the rank and file and of whether the limits of their loyalty are being approached. A more modern instrument for taking such soundings and for enabling leaders to anticipate disaffection is provided by the elaborate organization of back-benchers that has grown up in both parties in the past fifty years and especially since World War II. In both parties there are regular weekly meetings of what we could call the party caucus; in addition there are many specialized committees roughly corresponding in their subjects of concern with the main departments of state. In both parties leaders keep in touch with these meetings, and discussion at them can be fierce when the party is divided over some question of policy or leadership. If the ancient function of criticism is nowadays performed especially by the opposition, the more modern function of keeping the actions of government in line with its electoral commitments depends in no small degree upon such pressures from the back-benchers of the governing party.

As a model of what actually goes on, the notion of Parliament as chief law-maker, whether in its Liberal or Radical versions, is a gross distortion—a common fate of models. Yet it does give us a systematic insight into a function of the legislature that is a necessary supplement to the view that Parliament's role is to criticize and control. At times Parliament does behave as a deliberate body—for instance, when amending bills in the less partisan atmosphere of standing committee where the special knowledge of members has a chance of being attended to by civil servants, ministers, and other MPs.

Moreover, although pure mandate theory is an exaggeration, Parliament performs its criticizing and controlling function in the context of a lively system of democratic and party politics. It is the principal forum from which the parties appeal to voters for their support in the next general election. 'Governing', writes Professor Crick, 'has now become a prolonged election campaign.' 'Parliament', he goes on to observe, 'is still the agreed arena in which most of the continuous election campaign is fought,' and the principal device by which 'the Parties obtain something like equal access to the ear of the electorate in the long formative period between the official campaigns.'[8] One must not exaggerate the attention given to Parliament. Those newspapers that carry reasonably full reports of parliamentary debates are read by only 11 per cent of the population—that is, rather more than five million persons. About the same number (though not necessarily the same people) have been identified as the 'serious public' who declare themselves to be 'very interested' in political affairs and who follow them between elections.[9] These people are only a fraction of the total electorate, but as opinion leaders they play an important role in the formation of the opinion that is expressed at elections.

To mobilize consent. There are two aspects of this opinion that are of interest to us. On the one hand, it includes those 'electoral commitments' which were made by the leadership of the winning party and will be in some degree pressed on that leadership by their parliamentary followers. This aspect of the electoral process is a primary concern of traditional democratic theory which emphasizes the flow of public will into governmental action by means of such commitments. In this view, voters use elections to oblige government to follow their wishes.

For the purposes of this chapter however, another aspect of the electoral process is more important. This is the fact that these 'electoral commitments', so to speak, commit not only the government, but also the voters. They constitute a set of expectations—some specific, most rather vague—about the future course of government policy which the voters in substantial numbers have shown themselves to share. These expectations originated with the public itself probably in only a few instances and in a very distant sense. As our previous discussion suggested, they may well have been initially communicated to the electorate by means of the party battle in Parliament. The important point is that the expectations, however they originated, have laid a foundation of consent and acceptance for relevant government programmes in the future. A first step in mobilizing consent has been taken.

[8] Crick, *Reform of Parliament*, pp. 25–6.

[9] R. Rose, *Politics in England* (Boston, Mass., 1965), 89; id., *Influencing Voters: A Study of Political Campaigning in 1964* (London, 1967), ch. 11. n. 19.

With some stretching of democratic theory, we may say that this process is one way in which the legislature fulfils its representative function. The voters did not originate the commitments and there was perhaps some 'dependence effect'[10] in the way they were brought to accept them. Still, the electorate made the choice and the legislature, more or less faithfully, carries out its will. It is immediately clear, however, that such an expression of popular will—such a set of commitments and expectations—can realistically control the course of government in only the most limited sense. Many—and quite possibly the most painful—decisions will have to be taken after the election.

How to legitimize these decisions may be a problem for democratic theory. Our concern here is to point out that winning consent for them among the people they affect will certainly be a problem for the government. For modern government cannot and does not rely solely upon the legitimizing effects of periodic elections. It must make continuous efforts to create consent for new programmes and to sustain consent for old ones. *It must mobilize consent between as well as at elections.*

In so mobilizing consent, various elements of British government make a contribution. The 'exhortations' to which ministers resort from time to time in an effort to win voluntary co-operation with some painful policy have not been uniformly successful. Still, the kind of leadership ministers provide, and especially the confidence the prime minister is able to arouse, are vitally important. Likewise, the spirit and the incentives that government imparts to the bargaining process can make a difference. My concern here, however, is briefly to suggest the possibilities of an enlarged role for Parliament.

I do not know of a theoretical exploration of this function by a political scientist. It has, however, been recognized as an important function of the American Congress by one of the most effective and scholarly of the new generation in the US

[10] 'A society becomes increasingly affluent,' writes J. K. Galbraith, 'wants are increasingly created by the process by which they are satisfied.' e.g. 'producers may proceed actively to create wants through advertising and salesmanship'. Galbraith calls this 'the dependence effect': *Affluent Society* (Boston, Mass., 1958), 158.

House of Representatives. Writing of 'the emerging role of Congress', John Brademas has isolated and described an important aspect of the modern legislator's relationship with his constituents. Referring specifically to the recently enacted education, anti-poverty, and medicare programme, he reports that as he travelled around his district, he was constantly questioned by 'state and local authorities, officials and private organizations and individuals on how the programmes work'.

It is more than a question of red tape and filling out applications. Many local leaders may not understand the purposes of the legislation or see its relevance to their communities. The Congressman or Senator, by organizing community conferences, mailing materials and in other ways, can supply important information, interpretation, justification and leadership in his constituency. . . . These activities of explaining, justifying, interpreting, interceding, all help, normally, *to build acceptance for government policy*, an essential process in democratic government. . . .[11]

When Congressman Brademas writes of how the legislator can 'build acceptance for government policy' he means exactly what in this paper has been called mobilizing consent. In his illustration he refers to programmes which have already been enacted into law, but which are not understood or fully accepted even among those whom they benefit. That he sees the necessity to 'build acceptance' for these particular programmes is especially interesting, as they are concerned with direct 'welfare' benefits rather than more remote objectives, such as economic growth. Yet even in the case of such 'popular' programmes and among people who stand to benefit from them, he finds a need to 'build acceptance'.

The welfare state and the managed economy bring many benefits, but inevitably they also impose many new and complex coercions—often in the very process of conferring benefits. A great deal is expected of the citizen in the form of new necessities that oblige him to conform his behaviour to the complex requirements of economic and social policy. On the one hand, the burdens that government imposes on

[11] J. Brademas, 'Emerging Role of the American Congress', paper presented at the Conference on the Future of the Legislative Power, pp. 11, 12. My emphasis.

citizens are very demanding and, on the other hand, the reasons for these impositions are often highly complex and technical. To win both the mind and the heart of the citizen to an acceptance of these coercions is a major necessity, but a severe problem. And if, as Congressman Brademas shows, this problem is substantial in our own country, it is far more acute in Britain where welfarism and economic management have become more comprehensive and elaborate.

The democratic process, focused by the legislature upon periodic elections, can do a great deal to meet this problem. Yet much more is required—a more continuous, intimate interchange between authority and those subject to authority. The process of policy-making itself in so far as it is carried out in public, can be shaped as a means of winning consent to the very coercions then being explained, defended, and attacked. If I may again quote Professor Crick: 'The truth is that if anything useful and significant is to be done in a free society, it must be done publicly and in such a way as to consult, involve and carry with it those affected.'[12] *Consent in this instance does not spring from some previous interaction of government and voter at a general election, but is the constantly renewed product of a continual exchange of communications.*

In performing the function of winning consent in either of these modes, Parliament displays glaring inadequacies and as one goes through the current literature advocating reform of Parliament, one can catch many glimpses of how these inadequacies might be remedied. I refer those interested in the detail of these proposals to Professor Crick's excellent little book, *The Reform of Parliament.* Here I shall simply bring out a few main points.

In the first place, the level of secrecy should be reduced. It is not plausible to expect people to identify with the output of the governmental process when only the product and not the process itself is revealed to the public gaze. Defence matters no doubt require much secrecy. So also in Britain does the system of party government and cabinet responsibility by which sharp conflicts within a party, a cabinet, or the Civil Service are removed from public knowledge and scrutiny. Too

[12] Crick, *Reform of Parliament*, p. 177.

much public scrutiny could—as the example of Washington, DC, warns us—exacerbate personal relations and abrade the channels of communication and decision within the Whitehall machine.

Yet it is nevertheless clear to the growing body of British critics that the level of secrecy in British government is excessively high. The reporting of parliamentary news is faulty. Party leaders in office and in opposition hold too few press conferences. The restraints on reporters at Westminster are too strict. Another area in which the veil of secrecy could be lifted is the parliamentary party. Already the debates in meetings of the parliamentary parties seep out, often in distorted form. It would add greatly to the vitality of British government if the press were admitted on a regular basis to these debates.

If the public is to be given a greater sense of participation, not only must secrecy be reduced, but MPs must be given better instruments for understanding, explaining, and—inevitably—criticizing what the government is doing. A major reform toward this end would be to substitute for the present non-specialized committees of the House, a system of committees, each with a sphere of competence parallel to one or more ministries. Such committees would take the committee stage of bills, but more important they would have some of the functions of reviewing administration—'legislative oversight'—that the specialized committees of Congress perform. The essential point is that such a committee system would not only enable MPs themselves to gain some competence in a substantive field of government, but would also provide a focus for public attention upon government action in these fields. For the same general purpose, MPs need much more expert staff assistance. The specialist committees should have such staff and the House Library should be expanded.

A government today is strong for any purpose—economic, social, or military—only so far as it can mobilize consent among its citizens. As events of recent decades have shown, democratic governments are more likely to have this power than non-democratic governments. A leading instance is the comparative war effort of democratic Britain and Nazi Germany. Although it started far behind Germany in mobilizing its resources for war, Britain was much more successful in total mobilization. After the war, the German Minister for War Economy, Albert Speer, said: 'You won because you made total war and we did not.'

Today Britain confronts the political problem of breaking through the politics of stalemate and at once releasing and concerting untapped energies among her people. There is no simple solution to this problem and no single agency of government or politics can be expected to cope with it. It is, however, essentially a task of mobilizing consent in which the legislature could be given a much more important role.

5

LEGISLATURES AND POLITICAL DEVELOPMENT

ROBERT A. PACKENHAM

What Fenno[1] has written of studies of Congress applies also to the entire field of comparative legislative study: 'these are the best of times, these are the worst of times'. These are the best of times because there is greater interest in, and able attention to, some facets of legislative study than there has been in years, perhaps ever. These are the worst of times because these studies are disproportionately focused on American legislatures—especially the US Congress—and because even in these studies some of the most crucial questions (notably, the consequences for the rest of the political system of legislative activity) are virtually ignored. Outside the United States, and especially in the so-called Third World countries, knowledge of legislatures, and their relationship to other political institutions and processes, is extremely limited.

If one accepts for the moment the premiss that existing knowledge is limited, what does this admittedly limited knowledge suggest about the consequences—which I call the functions—of legislative activity for the political system? It suggests that the principal function of most of the world's legislatures is not a decisional function. Most of them, that is to say, do not allocate values, or at least do not have this as their principal function. Other functions—i.e. legitimation and recruitment and socialization to other political roles—

Robert A. Packenham, 'Legislatures and Political Development', in A. Kornberg and L. D. Musolf (edd.), *Legislatures in Developmental Perspective* (Durham, NC: Duke University Press, 1970), 521–37. Reprinted by permission of the publisher.

[1] R. F. Fenno, jun, Review, *American Political Science Review*, 58/4 (Dec. 1964), 975.

seem to be more important. Satisfactory concepts, methods, and data for determining with precision which functions are more and less important—and what important means—do not exist currently (or, if they exist, they are not used very much). But judgements, based on the best tools, data, and intelligent thinking available, can and must be made.

If one wants to 'do something' about legislatures as a means to promote political development, then one must know something about the relationship between legislatures and political development. In particular, it would seem crucial to know the likely consequences of 'strengthening' legislatures for other parts of the political system and for the capabilities of the political system as a whole. Yet it is precisely about these questions—the consequences of legislative activity—that existing knowledge is least impressive. Since knowledge of present and past consequences of legislative activity is, I believe, so imperfect, anyone seeking to change legislatures in any way has very little basis for predicting what the consequences of such changes will be for other parts of the political system and for total system performance. What little we do know suggests that strengthening legislatures in developing countries would, in most cases, probably impede the capacity for change which is often crucial for 'modernization' and economic development. . . .

[T]here seems to be no commonly accepted list of functions which legislatures perform quite aside from the issue of how to rank their importance in different countries. Thus, my functions are *ad hoc*, but no more so than those utilized by other scholars. The foregoing comment recognizes, incidentally, that everyone who has written about legislatures is, explicitly or implicitly, a functionalist. That is to say, everyone writing about legislatures says or assumes that legislatures have consequences for the political system at large and provides some indication of what he thinks those consequences are. In short, in *this* sense, we are all functionalists.[2]

[2] 'Function' has many meanings in the social sciences and even within political science. For example, Ernst Nagel cites six meanings of the term, only one of which is 'consequence', the meaning used throughout this paper: see *Structure of Science* (New York, 1961), 523–5. When I say 'we are all

THE FUNCTIONS OF THE BRAZILIAN NATIONAL CONGRESS

To begin with, I should like to specify . . . the functions of the Brazilian Congress from April 1964 to July 1965.[3] I must emphasize that what follows is an interpretation based mostly on impressionistic evidence of these functions. No more than this is possible at this time. To put this functional analysis in perspective, it may be helpful to recall very briefly the context of legislative activity during this period.[4]

The Brazilian Congress has seldom been a 'strong' legislature. Certainly this is true since 1930. During most of the period from 1930 to 1945 the personal apparatus of President Getúlio Vargas effectively contained the ability of the Congress to allocate values. From 1946 to 1964 Brazil formed a democracy, with a constitutional political system largely patterned after that of the United States. But the Brazilian Congress was seldom if ever as powerful as the US Congress, even though its influence varied during this period.

On 2 April 1964 the Government of João Goulart was toppled in a coup dominated by the military. On April 9 an Institutional Act was promulgated by a three-man military revolutionary council. Besides calling for the election by the Congress of a new president for Brazil—who turned out to be, under military pressure, Army Chief of Staff Humberto Castello Branco—this (first) Institutional Act had two provisions which restricted the legislative function of the Congress. First, it enabled the president to require any bill sent by him to the Congress to be considered within thirty days by each

functionalists', I mean functions as consequences, *not* as 'functional requisites', a concept and term I never imply in this chapter.

[3] The reasons for this is that between Sept. 1964 and July 1965 I lived in Brasilia, studying the Brazilian National Congress, esp. the lower house or Chamber of Deputies. This experience stimulated my interest in the questions treated in this chapter, and led to the research about other legislatures and to the analysis and critique of paradigms in the broad field of comparative legislative study which are reported here.

[4] For the most complete and well-documented treatment of Brazilian politics between 1930 and 1964, see T. F. Skidmore, *Politics in Brazil, 1930–1964: An Experiment in Democracy* (New York, 1967).

house (thus allowing a maximum of sixty days), or at his discretion within thirty days for both houses in joint session. Any bill not considered and rejected within the period specified automatically became law. Second, it provided that only the president could initiate bills creating or increasing public expenditures. Nor could either house add amendments to presidential bills which would increase expenditures.[5] These provisions substantially reduced the value-allocation function of Congress. Hitherto, the authority to take almost unlimited time to consider bills had given it a veto power of substantial weight; and the authority to raise public expenditures had enabled it to play a role, however limited, in the allocation of financial resources. With these two options closed, the Congress lost much of what genuine lawmaking function it had had. And it was to lose even more of this function after 27 October 1965.[6]

Some other features of the first Institutional Act deserve mention here. The proclamation which accompanied the text itself of the Act declared:

> The victorious revolution invests itself with the exercise of the Constituent Power, which manifests itself either through popular election or revolution. Thus the victorious revolution, like the Constituent Power, legitimizes itself. It destroys the former government and has the capacity to constitute the new government. In it is contained the normative strength inherent in the Constituent Power. The leaders of the victorious revolution, thanks to the action of the Armed Forces and the unequivocal support of the nation, represent the people and in their name exercise the Constituent Power, which only the people truly hold [*de que o Povo é o único titular*].
>
> The present Institutional Act can only be issued by the victorious revolution, represented by the Commanders-in-Chief of the three

[5] Text of the *Ato Institucional*, arts. 3–5.

[6] The second Institutional Act of 27 Oct. 1965, and subsequent amendments to the Constitution, further restricted the powers of the Congress. See Institute for the Comparative Study of Political Systems, *Brazil: Election Factbook Number 2* (suppl.; Washington, Nov. 1966), 3, 28. From that date to Mar. 1967, when a new Constitution took place in Brazil, the Congress was even less powerful than it had been from Apr. 1964 to July 1965. The Constitution of 1967 incorporated many of the main features of the Institutional Acts regarding presidential–congressional relations.

armed services . . . Only they can appropriately state the norms and processes for constituting the new government and provide for it [the new government] the powers and juridical instruments which may assure the exercise of power in the exclusive interest of the country. In order to demonstrate that we do not intend to radicalize the revolutionary process, we have decided to maintain the Constitution of 1946, restricting ourselves to modifying it only regarding the powers of the president of the Republic . . . In order to reduce still further the complete [*plenos*] powers of the victorious revolution, we equally resolve to maintain the National Congress, except for the reservations with respect to its powers contained in this Institutional Act.

It is thus quite clear that the revolution does not seek to legitimate itself through the Congress. It is rather the Congress which receives from this Institutional Act, the consequence [resultante] *of the exercise of the Constituent Power inherent in all revolutions, its legitimacy.* [My translation, emphasis added]

Two points may be noted about this passage. First, there is the attempt to justify, in terms of a democratic ideal and 'the people', what was obviously an unconstitutional seizure of power. Second, there is an explicit assertion, little emphasized in the subsequent rhetoric of the revolutionary government, that the revolution does not derive its legitimacy from the Congress, but rather vice versa. Both features warn both mass and élites alike that the revolutionary group in the military means to rule, constitutional traditions notwithstanding. But the references to popular sovereignty, and the fact that the substance of the final two sentences was seldom, if ever, publicly emphasized after the Institutional Act was issued, reveal that the revolutionary group did not want to push its point too far. For the maintenance of an active congress, even if that action had little consequence for the allocation of values in Brazilian politics, was an important determinant of the legitimacy of the revolutionary government, despite what the proclamation declares.

Now I may proceed to offer some hypotheses about the functions of the Brazilian Congress from April 1964 to July 1965. I shall discuss these functions roughly in the order of their importance, i.e. starting with the ways in which the Congress—especially the Chamber of Deputies, the lower house—had the greatest consequences for the Brazilian political system, and proceeding to the ways in which it had the least consequences.

Consider three processes in the Brazilian political system: legitimation, or the production of acquiescence in, and/or support of, the moral right to rule of the government by the members of the political system (including the population at large as well as political élites); recruitment, socialization, and training to élite political roles; and political decision making or influence. My hypothesis is that the Brazilian legislature accounted for, or caused, a higher proportion of this totality of legitimation than it did of either of the other two processes, and that it accounted for a higher proportion of the totality of recruitment, socialization, and training to élite political roles than it did of the totality of political influence.

Indeed, whenever anyone speaks of the more and less important functions of legislatures, he usually if not always employs this kind of construct, although it is seldom made so explicit. Different functions may be more important in different political systems: for example, in the US Congress, it may be that influence is a more important function than recruitment, socialization, and training to other élite political roles. Whenever functions are defined as consequences of legislative activity, however, characterizing any function as the most important one usually means that it is the process or set of processes—among all those processes for which the legislature has consequences—on which the legislature has its largest impact. That is, it causes a higher proportion of that total process than it causes of any other process. Note that this does not at all mean that the legislature produces or causes more of the process than any other institution or phenomenon. The comparisons are among the consequences of legislative activity, not between the consequences of legislative activity and the consequences of the activity of other institutions or phenomena.

THE LEGITIMATION FUNCTION

The legitimation function may be broken down into three types, all of which share the common characteristic of fostering acquiescence in, or support for, the moral right to rule of the government among the population at large as well as political élites.

Legitimation as a latent function. The Brazilian Congress during this period performed a latent legitimizing function in so far as its activities had the consequence of legitimizing the government in power at the time, even beyond what was intended or understood by the legislators. Simply by meeting regularly and uninterruptedly, the legislature produced, among the relevant populace and élites, a wider and deeper sense of the government's moral right to rule than would otherwise have obtained.

This was perhaps less well understood by legislators, journalists, and the populace at large, than by some élites in the military. It was in this sense an unintended consequence of the Congress's activity. For many legislators, the regular meetings of the legislature were perceived as a check upon the government in power. There was some small truth in this perception; but more important, and also more striking, was the tacit and dimly perceived sanctioning of the government which their very activity symbolized and nurtured. In short, the legislators, including and perhaps especially those in opposition, thought that their vigorous debates and the widely reported accounts of their activities in the press constituted a sharing of power with the military and the president. The fact, however, was that they were, even where their debate and activities had little or no consequence for élite decision-making, enhancing the power of the president in so far as congressional activity legitimized his role and thus provided him with a less costly means for exercising his power.

It is important to stress that this function was performed without many legislators and other élites being aware of it, no matter what decisions were taken by the legislature, and no matter how little or how much power was exerted by it. For the executive, backed by the military, there was always a way around a negative decision by the legislature in response to one of the executive's proposals. In fact, such negative responses seldom came, but even when they did, they were circumvented relatively easily. It seems fair to say that during this period the executive branch did not once fail to achieve its will on any crucial issue because of constraints imposed upon it by the legislative branch. This was true even though the legislators always had at least a minimal chance to reject the proposals of the executive and on some minor issues managed to do so. In light of this, it appears that the most important function of the Brazilian Congress during this period was to legitimize, both in this latent as well as in an overt or manifest sense, the actions of the government in power. Whether the legislature made decisions which appeared to have a significant impact upon recommendations from the executive, or whether in fact it had a relatively minor impact upon such recommendations, this function was being performed.[7]

Legitimation as a manifest function. A second important function of the Brazilian legislature was the familiar one of putting the legislative stamp of approval on initiatives taken elsewhere. This legitimizing function is distinguished from the previous function by the overt, conscious, and widely understood character of this legitimation, and by the fact that the Congress had to approve presidential initiatives for it to take effect. It is the legitimation function of legislatures as conventionally understood.

Like the latent legitimizing function, this manifest legitimizing function was performed not only in the domestic but also

[7] So far as I can tell from reading and discussions with Brazilians, the only times since independence that the Brazilian Congress has been totally and indefinitely closed down or dissolved—as opposed to temporarily suspended—were during the periods from 1823 to 1826; from 1891 to 1894; from 1930 to 1934; and from 1937 to 1945. The rest of the time the Congress has been open and active, even though sometimes limited by or under attack from presidential emergency powers under the Constitution, Institutional Acts, and other measures. It is noteworthy that these three periods are among the few in Brazilian history in which the federal government is regarded as having been controlled by a type of dictator (Dom Pedro I, Floriano Peixoto, and Getúlio Vargas), the present period excepted for the moment. The foregoing paragraph was written in 1967. In Dec. 1968 the Brazilian Government failed to gain legislative support for a measure to suspend the immunity of two critical legislators. It then suspended congressional sessions indefinitely and entered into a period of harsh authoritarian rule in which all pretence of democracy was abandoned. The indefinite suspension of Congress was one of a series of actions for which the regime paid dearly in the coin of legitimacy. Legislative sessions were resumed in 1970.

in the international sphere. Many Brazilian élites, including congressional élites, were aware that the Castello Branco regime acquired legitimacy in the international political system, and perhaps especially with respect to the United States, by virtue of allowing the Congress to remain open and carry on its activities at least formalistically.

The 'safety-valve' or 'tension-release' function. One of the most important functions of the Brazilian Congress was to provide 'safety-valves' for those tensions generated by the political process. Once again, completely aside from the decision-making powers which the Congress had, its activities had significant consequences for the political system in so far as they reduced tension, provided reassurance, and generally enhanced satisfaction with or acquiescence in the policies and programmes of the ruling government. In this sense, the Congress was a safety-valve or way of letting off steam in a political system where nobody got all he wanted and/or where the government was not willing to let everyone have what he wanted. This seems to be one important explanation for the strikingly large percentage of press space devoted to the activities of the Congress during a period when its decision-making power was extremely low. Plenary session debates, committee meetings, party and factional strategy sessions, individual legislators' statements—all these activities were widely reported in the press, even though they seemed to make little difference for the allocation of values in the Brazilian polity. But they were a device for the release of tensions among both the relatively impotent legislators (who debated, met, spoke) and various layers of the attentive public (who read about the activities and thus gained some symbolic reassurance that the government was 'democratic' and 'vital').[8]

THE RECRUITMENT, SOCIALIZATION, AND TRAINING FUNCTIONS

Another function of the Brazilian Congress, less important

[8] For some interesting theorizing about these and other symbolic uses of politics and political institutions see M. Edelman, *Symbolic Uses of Politics* (Urbana, Ill., 1964), esp. pp. 31–3.

than the ones just discussed but significant nonetheless, is that the legislature recruits, socializes, and trains politicians to and for other roles in the political system in which they may wield more power than they do as national legislators. For example, some politicians gain experience in the legislature which enables them to go on to other posts like governorships, national ministries, state ministries, and the like. They learn the norms of the élites, they learn political skills, and they acquire visibility and prestige resources which are useful to them in acquiring, maintaining and utilizing these other roles. In this sense, the activities of the Brazilian Congress constitute a training ground for Brazilian politicians. This activity has consequences for the political system at large which are significant and which are quite independent of any decision-making or influence functions which it may or may not have.

THE DECISIONAL OR INFLUENCE FUNCTION

The Brazilian Congress sometimes makes decisions that 'count'; it allocates values; it gets somebody to do something he otherwise would not do. In short, it sometimes has influence. What follows details some of the ways and some of the circumstances under which this takes place.

The law-making function. Occasionally, on some issues at some times, the legislature exerts power in the traditional sense of the term '*legislation*'. During the 1964–5 period, the activities of the Brazilian Congress produced little law-making in this sense. The proportion of bills initiated by the Congress which became enforced law was infinitesimal. The proportion was higher before 1964, though still small. From 1945 to 1964, particularly during the Governments of Getúlio Vargas (1951–4) and João Goulart (1961–4), the power of the Congress in terms of vetoing recommendations made by the executive branch was sometimes substantial. However, this power was drastically reduced after the 1964 coup.

In terms of modifications of recommendations from the executive branch, there have been some exceptions to the generalization above. Examples of these would be the congressional modifications of the Agrarian Reform Bill of 1964 and even of the new Constitution which was instituted in 1967. In both of these instances, as in a few others, significant modifications were made through negotiations with the Congress. But it seems fair to say that the executive branch had the power to override even the restrictions thrust up by the Congress. It could have closed down the Congress, passed the laws as originally formulated, and the government would probably have continued. The costs would have mainly taken the form of legitimacy costs for the Castello Branco administration.

The 'exit' function. Under certain specific, relatively infrequent, but recurring conditions in Brazilian politics, the National Congress performs what may be called an 'exit' function. When the political system seems to have reached an impasse and the mechanisms for decision-making which normally characterize Brazilian politics seem incapable of providing a way out of the situation, the élites sometimes turn to the legislature for either the substance or the form, or both, of a decision which will take the system out of the impasse. This 'exit' function is a special case of the decision-making function.

No such function was performed by the Brazilian Congress during 1964–5, but there are examples in recent Brazilian political history. In November 1955 the military and the nation were split over whether the president–vice-president ticket of Juscelino Kubitschek and João Goulart, which had won the election, should taken office. There were rumours that Acting President Carlos Luz, together with some other political and military officials, planned a preventive coup and were already taking steps toward this end. At about the same time other groups, also both military and civilian, but led by War Minister Henrique Lott, initiated a counter-coup to assure that Kubitschek and Goulart might take office. By November 11 it was clear that the latter group had won. Congress went into session that same day. By a strictly partisan vote, the Chamber of Deputies recognized Neren Ramos, the Speaker of the Senate and next in line according to the Constitution, as the new president. But it did not vote to impeach Luz the Acting President. Nor did it vote any sanctions against him or President Café Filho, who was then 'on leave' due to illness. It is a reasonable view that the coup and the vote of the Chamber were both wholly unconstitutional; at best, they were highly debatable. There was no attempt in the Congress to prove that 'either Luz or Café Filho or any of their ministers were guilty of the plot whose prevention was the justification of Lott's coup'.[9] Thus, it seems that the Congress had gone outside the Constitution, under military pressure, to help legitimize the victorious coup in the name of constitutionality. The ploy was not fully successful; the incident left a legacy of bitterness among the losers; and on 22 November when Café Filho announced that his illness was over and he was ready to reassume his presidential office, the Chamber of Deputies responded again to military pressure by voting to disqualify him (Café Filho) from office and by confirming Nereu Ramos as president until the following January. The Chamber's action, nevertheless, probably gave the coup greater legitimacy than it otherwise might have had, and the Congress may have made some small contribution to the decision itself.[10]

Another example is the decision to change from a presidential to a semi-parliamentary form of government in September, 1961. This decision, the idea for which apparently had its origins in the Congress, grew out of a conflict over whether João Goulart the Vice-President should be allowed to assume the presidency upon the sudden, unexpected resignation of President Jânio Quadros on 25 August. The controversy over this issue brought the nation literally to the verge of civil war. Because the military was divided, a compromise solution, proposed first by a congressional commission and then adopted by the whole Congress, carried the day. This solution provided that Goulart could assume the presidency, as the Constitution indicated, but it included also a constitutional amendment providing for a cabinet of ministers nominated by the president but serving at the pleasure of the Chamber of Deputies. Thus, the powers of the president were severely limited: this was the price demanded by the opposition to Goulart. Once in office, Goulart spent fourteen months

[9] Skidmore *Politics in Brazil*, p. 156.
[10] See ibid. 146–58 for details.

manœuvring himself into a position where he could reclaim the full powers of his office through a successful national plebiscite.[11]

The interest-articulation function. Debate in Congress, and press attention to this debate, do receive some attention from powerful Brazilian élites in the executive branch and the military. Although attention by these élites to such reflections of 'public' opinion is not nearly so great as the proportion of space devoted to them in the press would suggest, they do have consequences for the political system. By representing or articulating 'public' interests in some sense, Congressmen do exert a limited amount of influence. The linkages between Congressmen and wider publics in Brazil are, in general, extremely imperfect. Nevertheless, this 'interest-articulation' function is worth noting, even though it is less important than the ones mentioned so far.

The conflict-resolution function. Classically, legislatures are often thought of, especially in normative terms, as an ideal place for political interests to be presented, negotiated, and resolved. Any institution that could negotiate and resolve conflicts would be exercising a form of influence. The study of interest groups has shown that in many political systems such activities and functions occur much more in the bureaucracy and elsewhere, and less in legislatures, than had long been assumed. Nevertheless, the literatures on legislatures in the United States and elsewhere indicates that students of legislative behaviour still consider this function to be one of the most important ones which legislatures perform.

Such is not the case with respect to the Brazilian Congress since 1964. Legislators, as legislators, are not significant brokers for political interests. Since the Congress has little decision-making power as an institution, it makes little sense for interest group representatives to present their demands to Congressmen and to try to have political conflicts resolved in Congress. The Congress did play a role in this respect from 1945 to 1964, although it was a limited one. Even this role has been greatly reduced since 1964.

The administrative-oversight and patronage functions. The Brazilian

[11] Ibid. 200–23.

Congress is not very effective as a check upon the bureaucracy. Its political and other resources for exercising this kind of influence are extremely limited. This situation has been intensified by the physical shift of the Congress to Brasília, because 90 per cent or more of the administrative apparatus of the federal government has remained in Rio de Janeiro. Moreover, dismayed as American Congressmen may be by their inability to control cabinet secretaries and bureaucrats in the American political system, they would be appalled at the plight of their counterparts in Brazil. Brazilian ministers seldom testified before congressional committees, which are active but not in the sense of chastising cabinet ministers. On the few occasions when cabinet ministers presented themselves to Congress, they usually made formal appearances before plenary sessions. In these the ministers spoke from a rostrum ten feet above the floor of the Congress and delivered long initial speeches, which could not be interrupted by congressional questions, and which were subject to only a limited number of scheduled questions (resembling short speeches) after the formal address. Most important, the restrictions in the first Institutional Act of 1964 and the new Constitution of 1967 with respect to control of federal budgets virtually deprived the Congress of the most powerful tool, classically, for legislatures to control the executive branch.[12]

Legislators who have control over financial resources thus have an instrument—patronage—which can be used to exert influence. But since this control has been so severely restricted, the patronage function has not been very important either. Nor is 'errand-running'—casework, as it is called in the United States—translated into very much political influence. Congressmen in Brazil vary in the degrees to which they run errands to the bureaucracy for their constituents, but, in general, there was little of this activity during the period from 1964 to the present. Many deputies are indifferent about it and do it only for personal friends. Others make an effort but are severely limited in their capacity to carry on such activities by lack of staff and the capacity for indifference (which the

[12] For these provisions in the new Constitution of 1967 see O. D. Pereira, *A Constituicão do Brasil (1967); Introducão, Cotejas, e Anotacões* (Rio de Janeiro, 1967), 16–67.

legislators have little power to permeate) of the bureaucrats. This activity was considerably more important, it should be noted, during previous administrations when, among other differences, the Congress had the option of increasing the total size of the budget. This option was foreclosed by the first Institutional Act and the Constitution of 1967.

The foregoing account of the functions of the Brazilian Congress is designed to indicate the variety and, more importantly, the relative importance of the functions which the Congress seems to perform in the political system. These functions are derived inductively. They grow out of an examination of the Brazilian case. They are not 'functional requisites' for any legislature, although they are probably found in most of them. No claim is made for the special and unique correctness of this set of functions as opposed to another set which others might advance. However, what is emphasized here is that however the functions of the Brazilian Congress are defined or divided up, the influence function (or something like it) in its various forms is less important—and what 'important' means here was indicated above—than the other two functions (or something like them) in their various forms. Despite the fact that its power has been drastically reduced, in terms of decision-making, since 1964, it is too simple to characterize this Congress only as a 'rubber stamp' or 'notary public' to certify executive decisions, as journalistic and other accounts frequently do. In fact, even if it had no decision-making power whatsoever, the other functions which it performs would be significant. These other functions must, it seems to me, be taken into account in assessing the role of the legislature in political development in Brazil. They would also seem to be relevant to any assessment of technical assistance to legislatures as a means for promoting political development.

THE FUNCTIONS OF LEGISLATURES IN SOME OTHER DEVELOPING COUNTRIES

Is the Brazilian case between 1964 and 1965 unique? Is it one of only a minority of cases where the legislature does not allocate values but has other significant functions? Or is it more like most of the legislatures of the world than the US Congress?

Specialists in legislative studies have not studied the functions of legislatures very much, but what knowledge we have suggests that the Brazilian case is much closer to the mode than the US Congress. Moreover, the functions of most legislatures seem to be so different from those of the US Congress that it seems most unrealistic to expect that they can be made to operate even reasonably similarly in the foreseeable future. Perhaps more importantly, most of the legislatures of the world seem to have functions which do not fit at all closely the assumptions about functions adopted by most studies of legislatures. Although most studies use the working assumption that the principal function of legislatures is to allocate values, this seems not to be the case for the vast majority of the world's legislatures. . . .

6

POLICY DEMANDS AND SYSTEM SUPPORT: THE ROLE OF THE REPRESENTED

JOHN C. WAHLKE

Discontent with the functioning of representative bodies is hardly new. Most of them were born and developed in the face of opposition denying their legitimacy and their feasibility.[1] Most have lived amid persistent unfriendly attitudes, ranging from the total hostility of anti-democrats to the pessimistic assessments of such diverse commentators as Lord Bryce, Walter Lippmann, and Charles de Gaulle.[2] Of particular interest today is the discontent with representative bodies expressed by the friends of democracy, the supporters of representative government, many of whom see in recent history a secular 'decline of parliament' and in prospect the imminent demise of representative bodies.[3]

Much of the pessimism among the friends of representative government appears, however, to be very poorly grounded.

John C. Wahlke, 'Policy Demands and System Support: The Role of the Represented', *British Journal of Political Science*, 1 (1971), 521–37. Reprinted by permission of Cambridge University Press. This is a revised version of a paper originally presented at the 7th World Congress of the International Political Science Association in Brussels, Belgium, 18–23 Sept. 1967.

[1] The best analytical surveys of representation theory are those of A. H. Birch, *Representative and Responsible Government* (Toronto, 1964), and Alfred de Grazia, *Public and Republic* (New York, 1951).

[2] Bryce's views are expressed, e.g. in *Modern Democracies* (London, 1921), ii. 335–57. Lippmann's can be found in *Public Opinion* (New York, 1946), esp. pp. 216–20. While General de Gaulle has, of course, not contributed formally to literature of this kind, Gaullist views are well known from various speeches, debates, and publication preceding the creation of the Fifth French Republic. They are conveniently discussed in R. C. Macridis and B. E. Brown, *De Gaulle Republic* (Homewood, Ill., 1960), 124–31.

[3] J. P. Clark, *Congress: The Sapless Branch* (New York, 1964); *Senate Establishment* (New York, 1964).

The notion that we are witnessing 'the decline of parliament', it has been observed, 'has never been based on careful inquiry into the function of parliaments in their presumed golden age, nor into their subsequent performance'.[4] Neither has it rested on careful inquiry into the functions and roles of citizens, individually and collectively, in a representative democracy. Indeed, it is both possible and likely that, 'If there is a crisis . . . it is a crisis in the theory of representation and not in the institution of representation.'[5] This paper suggests how (and why) we might begin to reformulate representation theory and to identify the critical questions which research must answer.

Much of the disillusionment and dissatisfaction with modern representative government grows out of a fascination with the policy decisions of representative bodies which, in turn, reflects what may be called a 'policy-demand-input' conception of government in general and the representative processes in particular. Theorists and researchers alike have long taken it for granted that the problem of representative government centres on the linkage between citizens' policy preferences and the public-policy decisions of representative bodies. Almost without exception they have conceived of the public side of this relationship in terms of 'demands' and the assembly side in terms of 'responses'. Julius Turner, for instance, has said that, 'the representative process in twentieth-century America involves . . . the attempt of the representative to mirror the political desires of those groups which can bring about his election or defeat'.[6] Almond and Verba, in the course of explicating new dimensions of civic behaviour (to which we shall return) take the making of demands to be the characteristic act of citizens in democratic systems: 'The competent citizen has a role in the formation of general policy. Furthermore, he plays an *influential* role in this decision-making process: he participates through the use of explicit or

[4] G. Loewenberg, *Parliament in the German Political System* (1966; 2nd edn., Ithaca, New York, 1967), 1.

[5] H. Eulau, 'Changing Views of Representation', in I. de Sola Pool (ed.), *Contemporary Political Science: Toward Empirical Theory* (New York, 1967), 55.

[6] J. Turner, 'Party and Constituency: Pressures on Congress', *Johns University Studies in Historical and Political Science*, 69/1 (Baltimore, Md., 1952), 178. My emphasis.

implicit threats of some form of deprivation if the official does not comply with his demands.'[7]

THE SIMPLE DEMAND INPUT MODEL

The basic elements in the general policy-demand-input conception can be described, in necessarily over-simplified form, as follows. The principal force in a representative system is (as it ought to be) the conscious desires and wishes of citizens, frequently examined in modern research on representation under the heading of 'interests'. Interests are thought of as constituting 'policy demands' or 'policy expectations', and the governmental process seems to 'begin' with citizens exerting them on government. Government, in this view, is essentially a process for discovering policies which will maximally meet the policy expectations of citizens. There are several points at which emphases or interpretations may vary in important respects, but the critical assumptions of this view and the points at which such variations may occur can readily be outlined.

In the first place, the interests which constitute the fundamental stuff of democratic, representative politics are most often thought of in terms of specific policy opinions or attitudes, i.e. preference or dislike for particular courses of government action. But it is also common to envision citizens holding less specific policy preferences, in the form of ideological orientations or belief systems.

Although 'interests' are taken to be rooted in individual desires, they may be expressed in the form of either individual policy opinions (often aggregated by opinion analysts as 'public opinion' or the opinion of some segment of the public), or organized group or associational opinion, usually thought to be expressed on behalf of the individuals by group agents or spokesmen, or, of course, in both forms simultaneously.

[7] G. A. Almond and S. Verba, *Civic Culture* (Princeton, NJ, 1963), 214. More recently Almond has specifically identified this kind of model as a sort of paradigm for developed representative political systems, listing 'responsiveness' (to demand inputs) as a capability of the most developed political systems: G. A. Almond, 'Developmental Approach to Political Systems', *World Politics*, 17 (1965), 183–214, esp. pp. 197 ff.

Analytically, the core of the representative process is the communication of these various forms of interest to governmental actors, which is thought to occur in either or both of two principal ways. It may take place through constituency influence, i.e. the communication of aggregated individual views by constituents to their 'representatives'. (The latter term theoretically includes administrative agency personnel, police officials, judges, and countless other governmental actors, but we shall deal here only with members of representative bodies.) Communication may also occur through group pressure or lobbying activities, conceived of as communication by group agents who are intermediaries between representatives and the aggregates of citizens for whom they (the group agents) speak.

The critical process for making representative government democratically responsible is, of course, election of the representatives. Elections are the indispensable mechanism for ensuring a continuing linkage between citizens' public-policy views (interests) and the public policy formulated by representatives (in co-operation, needless to say, with executives and administrators). The mechanism works in one or both of two ways. It may provide representatives with a mandate to enact into public policy at an early date the policy views expressed in the elections. It may also serve to legitimize, by stamping the imprimatur of citizen acceptance on, the policies most recently enacted by the representatives.

However logical and obvious such a conception of democratic representative governmental processes may seem, the observed behaviour of citizens is in almost all critical respects inconsistent with it. Some of the more important established propositions about observed behaviour which conflict with assumptions about the role of policy-demand inputs in politics may be listed here, even though there is no room to list in detail the evidence supporting them. They are, in most instances propositions which are well known, although not normally brought to bear in discussions of representation:[8]

[8] See, e.g. the familiar discussion in B. R. Berelson, P. F. Lazarsfeld, and W. N. McPhee, *Voting* (Ch., Ill., 1954), 305–23. The particular propositions listed here are supported, in every instance, by survey data from various political systems collected at various different times. Although systematically

1. Few citizens entertain interests that clearly represent policy demands or policy expectations, or wishes and desires that are readily convertible into them.
2. Few people even have thought-out, consistent, and firmly held positions on most matters of public policy.
3. It is highly doubtful that policy demands are entertained even in the form of broad orientations, outlooks, or belief systems.
4. Large proportions of citizens lack the instrumental knowledge about political structures, processes, and actors that they would need to communicate policy demands or expectations if they had any.
5. Relatively few citizens communicate with their representatives.
6. Citizens are not especially interested or informed about the policy-making activities of their representatives as such.
7. Nor are citizens much interested in other day-to-day aspects of parliamentary functioning.
8. Relatively few citizens have any clear notion that they are making policy demands or policy choices when they vote.

analysed in the original research for this paper, the data are not reported here because of limitations of space. The more relevant compilations and commentaries include the following: H. Cantril, *Pattern of Human Concerns* (New Brunswick, NJ, 1965), 167–71; H. Cantril and M. Strunk, *Public Opinion 1935–46* (Princeton, NJ, 1951); A. Campbell, P. E. Converse, W. E. Miller, and D. E. Stokes, *American Voter* (New York, 1960); P. E. Converse and G Dupeaux, 'Politicization of the Electorate in France and the United States', *Public Opinion Quarterly*, 26 (1962) repr. in A. Campbell *et al.*, *Elections and the Political Order* (New York, 1966), 269–91; P. E. Converse, 'New Dimensions of Meaning for Cross-Section Sample Surveys in Politics', *International Social Science Journal* 16 (1964), 19–34; R. A. Bauer, I. de Sola Pool, and L. A. Dexter, *American Business and Public Policy* (New York, 1963); D. E. Stokes, 'Spatial Models of Party Competition', *American Political Science Review*, 57 (1963), repr. in A. Campbell *et al.*, *Elections*, pp. 161–79; R. Axelrod, 'Stucture of Public Opinion on Policy Issues', *Public Opinion Quarterly* 31 (1967), 51–60; E. Noelle and E. P. Neumann (edd.), *Jahrbuch für öffentliche Meinung*, iii (1958–64), (Allensbach and Bonn: Verlag fur Demoskopie, 1965); W. N. McPhee and W. A. Glaser (edd.), *Public Opinion and Congressional Elections* (New York, 1962); L. D. Epstein, 'Electoral Decision and Policy Mandate: An Empirical Example', *Public Opinion Quarterly*, 28 (1964), 564–72; and W. Buchanan, 'Inquiry into Purposive Voting', *Journal of Politics*, 18 (1965), 281–96.

None of this, of course, is new or surprising information. But it is sometimes forgotten when working from slightly less naïve models of the representational system than the one sketched out above. Each of the alternative models familiar to students of representative bodies, however, must sooner or later reckon with these facts.

A RESPONSIBLE-PARTY MODEL

Whatever else they are doing in the electoral process, voters in most political systems are certainly choosing between candidates advanced by political parties. It is therefore easy to assume that electoral choice between party candidates is the vehicle for making policy choices and to derive logically plausible mechanisms by which that choice might be made. For such mechanisms of demand input to operate, several requirements would have to be met. In the first place, there must be a party programme formulated and it must be known to the voters. Second, representatives' policy-making behaviour must reflect that programme. Third, voters must identify candidates with programmes and legislative records, and base their choices on reaction to them.[9] The arguments against the American party system and in favour of the British on grounds of systematic capacity for meeting these requirements are well known.[10]

In most American contexts, the failure of party and legislative personnel to provide appropriate policy cues makes the applicability of the responsible-party model dubious to begin with, no matter what voters might be doing. But there are also signs of voter failure to respond appropriately to whatever such cues might be available. In one American state (Washington), for example, far less than half the public knew which party controlled either house of the state legislature at its most recent session (41 per cent in the case of the lower,

[9] D. E. Stokes and W. E. Miller, 'Party Government and the Saliency of Congress', *Public Opinion Quarterly*, 26 (1962), 531–46, repr. in Campbell *et al.*, *Elections*, pp. 194–211.

[10] Committee on Political Parties of the American Political Science Association, 'Toward a More Responsible Two-Party System', *American Political Science Review* (suppl., 1950).

27 per cent for the upper house).[11] Shortly after the 1966 election in the United States, 31 per cent of the electorate did not know (or was wrong about) which party had a majority in Congress just before the election; more striking still, 34 per cent did not know which party had won most seats in that election and another 45 per cent misinterpreted Republican gains to believe the Republican Party had won a majority![12] With respect to public reaction to party at the national level, Miller and Stokes have demonstrated that party symbols are almost devoid of policy content, which is not surprising in view of what they call the legislative party 'cacophony'.[13] And Converse, in one of the few relevant studies using panel data, found that party identification was far more stable among American voters sampled in 1958 and 1960 than their opinions on any 'issues'.[14] We can only conclude, at least for the American case, that, with or without policy content, party symbols do not serve the American voter as the responsible-party model would wish.

Of somewhat greater interest, however, is the situation in those countries where it seems more likely that party and legislative leaders provide voters the conditions under which they could, if they chose, behave as the responsible-party model would have them. The British political system is usually cited as the classic example. What, then, are the facts about the connection between voting and policy preferences of British voters? Perhaps because it has been so commonly taken for granted that every general election in Britain constitutes an electoral mandate or at least an unfavourable judgment on past policy performance, surprisingly little evidence is available. The most direct testimony, from a nationwide survey of 1960, is that, given a question asking

[11] M. Showell, 'Political Consciousness and Attitudes in the State of Washington', *Public Opinion Quarterly*, 17 (1953), 394–400.

[12] University of Michigan Survey Research Center Study 0504, Preliminary Code Book, 1967, deck 02, col. 51, 52. I am grateful to Prof. W. E. Miller and the Inter-University Consortium for Political Research for their permission to cite this and other preliminary marginal tabulations.

[11] Stokes and Miller, 'Party Government and the Saliency of Congress', p. 209.

[14] P. E. Converse, 'Nature of Belief Systems in Mass Publics', in D. Apter (ed.), *Ideology and Discontent* (New York, 1964).

them to differentiate between the two major parties with respect to sixteen political ends or party traits, on only four of the statements did as many as two-thirds of the sample attribute a clear-cut goal to either party, and these were not stated in policy but in group (e.g. 'middle class') or personal terms; on four, some one-half or more were unaware of any difference between the parties, and on the remaining eight, between 33 per cent and 45 per cent detected no differences.[15] There is strong reason, then, to doubt the applicability of the responsible-party model even in Great Britain.

But the most persuasive reason for questioning that model is what we know about the phenomenon of party identification itself. For the mere fact that one political party (or coalition) is replaced in government by another as a result of changing electoral fortunes, together with the fact that voters are making electoral choices between parties, does not in itself demonstrate anything at all about the relationship between election results and the public's views about party programmes or policy stands. There is abundant evidence, on the contrary, that in many political systems voters identify with a political party much as they identify with a baseball or soccer team. Many voters in many lands are better described as 'rooters', team supporters, than as policy advocates or programme evaluators. The authors of *The American Voter* have acquainted us with the importance of that phenomenon in the United States.[16] Of special interest here is their finding that, far from serving as a vehicle for the voter to express prior formed policy views, it is more likely that 'party loyalty plays no small role in the formation of attitudes on specific policy matters'.[17] More recent studies seem to show that party identification of German voters is in some respects similar.[18] The very great

[15] M. Abrams, 'Social Trends and Electoral Behavior', *British Journal of Sociology*, 13 (1962), 228–42, repr. in R. Rose (ed.), *Studies in British Politics* (New York, 1966), (ed.), quotation from p. 136.

[16] Campbell *et al.*, *Elections*, esp. pp. 68–75.

[17] Ibid. 169.

[18] W. Zölnhofer, 'Parteiidentifizierung in der Bundesrepublik und den Vereinigten Staaten', in E. K. Scheuch and R. Wildenman (ed.), *Zur Soziologie der Wahl*, Sonderheft, 9 (edd.), (1965), *Kölner Zeitschrift für Soziologie und Sozialpsychologie* (Cologne and Opladen, 1965).

stability of party loyalties in Great Britain suggests strongly the operation of similar mechanisms there:

Not many people switch their votes in the course of their whole lives; therefore, the number changing in the short period between any two successive elections is necessarily small. On this definition, only 4 per cent of the electors in the Bristol sample [Bristol Northeast, 1951] were floaters . . .[19]

It can hardly be said, then, that the responsible-party model solves any of the theoretical problems encountered in the elementary atomistic model of representative democracy. If anything, it raises further and more serious ones.

POLYARCHAL AND ÉLITIST MODELS

Historically, the awareness that few human beings are politically involved or active was at the core of many anti-democratic theories. More recently it has been the starting assumption for various élitist conceptions of power structure, particularly at the level of local communities.[20] Still more recently the empirical accuracy of the assumption as well as the justifiability of 'élitist' conclusions drawn from it have been questioned and subjected to empirical research.[21]

Our concern here is not with the general theoretical problems raised by such approaches, however.[22] It is rather

[19] R. S. Milne and H. C. MacKenzie, 'Floating Vote', *Political Studies*, 3 (1955), 65–8, repr. in Rose (ed.), *Studies in British Politics*, pp. 145–9, quotation from p. 149.

[20] F. Hunter, *Community Power Structure* (Chapel Hill, NC, 1953). For a general commentary on this line of studies see N. W. Polsby, *Community Power and Political Theory* (New Haven, Conn., 1963).

[21] R. A. Dahl, *Preface to Democratic Theory* (Ch. Ill., 1956), esp. ch. 3; id., *Who Governs* (New Haven, Conn., 1961).

[22] Such problems are discussed in 'Electoral Studies and Democratic Theory', 1 'A British View', by J. Plamenatz, and 2 'A Continental View', by G. Sartori, *Political Studies*, 6 (1958), I–15; J. Walker, 'Critique of the Elitist Theory of Democracy', *American Political Science Review*, 60 (1966), 285–95, and the reply by R. A. Dahl, 'Further Reflections on "The Elitist Theory of Democracy" ', *American Political Science Review*, 60 (1966), 296–304; and P. Bachrach, *Theory of Democratic Elitism: A Critique* (Boston; Mass., 1967).

with their implications for the demand-input conception of representative processes. The chief implication, of course, is that policy demands and policy expectations are manifested by a relative few and not by citizens in general. This implication is hardly to be questioned. Summarizing relevant knowledge on the point, one article noted that 'Most recent academic studies of public attitudes . . . indicate differences between the political attitudes of elite groups and attitudes reflected in mass samples.'[23] And Converse and Dupeux have said that 'It appears likely that the more notable [Franco–American] differences stem from the actions of elites and require study and explanation primarily at this level, rather than at the level of the mass electorate.'[24]

The crucial question, then, concerns the extent to which and the mechanisms by which élites' policy-demanding activities are connected to the representational activities of the mass public. One possibility is that there is competition for different policy satisfactions among different élites, that this competition is settled initially in the governmental process, much as Latham has described the group process:

> The principal function of official groups is to provide various levels of compromise in the writing of the rules, within the body of agreed principles that forms the consensus upon which the political community rests. In so performing this function, each of the three principal branches of government has a special role.
>
> The legislature referees the group struggle, ratifies the victories of the successful coalitions, and records the terms of the surrenders, compromises, and conquests in the form of statutes.[25]

What Latham leaves unsaid is how members of the voting public enter into this process 'within the body of agreed principles that forms the consensus upon which the political community rests'. Does it, by electoral decision, provide the ultimate ratification of policies formulated in the process of compromise among élites (groups)? At the very most, one might look for some 'potential' power in the hands of the

[23] S. Verba, *et al.*, 'Public Opinion and the War in Vietnam', *American Political Science Review*, 61 (1967), 317–33, quotation from p. 318.

[24] Converse and Dupeux, 'Politicization of the Electorate', p. 291.

[25] E. Latham, *Group Basis of Politics* (Ithaca, New York, 1952), 35.

general public which it could use, if it wished, to ratify or reject policies and programmes thus put before it. But all the conceptions which made the simple atomistic and responsible-party conceptions implausible apply with equal force and in identical fashion against such an interpretation.

Thus, when we look for public participation through electoral choice among competing élites, we encounter the same difficulties we have encountered before. So-called polyarchal or élite–democracy models are no more helpful in connecting policy-making to policy demands from the public than were the atomistic and party models.

Demand-input emphases have tended also to colour our views of what constitutes responsible behaviour by elected representatives. Since the kind of findings just surveyed are well known, few modern studies consider Edmund Burke's 'instructed delegate model' appropriate for modern legislators.[26] Most report without surprise the lack of connection between any sort of policy-demand input from the citizenry and the policy-making behaviour of representatives.

Nevertheless, most empirical studies of representative behaviour accept the premiss that conformity between legislators' actions and the public's policy views is the central problem of representative government, usually envisioning some kind of role-conception or normative mechanism through which the agreement comes about. Thus Jewell and Patterson argue that high concern of representatives for their constituency is plausible in spite of the fact that legislators have low saliency in constituents' eyes.[27] And Miller and Stokes suggest still more specifically that, in spite of these facts, 'the idea of reward or punishment at the polls for legislative stands is familiar to members of Congress, who feel that they and their records are quite visible to their

[26] J. C. Wahlke, H. Eulau, W. Buchanan, and L. C. Ferguson, *Legislative System* (New York, 1962), 267–86; W. E. Miller and D. E. Stokes, 'Constituency Influence in Congress', *American Political Science Review*, 57 (1963), 45–56, repr. in Campbell *et al.*, *Elections*, pp. 351–73; and D. E. Stokes, 'A Variance Components Model of Political Effects', in J. Claunch (ed.), *Mathematical Applications in Political Science* (Dallas, Tex., 1965), 62.

[27] M. E. Jewell and S. C. Patterson, *Legislative Process in the United States* (New York, 1966), 351–2.

constituents'.[28] A study by John Kingdon suggests one interesting mechanism through which the moral obligation to represent constituency views might work: what he terms the 'congratulation–rationalization effect' leads winners of congressional elections to have higher estimates of voters' interest and information than do losers, and to attribute less importance to party label and more importance to policy issues in voters' actions at their election than do losers. Therefore,

> The incumbent is more likely than if he lost to believe that voters are watching him, that they are better informed, and that they make their own choices according to his own characteristics and even according to the issues of the election. Because of the congratulation–rationalization effect . . . [he] may pay greater attention to the constituency than otherwise, because he believes that his constituents are paying greater attention to him than he might think if he had lost.[29]

Perhaps the most persuasive explanation of the mechanism linking public views to legislative policy is that offered by Miller and Stokes. They compared representatives' votes in several policy domains to constituency opinion, representatives' personal opinion, and representatives' perceptions of their constituency's opinion, in order to determine the proportionate contribution of each to his voting. In brief, they found that constituency policy views play a large role for Congressmen in civil rights issues, but a negligible role in domestic welfare issues and no role in foreign-policy issues. Cnudde and McCrone, extending this line of research, demonstrated the primary importance of the Congressman's perceptions of his constituents' opinion in establishing whatever link there is from constituency through to legislative voting. That is, in civil-rights issues, Congressmen appear to shape their attitude to fit the opinions they think their constituency holds.[30]

[28] Miller and Stokes, 'Constituency Influence in Congress', p. 368.

[29] J. W. Kingdon, 'Politicians' Beliefs about Voters', *American Political Science Review*, 61 (1967), 144.

[30] Miller and Stokes, 'Constituency Influence in Congress'; C. F. Cnudde and D. J. McCrone, 'Linkage between Constituency Attitudes and Congressional Voting Behavior: A Causal Model', *American Political Science Review*, 60 (1966), 66–72.

These findings, while in some respects striking, are none the less ambiguous. From the standpoint of our understanding of representative government, the results of studies of the behaviour of representatives are as unsatisfactory as the studies of citizen behaviour seem disquieting. Many important questions are left unanswered, theoretically or empirically. Often the differences on which theoretically important distinctions are based are found to be small. Above all, in spite of the fact that legislative policy decisions are universally taken to be the most important type of legislative output, we know almost nothing about the character, let alone the conditions and causes, of how they vary in content. We now turn briefly to this problem.

'Policies' have been described as the most important variety of political output, and legislative policy decisions are commonly understood to be the most important type of legislative output.[31] It has been argued, therefore, that a major problem for legislative research is 'to achieve adequate conceptualization of legislative output, i.e. to specify the dimensions or variables of legislative output which are related to different consequences of that output'.[32] So it is rather startling to discover that the term 'policy' remains almost totally unconceptualized, i.e. that the literature provides 'no theoretically meaningful categories which distinguish between types of policies'.[33]

There is, however, a recent series of methodologically sophisticated but theoretically unstructured inquiries into possible variations in public policy which tends still further to challenge the relevance of demand-input conceptions to understanding the representative process. Most of these studies utilize the readily available masses of quantitative data about American states to analyse relationships among policy outputs and many possible correlates. Variations in policy output have usually been measured by the amount of

[31] D. Easton, *Framework for Political Analysis* (Englewood Cliffs, NJ; 1965), 125; id., *Systems Analysis of Political Life* (New York, 1966), 353 ff.

[32] Wahlke *et al.*, *Legislative System*, p. 25.

[33] L. A. Froman, jun., 'An Analysis of Public Policies in Cities', *Journal of Politics*, 28, (1967), 94–108.

money spent by a system on different categories of substantive policy or programmes such as public highways, health programmes, welfare, etc. Political variables investigated have usually been 'structural' in nature—for example, degree of two-party competition, degree of voter participation, extent of legislative malapportionment, and so on. Socio–economic environmental (or 'background') variables have included such things as degree of urbanization and industrialization, or education level.

It is the general import of these studies that, with only rare and minor exceptions, variations in public policy are *not* related to variations in political-structure variables, except in so far as socio–economic or environmental variables affect them and public policy variations together. Variations in policy output can be almost entirely 'explained' (in the statistical sense) by environmental variables, without reference to the variables supposedly reflecting different systems and practices of representation. Most far-reaching of such studies is Dye's examination of the effects of economic development (industrialization, urbanization, income, education) and political system (party division, party competition, political participation, and malapportionment) on ninety policy variables in four different policy fields. His conclusion:

> system characteristics have relatively little *independent* effect on policy outcomes in the states. Economic development shapes both political systems and policy outcomes, and most of the association that occurs between system characteristics and policy outcomes can be attributed to the influence of economic development.[34]

It is possible, of course, that these remarkable findings are unique to the American political system. That such is not the case, however, is strongly suggested by Cutright's discovery that variations in the national security programmes of seventy-six nations appear to be explainable directly in terms of economic-development level and to be unrelated to differences in ideology or type of political system (including differences between communist and capitalist systems).[35]

[34] T. R. Dye, *Politics, Economics and the Public: Policy Outcomes in the American States* (Chi., Ill., 1966), 293.

[35] P. Cutright, 'Political Structure, Economic Development, and National Security Programs', *American Journal of Sociology*, 70 (1965), 537–48.

There is a curious hint of similar findings in a study suggesting that changes in foreign policy do not seem to be associated with instances of 'leadership succession' so far as voting in the UN General Assembly is concerned; that is, there is apparently substantial continuity of foreign policy in any given system despite changes in political regime.[36]

In sum, then, the policy-environment correlation studies imply that stimuli which have been thought to be policy demands are really just automatically determined links in a chain of reactions from environment to policy output, a chain in which neither policy demands, policy expectations, or any other kind of policy orientation plays any significant role. There is no room, in other words, for any of the policy-related behaviours and attitudes of citizens which we examined in the preceding section of this paper to enter into the policy process.

The foregoing arguments are not especially 'anti-democratic' or 'anti-representative'. They are just as damaging to much anti-democratic theory and to élitist criticisms of representative democracy. It is not only policy-opinions of citizens in the mass public which are demoted in the rank order of policy determinants but policy opinions of élites and group leaderships as well. The principal implication is that 'policy-process' studies whose aim is primarily to discover the political bases of policy decisions conceived of as choices between policy alternatives contended for by divergent political forces, or to explain why a particular decision went one way instead of another, comprehend too little of the political life of man, and that the part they do comprehend is probably not its most vital. The appropriate conclusion is not the grandiose notion that representative democracy is chimerical but the limited recognition that our conceptions of government, politics, and representation are somewhat deficient, that 'policy-making' plays a different and evidently smaller role in the governance of society than we thought.

Precisely what role we cannot yet say, for neglect to study

[36] D. H. Blake, 'Leadership Succession and Its Effects on Foreign Policy as Observed in the General Assembly', mimeographed paper prepared for the Annual Meeting of the Midwest Conference of Political Scientists, Indiana, 27–9 Apr. 1967.

the political consequences of policy-making is 'a practice very much in line with the tradition of political science'.[37] Research on representation has tended toward preoccupation with the results of legislative roll-calls and other decisions, or the results of elections and series of them. It has concentrated on the antecedents of legislative 'output' and left unexamined the political 'outcomes' which above all make output an appropriate object of political study.[38] It has explored the possible sources of variations as small as a few percentage points in the influence of 'factors' influencing legislative and electoral decision, but ignored the relationship, if any, between legislative output and the incidence of discontent, riots, wars, civil wars, *coups d'état*, revolutions, and decay or integration of human groups. Its focus has been determined by 'political theories of allocation', in almost total disregard of the perspectives opened up by 'theories of systems persistence'.[39] This is an essential part of de Jouvenel's charge that political science has not so far had the 'dangerous' impact it might because it has so far been content to investigate only 'weak political behavior'.[40]

A plausible working hypothesis which directs the study of representation toward 'strong political behaviour' is provided by Easton's discussion of 'support'. Viewed from this perspective, previous studies are seen to presume that political systems stand, fall, or change according to the 'specific support' accorded them, the 'consent' granted 'as a consequence from some specific satisfaction obtained from the

[37] E. J. Meehan, *Contemporary Political Thought* (Homewood, Ill., 1967), 180.

[38] Easton describes this distinction as that between 'a stream of activities flowing from the authorities in a system' (outputs) and 'the infinite chain of effects that might flow from an authoritative allocation' (outcomes): *Systems Analysis*, pp. 349, 351.

[39] L. Lindberg, 'Role of the European Parliament in an Emerging European Community', in E. Frank, (ed.), *Lawmakers in a Changing World* (Englewood Cliffs, NJ, 1966), 101–28, quotation from p. 108. The same point has been made in J. Wahlke, 'Behavioral Analysis of Representative Bodies', in A. Ranney (ed.), *Essays in the Behavioural Study of Politics* (Urbana, Ill., 1962), 173–90, and is indirectly made by M. E. Jewell and S. C. Patterson, *Legislative Process in the United States* (New York, 1966), 528–31.

[40] B. de Jouvenel, 'On the Nature of Political Science', *American Political Science Reivew* 55 (1961), 773–9, quotation from p. 777.

system with respect to a demand that the members make.'[41] But the arguments above show that specific support, the support attaching directly to citizens' reactions to policy decisions, does not adequately describe the relationship between citizen and government. We must also recognize and take into account what Easton calls 'diffuse support', the support constituted by 'generalized attachment to political objects . . . not conditioned upon specific returns at any moment.'[42]

There is good warrant for the working hypothesis that,

> Except in the long run, diffuse support is independent of the effects of daily outputs. It consists of a reserve of support that enables a system to weather the many storms when outputs cannot be balanced off against inputs of demands. It is a kind of support that a system does not have to buy with more or less direct benefits for the obligations and responsibilities the member incurs. If we wish, the outputs here may be considered psychic or symbolic, and in this sense, they may offer the individual immediate benefits strong enough to stimulate a supportive response.[43]

The plausibility of such a starting-point has been intimated by other observers. Edelman's instructive discussion of the importance of 'symbolic' as compared with 'instrumental' satisfactions deriving from the administration of public policies clearly argues for it.[44] More directly concerning representative functions, Thomas Anton has shown, with respect to the roles of agency spokesmen, budget officers, legislators, and citizens in budgetary process of American states that 'what is at stake . . . is not so much the distribution of resources, about which state actors have little to say, but the distribution of symbolic satisfaction among the involved actors and the audiences which observe their stylized behavior'.[45] And Alfred de Grazia has discussed the ways in

[41] Easton, *Systems Analysis*, p. 268.

[42] Ibid., 272, 273. Easton himself later (note to p. 434) makes the much stronger assertion still that, 'Under some circumstances the need for outputs to bolster support may be reduced to the vanishing point.'

[43] Ibid., 273.

[44] M. Edelman, *Symbolic Uses of Politics* (Urbana, Ill., 1964).

[45] T. J. Anton, 'Roles and Symbols in the Determination of State Expenditures', *Midwest Journal of Political Science*, 11 (1967), 27–43, quotation from p. 39.

which 'the election process is symbolic and psychological in meaning, rather than a device for the purpose of instructing delegates'.[46]

That the problem of support is a proper springboard for representation research is suggested also by some commentators on the functions of representative bodies. Almost thirty years ago, T. V. Smith spoke of the 'cathartic function' of legislatures, which by themselves appearing as scapegoats, harmlessly conduct away disaffections that otherwise 'might well totalize into attacks upon public order'.[47] More recently, Eulau and Hinckley have pointed out that representative bodies perform 'such latent functions . . . as consensus-building, interest aggregation, catharsis for anxieties and resentment, the crystallization and resolution of conflicts, and the legitimization of decisions made elsewhere in the political system'.[48] With respect to Great Britain, Beer has described the main parliamentary task as that of 'mobilizing consent', 'certainly not the representative function by which in greater or lesser degree the legislature brings the grievances and wishes of the people to bear upon policy-making'.[49] And Patterson has asserted that,

> A legislature is much more than a law-making factory. It is a symbol of representative, democratic government. Its symbolic 'output' may be related to the kinds of policies it makes, but it is related also to the representative adequacy of the legislature, to the respect citizens can have for individual legislators, and to the pride citizens can take in their legislatures.[50]

David Truman has drawn important implications from such a view for the behaviour of representatives, arguing that the primary skill lying at the heart of representative government is not substantive, technical skill, but in combination with that,

[46] de Grazia, *Public and Republic*, p. 170.

[47] T. V. Smith, 'Two Functions of the American State Legislator', *Annals of the American Academy of Political and Social Science*, 195 (1938), 187.

[48] H. Eulau and K. Hinckley, 'Legislative Institutions and Processes', in J. A. Robinson, (ed.), *Political Annual*, 1 (1966), 85–6.

[49] S. H. Beer, British Legislature and the Problem of Mobilizing Consent', in Frank (ed.), *Lawmakers in a Changing World*, p. 31 [see pp. 62–80 in this volume—Ed].

[50] S. C. Patterson, 'Midwest Legislative Politics', paper presented at Mid-America Assembly on State Legislatures (1966), 114.

a special skill. This is skill in assaying what is asked or done in the name of substantive expertise and in reconciling or combining such claims or acts with the feasibilities that exist or can be created in the electorate, in the extra-governmental world in all its configurations.[51]

The shift of attention from 'demands' to 'support' which all these insights suggest calls for a corresponding shift of research emphasis from the behaviour of representatives which has hitherto preoccupied most of us, to the perceptions, attitudes, and behaviours of the people whom representatives collectively represent, about which as yet we really know very little. The most immediate task is a primarily conceptual one—to identify the dimensions of support behaviour, to map the incidence and variations of support in specific systems, and through comparative analysis of support mechanisms in different systems, to formulate hypotheses about its conditions and correlates.

David Easton's definition of support as affective orientation toward political objects, and his analytical distinction of political community, political regime, and political authorities as the three principal categories of such political objects is a useful starting-point.[52] We can probably assume, to begin with, that support for the political community is the most pervasive, general (diffuse), and stable element in the overall support-mechanism of any political system. Basic group-identification, the sort of 'pre-political' sentiment giving all segments of the community 'a we-feeling . . . not that they are just a group but that they are a political entity that works together and will likely share a common political fate and destiny',[53] is surely a major dimension of this level of support.

[51] D. B. Truman, 'Representative Function in Western Systems', 84–96 in E. H. Buehrig (ed.), *Essays in Political Science* (Bloomington, Ind., 1966), 90.

[52] 'Political community', refers to 'some minimal readiness or ability (of a group of people) to continue working together to solve their political problems'. (Easton, *Systems Analysis*, p. 172). 'Political Regime: refers to the values and principles, norms ("operating rules and rules of the game") and structures of authority (authority-*roles*) by which, over a period of time authoritative decisions are made in the political community.' (Ibid. 190–211). Political authorities are the persons who occupy the authoritative roles at any given point in time (ibid. 212–19).

[53] Ibid. 332.

Everything we know about the historical evolution of nation-states, tribal societies, and all other political forms, as well as everything modern research tells us about the processes of political socialization indicates that the loyalties, identifications, and cognitive-affective structures which make up this communal-loyalty dimension are acquired and shaped in early childhood and are affected little, if at all, by any political events, let alone such little salient events as the functioning of representative bodies. The indispensability of this kind of support for any political system was noted by V. O. Key: 'A basic prerequisite is that the population be pervaded by a national loyalty. Or perhaps, more accurately, that the population not consist of segments each with its own sense of separateness.'[54] Almond and Verba, whose concept of 'systems affect' approximates the concept of support for political community, likewise appear to take for granted (at least in the five countries they studied) the existence of a nationality sentiment or similar community sense defining a political community toward which members respond with varying effect.[55]

But what if no sentiment of political community binds together a group of people who are, in fact, being governed (as is the case in many new African nations, to give an obvious example)? Or if segments seem increasingly to develop 'each with its own sense of separateness' (as may well be the case in Canada or Belgium)? Can we be sure that 'the sense of community must also be in part a product of public policy?'[56] If not 'policy', what aspect then of governmental activity, and especially of representative bodies' activity, affects it? At this stage we can only wonder—and begin to design research to find out.

A second major dimension of political community support is suggested by Almond and Verba's typology of political cultures, comprising what we may interpret as the political roles of 'parochial', 'subject', and 'participant'. The authors' original formulation differentiates these three types primarily in terms of their relative participation in demand-input

[54] V. O. Key, *Public Opinion and American Democracy* (New York, 1961), 549.

[55] Almond and Verba, *Civic Culture*, pp. 101–5.

[56] Ibid. 551.

activities.[57] There is justification even in the original formulation, however, for viewing these roles as differentiated also by the extent of conscious support for the political community, or 'the gradation from "public" to "private" ': 'The overwhelming majority of the members of all political systems live out their lives, discover, develop, and express their feelings and aspirations in the intimate groups of the community. It is the rare individual who is fully recruited into the political system and becomes a political man.'[58] Viewed this way, the second component of community support, which might be labelled 'political commitment', appears as an autonomously defined political variable, a kind of participation through sensitivity and alertness to political events and objects as well as participation in civic and political roles—participation in politics *per se*, not necessarily in the sense of power seeking, however, and not participation in primarily instrumental activities. It is a kind of 'political interest', but, 'it is interest not in the form of gains in material well-being, power, or status, but it is rather in personal satisfaction and growth attained from active engagement in the political process'.[59]

A number of familiar concepts bear on this second dimension of political-community support. Most of the phenomena usually treated under the heading of 'political alienation', for example, represent an extreme negative value, ranking above only such anti-supportive positions as rebellion itself. 'Political apathy', in a sense related to Almond and Verba's 'parochialism', is more supportive than alienation but less so than 'compliance'. More supportive still is active 'interest and involvement', although one must be careful to remember that support for the political community here is perfectly compatible (perhaps often associated?) with failure of support for regime or authorities. Beyond active spectator interest there is participation of varying degrees—ranging

[57] The 'participant' is 'an active participant in the political input process', the 'subject' hardly at all oriented toward input objects but positively (if passively) oriented affectively 'toward the output, administrative, or "downward flow" side of the political system', and the 'parochial' detached from political roles of every sort, on both input and output sides. Ibid., 161, 19, 17 respectively.

[58] Ibid. 143.

[59] P. Bachrach, *Theory of Democratic Elitism*, p. 38.

from nothing more than sporadic voting to regular and intensive political communication, to participation in authority or other 'trans-civic' roles.

Such a conception of supportive political commitment seems perfectly consistent with what we do know about the relevant behaviour of citizens. For example, once-depressing statistics about 'low levels' of citizen interest take on quite different meaning in this light. The finding that 'only' 27 per cent of the American public could be considered politically active,[60] that during 1945 and 1946 sometimes 'as few as' 19 per cent and 'never more than' 36 per cent of the American Zone population in West Germany claimed to be personally interested in politics,[61] that in 1958 35 per cent of the West Germans had no interest at all in attending Bundestag sessions even if it cost them nothing,[62] or the countless similar readings of political interest and involvement in other political systems, must now, if there is no other different evidence on the point, be read not as sure signs of 'apathy' or 'negativism' but as probable indications of moderate support for the political community.

Still, on balance, we know much less than we should about the dynamics of support for the political community. Though we can recognize that communal loyalty and political commitment constitute important dimensions of it, we do not know how one dimension relates to the other, or how the day-to-day functioning of government, including the input–output functioning of representative institutions, relates to either.

The situation is not much different when we consider the problem of support for the 'political regime'. One major dimension here appears to be the level of conscious support for broad norms and values which apply to the political world generally, i.e. to 'rules-of-the-game', or standards by which regimes are judged. But the meaning of what information we have here is ambiguous. How much consensus, in the sense of 'agreement on fundamentals', may vary, and what is the effect

[60] J. L. Woodward and E. Roper, 'Political Activity of American Citizens', *American Political Science Review* 44 (1950), 872–85.

[61] OMGUS, 26 Oct., 13 Dec., 1945; 31 Jan. 7 June, 9 Aug. 3 Sept. 1946. Reported in Cantril and Strunk, *Public Opinion 1935–1936*, pp. 582–3.

[62] Noelle and Neumann, *Jahrbuch für öffentliche Meinung* (July 1958), 265.

of such variation, are questions which do not yet have clear answers.[63]

The level of support for the institutional apparatus of government seems to be another major dimension of regime support, empirically distinguishable from generalized 'agreement on fundamentals'. Citizens are apparently able to dislike something or other about the actions of government and at the same time support its continuation institutionally unchanged, and their levels of support in this respect apparently fluctuate over time. An instructive example is the differences in French responses to identical questions put at different times concerning which political regimes seemed to be functioning better or worse than the French regime. From January 1958 to January 1965 the percentage saying each country named worked better than the French dropped in every case and the percentage saying the French regime worked better increased in every case.[64] Again, although 41 per cent of a sample in a small midwestern American city said, in 1966, that there were things Congress had done which they did not like (about some of which they claimed to feel strongly), only 20 per cent of them thought any proposals for changing Congress should be given serious attention; although 44 per cent said the city council had done something they particularly disliked, and only 20 per cent thought the council was doing a good or excellent job, less than a third thought the form of government should be changed.[65] This perspective also leads us to view not as deviant, undemocratic views, but as probable indicators of probably normal regime support, the fact that more Americans think the majority of people usually *in*correct in

[63] Key's discussion (*Public Opinion*, p. 30 ff.) of 'supportive', 'permissive', 'negative', and 'decisional' consensus is most instructive here. See also H. McClosky, 'Consensus and Ideology in American Politics', *American Political Science Review* 58 (1964), 361–82, and J. W. Prothro and C. W. Grigg, 'Fundamental Principles of Democracy: Bases of Agreement and Disagreement', *Journal of Politics*, 22 (196), 276–94.

[64] Drop in proportion saying other regime better than France; 26 per cent for GB; 28 per cent for US; 7 per cent for Italy; 31 per cent for West Germany; 16 per cent for USSR. Increase in proportion saying French worked better: 15 per cent for GB; 13 per cent for US; 1 per cent for Italy; 14 per cent for West Germany; 9 per cent for USSR. See *Sondages*, 26/1 (1966).

[65] Iowa City Form of Government Study, 1966, Code Book. University of Iowa Laboratory for Political Research.

their ideas on important questions (42 per cent) than think the majority correct (38 per cent), or that Congress is thought more correct than 'the people' in its 'views on broad issues', (42 per cent as against 38 per cent).[66] Similarly, it becomes understandable why, when only half the American public thinks it makes much difference at all which party wins the election, some two-thirds to three-fourths of them make a point of voting at all elections, whether or not they have any specific interest in them,[67] and almost nine-tenths of them (87 per cent) think having elections makes government pay some or a good deal of attention to what the people think.[68] Although Almond and Verba consider such indicators as these under the heading of 'input affect', meaning essentially demand input ('the feeling people have both about those agencies and processes that are involved in the election of public officials, and about the enactment of public policies'),[69] they seem much more intelligible viewed under the heading of regime support, i.e. support for the apparatus of government in general.

Our information about regime-support phenomena, then, is no more adequate or satisfactory than our information about support for the political community. What there is of it, however, does seem to indicate that symbolic satisfaction with the process of government is probably more important than specific, instrumental satisfaction with the policy output of the process. Thus Thomas Anton has noticed, concerning the budget process, that 'it is not the document which creates satisfaction, but the process of putting it together . . . [The] budget, as document and process, creates symbolic satisfaction built upon the idea that affairs of state are being dealt with, that responsibility is being exercised, and that rationality prevails.'[70] Dye's conclusion after studying a voluminous array of the content of policy outputs, was that 'The *way* in

[66] AIPO 17 July 1939 and 8 August 1939, reported in 'Quarter's Polls', *Public Opinion Quarterly*, 10/4 (1939), 632. The remainder of responses in each instance were DK and NA.

[67] 49 per cent and 51 per cent in two separate polls in Sept. 1946, e.g. AIPO reported in 'Quarter's Polls', *Public Opinion Quarterly*, 3/4 (1946), 580.

[68] Survey Research Center, 1966, SRC Study 0504, ICPR Preliminary Code Book.

[69] Almond and Verba, *Civil Culture*, p. 101.

[70] Anton, 'Roles and Symbols', pp. 39–40.

which a society authoritatively allocates values may be an even more important question than the outcomes of these value allocations. Our commitments to democratic processes are essentially commitments to a mode of decision-making. The legitimacy of the democratic form of government has never really depended upon the policy outcomes which it is expected to produce.'[71] And de Grazia has said, more poetically, 'the whole *process* of representation becomes an acting out of a play in which the actors are independent within the limits of the state, the setting, and the changing tastes of the audience. Their role is meaningful but it has no direct connection with the ticket the audience files for admission.'[72]

Whereas political research has by and large neglected to study support for the political community and the political regime, it has paid considerable attention to support for 'political authorities'. Elections, of course, are considered an indispensable feature of representative government by anybody's definition, and election results in representative systems are almost universally interpreted as indices of support for incumbent authorities. The innumerable public opinion polls between elections which ask the level of voters' satisfaction or dissatisfaction with the ruling government's performance in general, with the performance of various individual office-holders or agencies, or with the handling of particular problems, are likewise taken as indicators of the rising and falling level of support for authorities.

No doubt such data are properly interpreted as measures of such support. But the question is, what should be read into them beyond that simple indication? 'Democracy', says Schumpeter, 'means only that the people have the opportunity of accepting or refusing the men who are to rule them.'[73] Our earlier discussion of the role of issues and policies in elections cautions us not to hastily assume voters are voting up one set of policies and voting down another when they go to the polls.[74] A unique series of data about British opinion in 1966 strongly intimates we ought not even assume that they are

[71] Dye, *Politics, Economics and the Public*, p. 30.

[72] de Grazia, *Public and Republic*, p. 170. My emphasis.

[73] J. A. Schumpeter, *Capitalism, Socialism, and Democracy* (New York, 1947), 285.

[74] See text above, pp. 102–7.

voting up one set of office-holders and voting down another in quite the simple, straightforward, preferential fashion we have always taken for granted. The data shown in Fig. 6.1 clearly demonstrate that, at least in Britain in 1966, many voters seem to be giving or withdrawing support from the whole apparatus of government officialdom and not, as one might at first think, transferring support from one set of authorities to another. To a remarkable degree, support for Government goes up as support for Opposition goes up, and support for Opposition goes down as support for Government goes down.

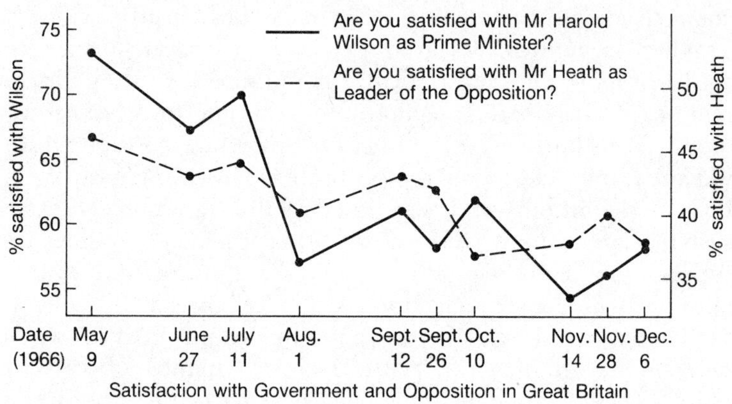

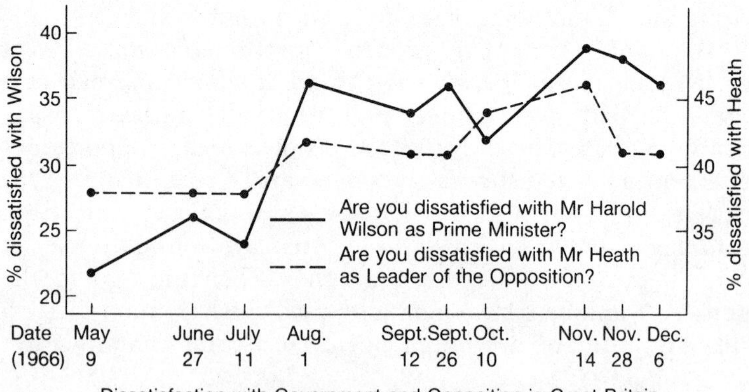

FIG. 6.1. Trends in Support for British Government and Opposition Leaders, 1966

One is strongly tempted to conclude, though it may be premature, that the support for authorities is much more closely related to regime support and much less related to individual voter preferences for individual authority figures than anyone has hitherto suspected.[75]

The conceptualization of support sketched out here is only that. It is not a theory, nor even a few hypotheses. Indeed, it is not even a very complete conceptualization, since many important questions are left open—how do we visualize support in a complex, multi-level, pluralistic government? What is the connection between support for local as against national (and, in federal systems, intermediate) authorities, regime, and political community? Between support for different segments of the regime at different levels? What is the relevance of the notion to supra-national and intergovernmental politics?

What bearing has all this on representative government? Surely it does not suggest that to maintain representative democracy is more difficult, or that representative democracy is less desirable, just because it might seem to depend less on support deriving from mechanically satisfying demand inputs than it does on the generation of support through quite different mechanisms. The question still is, how do representative bodies contribute to the generation and maintenance of support? In what respects and for what particular aspects of the task are they superior to non-representative institutions? These are questions to be answered by empirical research.

[75] For a summary of the implications of available studies on the dynamics of support and suggestions for further cross-national study of the problem see G. R. Boynton, S. C. Patterson, and J. C. Wahlke, 'Dimensions of Support in Legislative Systems', paper prepared for the Quail Roost Conference on Comparative Legislative Research, Rougemont, NC, 25–7 Feb. 1970.

PART III

NEW DIMENSIONS

CLASSIFYING LEGISLATURES

INTRODUCTION

Recognition that legislatures fulfil several functions, enjoying a significance beyond that of what Packenham terms the decisional or influencing function, has enabled political scientists to explore legislatures at a new level: beyond that of the individual legislature and below that of legislatures *qua* legislatures. It has been possible to identify different types, or categories, of legislature.

Two of the most important classifications have been provided by US scholars Nelson Polsby and Michael Mezey. In his substantial article, published in 1975, Polsby identifies what he terms the legislative forms that exist in four different political systems (derived from whether a system is closed or open, and whether governmental activity is specialized or unspecialized): where one has a closed system with unspecialized governmental activity, there is no legislature (laws are promulgated by juntas or cliques); where the system is closed and specialized, legislatures are of the 'rubber stamping' variety (as, for instance, the Supreme Soviet in the USSR and the Cortes in Franco's Spain); where the system is open but governmental activity unspecialized, rules are formulated by town meetings, tribal gatherings, and the like (appropriate, as Polsby notes, to small-scale political systems); and where one has an open system and specialized governmental activity, then one has a legislature to be found somewhere on a spectrum of legislatures, ranging from arena to transformative legislatures. It is this spectrum that has attracted particular attention, Polsby noting that the contrast between the two ends of the spectrum captures the distinction between the British (arena) and US (transformative) legislatures, with others falling either in between or on the arena end of the spectrum. Transformative legislatures possess the independent capacity, frequently employed, to mould and transform proposals into law; arena legislatures are settings for the interplay of significant political forces. With the former, it is important to analyse what is *done*; with the latter, more significance attaches to what is *said*—and by whom.

In *Comparative Legislatures*, published four years after Polsby's work, Michael Mezey provides a more clearly differentiated classification, derived from both the position of the legislature in relation to the making of public policy and the degree of support that it enjoys. In terms of the former (position in the making of public policy), he stipulates three levels of policy-making power: strong, modest, and little or none. In terms of the latter (support), he recognizes the problems inherent in measuring levels of support among élites (of particular importance in maintaining the position of a legislature) and the mass public, and so contents himself with the simple dichotomy between 'less supported' and 'more supported' legislatures. Cross-tabulating policy-making power with levels of support, he generates a six-box classification of legislatures, though only five of the six boxes are actually occupied.

The classification provided by Mezey is probably the most sophisticated and useful now available. However, one problem is apparent in his definitions of strong and modest policy-making power. Legislatures with a capacity to modify and reject executive proposals are deemed to enjoy strong policy-making power, whereas those that can modify but not reject are deemed to have modest policy-making power. In the 1970s, the British Parliament exercised—and in the 1980s continued to exercise—its power variously to reject government proposals. On the definition stipulated by Mezey, this would place Parliament in the category of an 'active'—rather than a 'reactive'—legislature and on a par with the US Congress. Given that such a categorization is largely untenable (and unintended), this writer in 1984 generated a new trichotomy of legislatures, distinguishing policy-making legislatures, policy-influencing legislatures, and legislatures with little or no policy affect. An extract from the article in which this trichotomy is identified is included in this section. The definitions stipulated for policy-making and policy-influencing serve to prevent Polsby's archetypal arena and transformative legislatures being classed as occupants of the same category.

7

LEGISLATURES

NELSON W. POLSBY

Legislatures may resemble one another in that they assemble, conduct business by means of spoken deliberation according to parliamentary rules, and vote in order to express their official will. But these acts, because they contribute to the outputs of organizations differently embedded in their respective systems, are arrived at in vastly different ways.

ARENAS VERSUS TRANSFORMATIVE LEGISLATURES

Upon what do these differences depend? The central distinction I shall propose describing these differences . . . posits a continuum of legislative power which expresses variations in the legislature's independence from outside influences. At one end lie legislatures that possess the independent capacity, frequently exercised, to mould and transform proposals from whatever source into laws. The act of transformation is crucial because it postulates a significance to the internal structure of legislatures, to the internal division of labour, and to the policy preferences of various legislators. Accounting for legislative outputs means having to know not merely who proposed what to the legislature and how imperatively but also who processed what *within* the legislature, how enthusiastically—and how competently.

Such legislatures—which I shall call *transformative legislatures*—can be contrasted with their fellows at the other end of the continuum. These latter I think of as *arenas*. Arenas in specialized, open regimes serve as formalized settings for the

Nelson W. Polsby 'Legislatures', in F. I. Greenstein and N. W. Polsby (edd.), *Handbook of Political Science*, v (Reading, Mass.; Addison-Wesley, 1975), 277–96. Reprinted by permission of the publisher.

interplay of significant political forces in the life of a political system; the more open the regime, the more varied and the more representative and accountable the forces that find a welcome in the arena. These forces may originate in the stratification system of society or even, as in medieval times, in estates of the realm. The crucial question we must ask of arenas is exemplified by Sir Lewis Namier's celebrated inquiry about eighteenth-century Britain—why men *went into* Parliament—in short, the question of political recruitment, which significantly is not a study of the acquisition or exercise of power once they got there.

The existence of legislative arenas leaves unanswered the question of where the power actually resides that expresses itself in legislative acts—whether (as is palpably the case in many modern democratic systems) in the party system, or the economic stratification system, the bureaucracy attached to the king, the barons and clergy, or wherever . . .

The contrast between arenas and transformative legislatures captures many of the differences that scholars customarily note in their discussions of the two great legislatures on which legislatures in most of the rest of the world are modelled—the British and the American. Because legislatures elsewhere are more often adaptations than carbon copies, I find it useful to contemplate these two classic cases as tending toward the ends of a continuum rather than as halves of a dichotomy, as is often proposed.

Britain, at any rate, is customarily, and understandably, identified as the home of an arena-like legislature. The truncated character of parliamentary committees, already mentioned, is one indication of this condition. Another is the long-standing preoccupation of observers of Parliament with the social composition of the membership.

It is entirely unnecessary for our purposes to enter into the dispute that has raged among historians of early modern England about how much weight to place upon the selfish, or class-oriented, as contrasted with altruistic, or state-oriented, impulses of the principal actors in English politics during the formation of the modern Parliament. For our purposes it suffices to note that none argue the view that a man's position or role within the parliamentary structure had a significant impact upon his attitudes or his influence. A politician's bearing, his 'personality, eloquence, debating power, prestige'[1] might weigh heavily, but these are personal, not organizational, attributes and further suggest the basic permeability of the parliamentary arena.

Consider also the concern students of Parliament have shown with the process and content of debate, including the well-known English obsession with the shape of the legislative chamber and its alleged effects upon oral exchange.[2] Debate means the ventilation of opinion for the education of the country at large. It also functions to mobilize interest groups and to proclaim loyalties not only within the chamber but also between those inside Parliament and their allies outside. As an aid to deliberation, debate is especially useful when the alliances that are most salient to politicians lie beyond the four walls of the chamber from which words are launched. And debate may be contrasted, as Woodrow Wilson did so favourably, with forms of deliberation that are more consultative or negotiatory in spirit and hence more suited to the private politicking of the committee room, the cloakroom, or even the smoke-filled room. . . .

The British Parliament came by its oral style, which persists to this day, in a historically explicable fashion. The traditional role of Parliament was from the beginning less to forge the details of legislation than to assert certain rights against the sovereign—early in the name of the people as organized into estates (economic-status groupings), later as organized into parties. This is characteristic of many parliaments. 'The standard pattern,' says Peter Gerlich, 'especially in the central European countries, was one of Crown plus bureaucracy against loosely organized representatives of the main societal classes or groups (nobility, bourgeoisie, peasantry).'[3]

[1] L. Namier, *Structure of Politics at the Accession of George III* (1929; London, 1963), 7.

[2] See K. C. Wheare, *Legislatures* (1st edn., Oxford, 1963); W. I. Jennings, *Parliament* (New York, 1940); E. Taylor, *House of Commons at Work* (Baltimore, 1951).

[3] P. Gerlich, 'Institutionalisation of European Parliaments', in A. Kornberg (ed.), *Legislatures in Comparative Perspective* (New York, 1973), 96.

The historical fulcrum around which centralized government—both bureaucracy and legislature—pivoted was the issue of taxation. Kings needed to devise means to raise the money to protect themselves, to go on crusades and other foreign adventures, to build public works and pay armies. In return they offered to the domestic populace a measure of protection: recourse for the enforcement of obligations, a means of mobilizing against foreign invaders, the rudiments of law and order in public places. A legislature was a useful tool of central government because it served as an arena for the establishment of tax obligations and legitimized the raising of money. In return, legislatures set constraints on the central government.

What determined the balance of power between the legislature and the sovereign, once both were in place? Essentially, the balance of power was determined by who controlled the greater armed force—king or barons, king or militia. Many of the armed conflicts of European history come down to a test of this question, and the agreements that followed upon these conflicts were arms control agreements and agreements about levels and distributions of taxation.

Thus the prerequisites of a central legislature, glimpsed in historical perspective, are (1) the spread of prosperity sufficient to make widespread taxation feasible as a method of supporting central government; (2) the spread of arms sufficient to make it necessary for the central government to bargain over, rather than unilaterally impose, tax burdens; and (3) some readiness to bargain about the rational restriction of arms and the supply of services to the populace.

The British Parliament did not develop an internal structure that took significant legislative prerogatives unto itself. Rather, such meagre internal differentiation as it has developed has been imposed for the convenience of the political parties in operating Parliament as a necessary tool of the government of the day. And in so far as internal differentiation and structure has been resisted it has been likewise because of the resistance of the leaders of the government, who saw that to empower Parliament as a transformative body was to empower their party opposition. The growth of the parties has provided one element in the superimposition of modern British democracy (in the form of a legislative Parliament) on the institutions of English feudalism; the other crucial element was the growth of the Civil Service, the modern technocratic successors to the centralized, executive monarchy.

More than a word should be spent on the significance of British parliamentary parties in the workings of Parliament. These parties' central role is to provide a talent pool of decision-makers from which the government of the day is staffed; but little is known about how the parliamentary party operates as a collective entity so as to aid in the selection and winnowing of governmental leaders and in constraining their policy options by carrying and amplifying public and élite opinion. The suspicion persists that while the influence of the parliamentary party is far from negligible, the expression of that influence is to be found not in structural features of Parliament but in extra-parliamentary forces and in the characters and the connections of individual members. Nevertheless, it is true that careers in future governments of the day are made and broken in the parliamentary party. Thus, because the reputations individuals make for themselves in the House are highly significant for their careers, there is a sense in which the real constituents of cabinet officials are their own back-benchers. As informed parliamentary opinion influences careers, so also does it frequently constrain the options of public policy. But here, again, it is difficult to pierce the veil and determine how much of this opinion arises within Parliament alone and how much is the product of the broader élite subculture of British governing circles.

Students of the Parliament urge on us the proposition that 'the true function of the House is to question and debate the policy of the government'[4] and that consequently to understand the policy-making of Parliament one must look elsewhere—to the social origins of members, especially in an earlier day, to the interests they represented, to the strength in society of interest groups themselves, to the plans of the government and civil service, and to the strategies and the institutions of the party system. Students of the US Congress have likewise looked to these very same influences and have often enough

[4] Jennings, *Parliament*, p. 8.

found ample evidence of their importance in explaining the emergence of policy.

Yet these factors, powerful as they have been, have time and again fallen short of satisfying students of American policy-making processes. For time and again a crucial transformation has occurred between 'inputs' from the rest of the political system and the final result of the legislative process. This transformation is not universally admired. For years on end, proponents of various progressive measures, for example, were convinced that they could enact new and useful laws by substantial majorities if they could only bring their proposals to a vote on the floor of both chambers of Congress. In the Senate their hopes were occasionally frustrated by skilful exploitation by minorities of an item of internal structure—a rule ordaining that debate could be terminated only by an extraordinary majority. In the House of Representatives the cards were stacked in even more complex ways: no bill can reach the floor save by a number of alternative clearance systems, each a yellow-brick road strewn with pitfalls and tended by trolls. The main route is through the Committee on Rules, for years controlled by a bipartisan conservative coalition. Short of structural reform, to revamp this—or any—committee meant waiting until the years took their toll of senior members, who otherwise served by a custom of reappointment ranked by party in order of committee service. When committee vacancies occur, a complex process of musical chairs takes place, moving newer members into coveted positions. This process of committee assignment engages the efforts of party leaders within the House and frequently entails competition among state delegations and bargaining within the party committees on committees. . . .

Late or soon, structural considerations take their toll: the simple and straightforward desire to pass this or that item of legislation through Congress must give way to a more cunning calculation of strategy based on detailed knowledge of structure.

This realization did not come early or often to political observers . . .

The tiny trickle of resolutely empirical studies on Congress, however, has all the staying power of good brandy. All grasp the central signficance in understanding Congress of internal structure. It is worth dwelling for a moment on these studies and their successors. If the identification of a legislature as an arena points the scholar away from the detailed examination of the legislature per se and toward the study of outside institutions such as party or stratification systems, the reverse holds for transformative legislatures, the most significant example of which is the Congress.

In the last fifteen years it is generally observed that the study of Congress has taken major strides. In part this phenomenon can be accounted for by calling it a scholarly reaction to the developing tension in the polity at large between increasingly importunate liberal—and mostly Democratic—electoral majorities and a long-standing conservative cross-party majority coalition that for thirty years dominated Congress. . . .

Most researchers would undoubtedly concede to Ralph Huitt of the University of Wisconsin the principal intellectual paternity of this new mood among political scientists who study Congress. In a series of articles that were persuasively written, thoroughly grounded in empirical research, and theoretically sophisticated, Huitt brought the internal structure and culture of Congress to the top of the academic agenda.[5]

It is clear from his more general, theoretical efforts that Huitt's appreciation of Congress as a political subculture is the product of a larger vision of human nature and human interaction under specified structural constraints. What gave Huitt's view its special interest, however, was his demonstration of its utility in the explication of empirical events. An early article,[6] showing how the record of committee hearings could be read to reveal the operation of congressional norms, was a kind of finger exercise. Then came three important case studies: one on the ways in which internal senate norms limited the application of sanctions to Wayne Morse when he changed his party affiliation, one on the ways in which

[5] These articles are collected in R. K. Huitt and R. L. Peabody, *Congress: Two Decades of Analysis* (New York, 1969).

[6] Ibid. 77–112.

Lyndon Johnson gathered up and deployed the resources available to party leadership within the highly structured confines of the Senate, and one on the ways in which boundaries of acceptable senatorial behaviour were tested by William Proxmire and Proxmire's adaptation to these boundaries was assimilated by the social system of the Senate. . . .

If, as Wilson long ago insisted, the committees of Congress were where the action (as well as the inaction) really was, it followed that ultimately scholars would have to learn in detail about committees and their work. One of the first committees to engage the sustained scrutiny of scholars was the House Rules Committee, which had long been the most troublesome one to liberal presidents and to the majority of the majority party.[7] Other committee studies soon followed: Richard Fenno's compendious examination of the Appropriations Committees[8] made the explicit argument that the pattern of committee activity—how the division of labour was arranged and what expectations and constraints members felt in the conduct of their work—was directly related to the nature of the committee's tasks and to its status in the congressional system. In a follow-up comparative study of six congressional committees,[9] Fenno elaborated upon this central insight, showing how different committees gratify different ambitions of congressmen and tend over time to do their work in different ways.

Nowhere is the significance of internal standards more apparent in the US Congress than in the ways in which the congressional parties select their leaders. Since 1960, half a dozen opportunities have arisen to watch the process of leadership selection in action. In the first of these, a battle for the majority leadership of the House in 1962, a candidate employing what was called an 'inside' strategy of campaigning for the office—stressing personal relations, friendship, the legitimacy of established internal arrangements—was thrown

[7] J. A. Robinson, *House Rules Committee* (Indianapolis, 1963); R. L. Peabody, 'Party Leadership Change in the United States House of Representatives', in R. L. Peabody and N. W. Polsby (edd.), *New Perspectives on the House of Representatives* (2nd edn., Chi. Ill., 1969).

[8] R. F. Fenno, *Power of the Purse* (Boston, Mass., 1966).

[9] Id., *Congressmen in Committees* (Boston, Mass., 1973).

up against a candidate employing an 'outside' strategy—stressing ideology, party programmes, and constituency pressures. The 'inside' candidate won handily.[10]

In general, 'outside' criteria enter only intermittently into the congressional leadership-selection process of either party; this is one secure conclusion that can be derived from Robert Peabody's meticulous reconstructions of leadership contests since 1962. It is noteworthy, moreover, that to do these studies, Peabody reversed the research procedure as Woodrow Wilson, that admirer of the legislature as arena. Where Wilson prided himself on never leaving the Baltimore campus of the Johns Hopkins University to study Capitol Hill at first hand, Peabody, a Hopkins professor, has virtually camped out in the halls of Congress for over a decade.

The strength of the internal structure of Congress and the significance of its imprint on legislative outcomes have led students to ask how long this has been going on. For different purposes, different answers are possible. Some might argue, for example, that James Sterling Young's demonstration[11] that at the dawn of the nineteenth century, boarding-house cliques had a significant impact on voting in Congress shows that internal congressional groupings have always dominated the affairs of Congress. Young's larger argument, however, is that the national government did not matter very much in those days, that national parties had not yet truly come into being, and that Congress was significant both as arena and as legislature.

A more intriguing case, first—and not too successfully—argued about the US Senate by David Rothman in his Harvard doctoral dissertation[12] and shortly thereafter suggestively elaborated for the House by H. Douglas Price,[13] places the probable turning-point at some place between 1870

[10] N. W. Polsby, 'Two Strategies of Influence: Choosing a Majority Leader, 1962', in Peabody and Polsby (edd.), *New Perspectives*, pp. 237–70.

[11] J. S. Young, *Washington Community 1800–1828* (New York, 1966).

[12] D. Rothman, 'Party, Power and the US Senate 1869–1901', Ph.D. Diss. Harvard University, 1964 (later published as *Politics and Power: The US Senate 1869–1901* (Cambridge, Mass., 1966)).

[13] H. D. Price, 'Congressional Career Then and Now', in N. W. Polsby (ed.), *Congressional Behavior* (New York, 1971), 14–27.

and 1910. Although there is a growing tendency in political science to assign responsibility for nearly everything—including congressional modernization—to the party realignment that took place in the national election of 1896, careful inspection of at least some congressional empirical indicators in time series does not appear to support this proposal.[14] It is much too soon, however, to rule out the suggestion that significant changes in Congress were indeed the product of the 'System of 1896'.[15] For the time being, evidence does at a minimum suggest that in the last decade of the nineteenth century something like 'institutionalization' was taking place in the House of Representatives: a strengthening of boundaries, a growth of internal complexity, and a marked shift from discretionary to universalistic norms of decision-making in the conduct of internal business.

One of the things that unobtrusive measures such as were employed in the institutionalization study are unsuccessful in elucidating is how actors feel about structural changes that go on around them. It is possible, by looking backward at the end of a long span of time, to see that some Congressmen were beginning at the very end of the nineteenth century to embark on careers as representatives that would stretch far into the twentieth century. This was much less common a generation before. And so it is worthwhile to ask how aware Congressmen were of the changed opportunity structures that governed their life chances and how these patterns of awareness affected their behaviour within the institution. If it is plausible to argue that some Congressmen became aware fairly early in the game that their careers would be tied to Congress in ways unimaginable to their predecessors, then it is also plausible to guess that changes in congressional behaviour appropriate to

[14] N. W. Polsby, 'Institutionalisation of the US House of Representatives', *American Political Science Review*, 62 (1968), 144–68.

[15] See E. E. Schattschneider, 'United States: The Functional Approach to Party Government', in S. Neumann (ed.), *Modern Political Parties* (Chi., Ill., 1956); W. Shannon, *Party, Constituency and Congressional Voting* (Baton Rouge, 1968); W. D. Burnham, *Critical Elections and the Mainsprings of American Politics* (New York, 1970); D. Brady, *Congressional Voting in a Partisan Era* (Lawrence, 1973); D. Ray, 'Membership Stability in Three State Legislatures: 1893–1969', *American Political Science Review*, 68 (1974), 106–12.

the new set of expectations (e.g. drives toward professionalization and subject-matter specialization) might have appeared in Congress well in advance of the evidence of structural changes that are capable of being registered by aggregate measures of such things as mean terms of service, which tend to build up into impressively high numbers only after a substantial portion of incumbent congressmen have served out the bulk of their careers. So the fact that measures currently in hand do not support the 'System of 1896' hypothesis (or for that matter a hypothesis tracing the responsibility for the transformation of this sector of American politics back to the Depression of 1893) cannot yet be taken as conclusive evidence that these hypotheses are incorrect.

Similar patterns of institutionalization have been observed by American historians of other institutions during the same period. . . . But to observe these similarities is not to account for them. It nevertheless seems reasonable to suppose that when the historical accidents responsible for the modern institutional structure of Congress are uncovered, what is attributed to them will not be inconsistent with whatever is asserted of historical causes that are ultimately assigned for the modernization of these other American institutions.

Students have argued that institutionalization is both a good thing and a bad thing, an indication of high social development and of institutional 'integrity' on the one hand and of organizational retrogression, insulation, and lack of initiative on the other.

During the twentieth century [says one writer] Congress has insulated itself from the new political forces which social change has generated. . . . Hence the leadership of Congress has lacked the incentive to take the legislative initiative in handling emerging national problems. . . . The members of Congress are 'isolated' from other national leaders. At gatherings of national leaders, 'members of Congress seem more conspicuous by their absence than by their presence.' One piece of evidence is fairly conclusive: of 623 national opinion-makers who attended ten American Assembly sessions between 1956 and 1960, only nine (1.4 per cent) were members of Congress! . . . On Capitol Hill the nineteenth-century ethos of the small-town, the independent farmer, and the small business man is still entrenched behind the institutional defenses which have developed in this century to insulate Congress from the new America.[16]

And yet:

> In a highly developed political system, political organizations have an integrity which they lack in less developed systems. In some measures, they are insulated from the impact of non-political groups and procedures. In less developed political systems, they are highly vulnerable to outside influences.
>
> At its most concrete level, autonomy involves the relations between social forces, on the one hand, and political organizations, on the other. . . . Political institutionalization, in the sense of autonomy, means the development of political organizations and procedures which are not simply expressions of the interests of particular social groups. . . . A judiciary is independent to the extent that it adheres to distinctly judicial norms and to the extent that its perspectives and behaviour are independent of those of other political institutions and social groupings. . . . So also with legislatures.[17]

It would no doubt be presumptuous for an outsider to join this debate. The contradictions it discloses may in any event be resolvable—or if not resolvable, at least ignorable—through the adoption of more adequate and operational indices of the underlying phenomena. Some of these have in fact been provided in the case of the US House of Representatives[18] and for other institutions the possibilities seem promising.

It is certainly not the case that institutionalization is an inevitable process, nor is it irreversible, uni-directional, or monotonic. When it occurs it may do so in a variety of patterns. Nevertheless, when we look for the causes and effects of institutionalization in any one sector, it seems reasonable to ask whether the explanations we formulate are compatible with what we know of circumstances elsewhere. It seems most implausible that there should be one set of laws governing human behaviour in business corporations, another set for

[16] S. P. Huntington, 'Congressional Responses to the Twentieth Century', in D. B. Truman (ed.), *Congress and America's Future* (Englewood Cliffs, NJ, 1965), 8, 15, 16.

[17] Id., 'Political Development and Political Decay', *World Politics*, 17 (1965), 401.

[18] Polsby, 'Institutionalisation of US House of Representatives'.

legislatures, still another set for institutions of higher education, another for the legal profession, and another for the military. Underlying all sectors there should be, if not uniformity, at least kinship in the propositions that purport to explain growth and change. When this kinship is made explicit, examples from one sector may strengthen or weaken propositions of another. When it is not, propositions are unlikely to possess sufficient generality to arouse much interest.

It is possible to summarize characteristic problems of studying arenas and to contrast them with characteristic problems of studying transformative legislatures. For arenas the impact of external forces is decisive in accounting for legislative outcomes. For transformative legislatures, what is decisive are variables depicting internal structure and subcultural norms. The student of arenas is perforce the student of social backgrounds of legislators, of legislative recruitment, of 'pressure' groups, of extra-parliamentary party politics, of the organization of parliamentary parties, and of debate. The student of transformative legislatures must consider committee structure and appointment processes, institutional socialization processes, the perception and regulation of interests by legislators, the dispositions of informal legislative groups such as state delegations in the case of the American Congress,[19] the operations of rules of internal procedure, and customs such as seniority.[20]

Between the pure cases of arenas and transformative legislatures there stretches a continuum whose breadth and main features are not well understood. In part this under-

[19] A. Fiellen, 'Functions of Informal Groups: A State Delegation', in Peabody and Polsby (edd.), *New Perspectives*; J. H. Kessell, 'Washington Congressional Delegation', *Midwest Journal of Political Science*, 8 (1964), 1–21; C. L. Clapp, *The Congressman: His Work as He Sees It* (Washington DC, 1963); B. Deckard, 'State Party Delegations in the US House of Representatives: A Comparative Study of Group Cohesion', *Journal of Politics*, 34 (1972), 199–223; id., 'State Party Delegations in the US House of Representatives: An Analysis of Group Action', *Polity*, 5 (1973), 311–34.

[20] N. W. Polsby, M. Gallaher, and B. S. Rundquist, 'Growth of the Seniority System in the US House of Representatives', *American Political Science Review*, 63 (1969), 787–807; M. E. Abram and J. Cooper, 'Rise of Seniority in the House of Representatives', *Polity*, 1 (1968), 52–85.

standing is hampered by the occasional impurity of even the supposedly pure types as, for example, when Congress obeys clear and urgent signals from its electorate on such issues as busing or when British MPs stir in the ranks as, for example, a few did on Suez, thus giving the legislative body for at least a short time an independent life of its own although this is not frozen into structural features of the system.[21]

Despite these problems, can we find some reasonably clear-cut intermediate cases? One hypothesis that has some plausibility proceeds from the observation that the main influence on the independence and hence the transformative capacity of the legislature in modern democratic political systems lies in the character of parliamentary parties. And this in turn refers to a number of separate variables. It is easiest simply to state, in bald propositional form, the influence these variables are hypothesized to have.

1. The broader the coalition embraced by the dominant parliamentary group that organizes the legislature, the more transformative the legislature. (The independent variable is indexed, e.g. by homogeneity of class and group composition of party electorates.)
2. The less centralized and hierarchical the management of legislative parties, the more transformative the legislative. (The independent variable is indexed, e.g. by locus of control over the nomination process.)
3. The less fixed and assured the composition of legislative majorities on successive specific issues, the more transformative the legislature. (The independent variable is indexed, e.g. by bloc structure analysis for successive votes and by the congruence of blocs with party labels.)

Not all of these independent variables run together along the same set of tracks, although at the extremes their influence is fairly plain. American legislative parties are extremely coalitional, decentralized, and flexible; British legislative parties are somewhat less coalitional, hierarchical, and fixed. Systems

[21] L. Epstein, *British Politics in the Suez Crisis* (Urbana, Ill., 1964); J. P. Mackintosh, 'Parliament Now and a Hundred Years Ago', in D. Leonard and V. Herman (edd.), *Backbencher and Parliament* (London, 1972).

that lie between the two in their transformativeness show a variety of patterns.

Netherlands. The Dutch political system provides for a modified separation of powers between the executive branch and the parliament, the States General. Cabinet members may speak in the States General but are not members and do not vote there, and most are not recruited from the Parliament. Parliamentary service is not a full-time occupation, and since the Netherlands is a small country, MPs commonly live at home and commute to the Hague. Members are elected not from their home towns but at large, in one of eighteen electoral districts, and they belong to well-organized but not well-disciplined parliamentary parties. Legislative initiative is in the hands of cabinet ministers, who work in collaboration with the large and powerful civil service, but the States General retains significant rights of amendment. The more powerful second chamber has in the last twenty years developed a specialized committee system, and there is also a parliamentary privilege to question individual ministers on specific subjects. In addition the Parliament occasionally undertakes inquiries analogous to congressional investigations.

Dutch parliamentary parties are small and must form coalitions to govern. They are somewhat decentralized and moderately flexible in their creation of successive parliamentary majorities. Lijphart says, 'Major pieces of legislation are often passed with the help of some "opposition" parties and with a "government" party voting against.'[22] This results in a less transformative legislature than the American case but a more transformative legislature than in most parliamentary democracies.[23]

Sweden. Policy-making in the Riksdag of Sweden is dominated by three interacting forces: the cabinet and Civil Service, which provide much of the agenda and staff work of the Riksdag and hence are powerful external influences on outcomes; the parliamentary parties; and the Riksdag's own committee system. Parliamentary parties caucus, provide

[22] A. Lijphart, *Politics of Accommodation* (Berkeley, Calif., 1968), 136–7.
[23] G. L. Weil, *Benelux Nations* (New York, 1970).

background research material on specific issues to their members, select leaders, who are important figures in the bargaining process that goes on for all major questions, and work out parliamentary strategy. But they do not deliver the votes of their members *en bloc*. Joseph Board says, 'There are forces other than party membership which may tug at the loyalties of an individual Riksdagsman. Among these are the sense of the Riksdag as a whole, the integrity of a particular committee, membership in a particular interest organization, or the demands of the national party and different factions within it.'[24] All legislation of any significance is routed through committees. Although their powers of initiative are sharply limited, they meet privately and hammer out the details of legislation that is set before them from the government (principally) or private members. Committee members tend to specialize in their committee service and build up seniority. Committee leadership is far less significant than in the American Congress, owing to the influence of staff work by the government and civil service and the weakness of independent committee staffs. Floor debate is far less significant than in pure arenas. 'Decisions on important issues are likely to have been made in committee or by inter-party agreement, and thus debate is more or less superfluous'.[25] Thus the Swedish Parliament appears to satisfy perfectly the legendary tropism of the Swedish national character toward moderation, producing a moderately transformative legislature, out of moderately coalition parliamentary parties, with moderately centralized party management, and moderate differences in the composition of successive legislative majorities.

Germany. In Germany there has been a slow increase in the power and significance of parliamentary committees, more or less concomitant with the increase in the coalition character of the major parties, especially the Socialists.[26] Party discipline remains relatively high, although more so for the Socialists (SPD) than for the Christian Democrats (CDU/CSU).

[24] J. B. Board, *Government and Politics of Sweden* (Boston, Mass., 1970), 137.

[25] Ibid. 140.

[26] G. Loewenberg, *Parliament in the German Political System* (1966; 2nd edn., Ithaca, New York, 1967), 151–2.

Christian Democratic deputies do defect in some numbers, although not on matters that would 'embarrass' the government of the day. The trend is clearly toward increased influence for specialized committees of the Bundestag and increased log-rolling among subgroup representatives within the parliamentary parties (who are aided by any trend toward committee independence). Scholars increasingly note the trappings usually associated with transformative legislatures—for example, private offices and staffs for legislators, a decline in the significance of floor debate, and more and more cases of cross-party voting within committees.

Italy. In Italy the dominant party—which organizes Parliament—is highly coalitional, the other parties much less so. Italy falls somewhere in the middle on all three of the scales proposed here. All parties strive to maintain a strong discipline over their members, and party leaders do succeed in fixing legislative majorities on a few major policy issues once they assemble the government—although the ability to do so is conditioned by the party balance in Parliament and is often in danger of evaporating as the concrete details of policy must be hammered out. In matters of lesser importance, however, party control is continually threatened by the existence of a full slate of committees in both houses (fourteen in the Chamber of Deputies, twelve in the Senate) and the constitutional provision that allows these committees to *adopt* laws independently under some conditions. These structural features, plus the highly fragmented party system, plus the factional, comparatively undisciplined nature of the largest party, sometimes combine to give the legislature important transformative opportunities even when the legislature is not directly threatening to the government of the day.[27]

France. Fourth-Republic France must be classed as a modified arena. It did develop narrowly focused, occasionally powerful committees (and hence some transformative capability) owing to the instability of governments. With the exception of the Communists, parliamentary parties were

[27] A. Manzella, 'Role of Parliament in Italy'. Paper prepared for the European Parliament Symposium on European Integration and the Future of Parliaments in Europe.

strongly decentralized and non-hierarchical, and this became more true as one moved toward the centre of the ideological spectrum—where all governmental coalitions had to be built. The combination of this instability in internal party cohesion with the large number of parties and the large size of the anti-system parties (which were always available to help break up legislative majorities) meant that there were few fixed majorities for dealing with successive major issues.

Such a situation might, in other circumstances, favour the evolution of a transformative legislature. However, because of the coexistence of undisciplined parties, few fixed legislative majorities, and a third element running in the opposite direction—that is, because of the lack of one or two broad-based, dominant parliamentary parties capable of organizing Parliament—the only transformative characteristic that emerged was the legislature's continuing ability to bring down the government. In an indirect way, the exercise of this power gives the legislature independent opportunities to influence policy, since the government is the body that originates policy. But in the sense that the Parliament itself alters the details of specific policies to suit imperatives internal to its own operation, there is little transformative effect.

This mild departure from the pure arena model—the ability to alter the identities of those who make policy without the ability to alter the details of policy itself—is what students of Fourth-Republic France apparently mean when they assert that internal legislative politics was important, that structural factors in the legislature (e.g. committees) had impact, but that Parliament was at the same time impotent.

To deal with this dilemma (among others), the Constitution of Fifth-Republic France proposed to make the legislature an arena mainly for the use of the separately elected president of the Republic and secondarily for his party. The possibility that the legislature would retain any transformative characteristics was, the framers hoped, crushed out through constitutional engineering. The parliamentary agenda was turned over entirely to the government, as was the ability to determine the form of the vote. Only the government can initiate appropriations measures, and parliament can neither cut taxes nor raise expenditures. Each chamber is limited to a maximum of six standing committees, which guarantees that they will be too large to make independent legislative inputs. The government is free to make any piece of legislation a question of 'confidence', but Parliament cannot 'dissolve' the president by voting 'no confidence'; all that will happen is that *Parliament* will be dissolved.

Belgium. In Belgium the three main parliamentary parties are centrally disciplined, and voting in Parliament is, on most issues, highly predictable. Moreover, parliamentary parties, never broadly based, have become less coalitional as the language question has increased in salience. This is the classic recipe for a non-transformative legislature, and indeed we find that the formula that creates the cabinet dominates the legislative process. The cabinet initiates virtually all proposals considered by the Parliament, and deviation from party expectations in voting on particular measures jeopardizes the governing coalition. Although committees exist, the real work of negotiating among interest groups and party leaders goes on elsewhere. 'If the Cabinet, majority parties, and interest groups can come to terms', says Gordon Weil,[28] 'there is little doubt that the proposed legislation will pass Parliament.'[29]

Table 7.1 summarizes the results of this brief European travelogue. It suggests that the legislatures surveyed fall into four main clusters, varying in their transformativeness more or less in accord with the three propositions earlier suggested. These 'findings' are, of course, to be taken with more than a grain of salt, and not only because they are based on rough-and-ready classification and superficial knowledge of the politics of the individual countries. At best, this exercise can serve as an illustration of the sort of variables that ultimately may explain variations in the independent capacities of legislatures to affect outcomes.

[28] Weil, *Benelux Nations*, p. 170.

[29] V. R. Lorwin, 'Belgium: Religion, Class and Language in National Politics', in R. A. Dahl (ed.), *Political Oppositions in Western Democracies* (New Haven, 1966).

TABLE 7.1. Determinants of Transformativeness in Legislatures

Independence of legislature	Example	Parliamentary organizing majorities	Parliamentary party management	Successive policy majorities
Highly transformative	United States	Highly coalitional	Very decentralized	Very flexible
Modified transformative	Netherlands	Coalitional	Decentralized	Flexible
	Sweden	Moderately coalitional	Moderately decentralized	Moderately flexible
Modified arena	Germany	Coalitional	Moderately decentralized	Moderately flexible
	Italy	Coalitional	Moderately centralized	Moderately fixed
	France (Fourth Republic)	Unstable	Decentralized	Flexible
Arena	United Kingdom	Moderately coalitional	Centralized	Fixed
	Belgium	Narrowly based	Centralized	Fixed
	France (Fifth Republic)	Narrowly based	Centralized	Fixed

8

CLASSIFYING LEGISLATURES

MICHAEL MEZEY

The literature in the field of legislative behaviour has been frequently and correctly criticized for its failure to be truly comparative.[1] Most research undertakings, with only a few exceptions, have focused on single legislatures. Each researcher has adopted techniques and developed concepts suitable or convenient for a particular legislature under study. Thus while we have been told a great deal about *individual* legislatures, we have been told very little about legislatures.

Hard practical realities are basically responsible for the state of the art. Comparative studies are more expensive and more difficult to execute, especially if they are designed collaboratively with the participation of researchers from several countries. Certain legislatures are studied simply because it is easier to study them; language problems may be acute at one research site and absent at another, while legislators may be open and co-operative in one country and secretive and inaccessible in another. Or it has been argued that detailed knowledge of a country is necessary before you can say anything about its legislature, and thus legislative studies should be done by country experts who, not surprisingly, will write only about that one legislature with which they are familiar.

These practical considerations clearly dictate most research decisions. Once these decisions are taken, they are often justified with elaborate rationalizations. For some period of

Michael Mezey, 'Classifying Legislatures', from *Comparative Legislatures* (Durham, NC: Duke University Press, 1979), 21–44. Reprinted by permission of the publisher.

[1] G. Loewenberg, 'Comparative Legislative Research', in S. C. Patterson and J. C. Wahlke (edd.), *Comparative Legislative Behavior: Frontiers of Research* (New York, 1972).

time it was asserted that any information on any legislature in the world was valuable simply because 'so little is known about legislatures'. As we came to know more, we were told that studying one particular legislature was worthwhile because that legislature was unique, important, or especially interesting. Or studying a legislature could be defended by asserting that it was 'broadly representative' of a nebulous larger class of legislatures, but most researchers who used this rationale did not make the effort to define that larger class clearly or demonstrate how it was related to the legislature in question. Some people, of course saw no need for rationalization; taking the idiosyncracies of each country seriously, they proceeded on the assumption that every legislature was entirely different from every other legislature and therefore any attempt at generalization would be both futile and wrong-headed.

Without passing judgement on the good faith with which these claims are made, it is none the less clear that there is a sizeable segment of the political science discipline that expects more than just a series of studies of single legislatures. If the institutional construct that we have called 'legislature' means anything at all, then we must be able to make some general statement about these institutions. If one recognizes that need, then the problems alluded to before must be dealt with: how can we study legislatures comparatively given the constraints of money and the other impediments to cross-national research?

One answer is to exploit the country studies already done. Instead of collecting new data, the findings of previously executed scholarly research can form a data base from which generalizations can be made. While such 'library' work is often denigrated in the profession, the fact is that if our colleagues are doing their field work well (and there is no reason to expect that they aren't) then the fruits of their labours can and should be used.

One problem with this method is that it is extremely unlikely that comparable data will be covered for a wide range of legislatures. This is especially true if one is dealing with questions of major political moment; the only easily available data for all legislatures are simple constitutional and historical facts.[2]

[2] J. Blondel, *Comparative Legislatures* (Englewood Cliffs, NJ, 1973).

The problem can be met in part by developing a classification scheme for legislatures. Such a step is long overdue in comparative legislative research. By taking that step, it then becomes possible to merge information on all legislatures located in the same class and thereby produce categorical statements which can then be compared to yield even more general statements.

There are some obvious drawbacks. All legislatures will not fit neatly into one category or another; undoubtedly there will be some degree of intracategory variation. Also the categories may be defined somewhat arbitrarily. Because classifications depend on concepts, and different concepts produce different categories, one researcher's categories may be inappropriate or unacceptable to other researchers. These quite relevant arguments are countered by the simple fact that there now appears to be no ready alternative short of a massive collection of new, original data that would start us toward generalizations about legislatures. While some may wish to wait for the happy moment of plentiful, representative, and strictly comparable data, others will wish to move tentatively along the road to generalization, comforted by the knowledge that when all the data are in, all of the errors of omission and commission will be corrected.

THE POLICY-MAKING STRENGTH OF LEGISLATURES

The simplest and most common comparative statements about legislatures relate to the strength or weakness of particular legislative institutions. Although not always stated explicitly, such statements usually refer to the importance of the legislature in the policy-making process relative to the importance of non-legislative institutions, commonly those operating through the executive branch of government.

Although there may well be some disagreement on whether or not a legislature's relative importance in policy-making should be the sole criterion for judging its strength,[3] there

[3] M. Mezey, 'Support for the Legislature: Clearing away the Underbrush', paper prepared for the Annual Meeting of the American Political Science Association, Washington DC, 1977.

seems little doubt that it can be an appropriate criterion for distinguishing legislatures from one another. However, classifying legislatures on the basis of their policy-making importance is not as easy as it may seem to be.

Jean Blondel[4] has pursued this point in greater depth and with more vigour than most other scholars. He develops a five-point scale that assesses the strength of the legislature compared to that of the executive on the basis of whether or not the right of censure is in the hands of the legislature and whether or not the executive has the power to dissolve the legislature. In addition to these constitutional variations, Blondel discusses the limits on legislative influence in terms of internal and external constraints operating on the institution. Internal constraints subsume several variables relevant to the internal organization of the institution, while external constraints refer to both the strength of the executive and the nature of the constitutional provision previously included in the five-point scale.

While Blondel's formulation is important, it is of only limited utility for analyzing the involvement of legislatures in the policy-making process. As he suggests, 'very strong executives are likely to be found at both ends of the continuum of constitutional powers'.[5] Communist systems, for instance, give wide grants of constitutional power to the legislature, yet real power resides in the executive branch. Such anomalies are inevitable when one becomes overly concerned with constitutional provisions rather than with political realities, particulary when dealing with rapidly changing political systems in which written constitutions often obscure more than they reveal.

An earlier formulation of Blondel's gets closer to the problem. Blondel introduces the concept of 'viscosity' as an indicator of the legislature's role in law-making. Viscosity reflects the degree to which legislatures are 'free' or 'compliant': 'where the legislature is very compliant [government] bills do not merely pass, they pass very easily and . . . the time spent or the number of speakers engaged is very small. As the

[4] Blondel, *Comparative Legislatures*.

[5] Ibid. 45.

legislature becomes freer, the time spent increases and amendments are discussed and indeed passed'.[6]

Nelson Polsby writes in similar terms when he distinguishes between 'transformative' and 'arena' legislatures, with the former possessing 'the independent capacity, frequently exercised, to mould and transform proposals from whatever source into laws', while the latter serve primarily as 'formalized settings for the interplay of significant political forces in the life of a political system'.[7] Marvin Weinbaum suggests the things that a transformative legislature might do when he says that as evidence of a legislature's 'decisional' role, we should look at its capacity 'to initiate legislation, to modify, delay, or defeat bills, to influence administration through parliamentary questions, interpellations, and investigations, and to alter departmental budgets, authorizations, and personnel'.[8]

These perspectives are useful because they direct our attention to the influence that legislatures have on the policy-making process and suggest a means for classifying legislatures on the basis of the extent of this influence. The key term is Blondel's concept of 'constraint', but not, as he says, constraints placed on the legislature that prevent it from influencing the policy-making process, but rather the constraints that the legislature is capable of placing on the policy-related activities of the executive.

In my view a constraint is a limitation that the legislature can place upon the executive branch of government that would not make it—the legislature—directly vulnerable to dissolution, proroguing, or closure. A constraint restricts the action of the executive branch and prevents it from making policy unilaterally. Legislatures will be salient in the policy-making process to the extent that their presence and prerogatives act as a constraint on the executive. If the

[6] Blondel, 'Legislative Behavior: Some Steps towards a Cross-National Measurement', *Government and Opposition*, 5 (1970), 80.

[7] N. W. Polsby, 'Legislatures', in F. I. Greenstein and N. W. Polsby (edd.), *Handbook of Political Science*, v (Reading, Mass., 1975), 277, [pp. 129–48 in this volume—Ed.]

[8] M. G. Weinbaum, 'Classification and Change in Legislative Systems', in C. L. Kim and G. R. Boynton (edd.), *Legislative Systems in Developing Countries* (Durham, NC, 1975), 43.

constraints at the disposal of the legislature are weak, then the institutions will be a correspondingly weak element in the policy-making process. The existence of substantive constraints brings with it a salient policy-making role.

It may strike some as prejudging the nature of the legislature's policy-making role to phrase an assessment of that role in negative terms—whether or not the legislature can stop things from happening. However, this conceptualization should not lead to the facile conclusion that legislatures are institutions designed to say no. Rather the argument is that the saliency of the legislature's policy-making role, whether ultimately evaluated as positive or negative, stems at base from its capacity to restrict the process, because that capacity is what compels other institutions to deal with it when they seek to make policy.

The most telling constraint that the legislature can place on the policy-making process is the veto. This means that the legislature can reject any proposal, no matter from which political actor or institution it emanates, without having to face new elections or some other form of disbandment. Constitutionally, almost every legislature in the world has this power, but we are concerned here with real rather than paper powers; a legislature that has a constitutional power to reject that it can never use does not in fact have the power.

A weaker constraint exists when the legislature can exact modifications or compromises in policy proposals even in the absence of a viable power to reject a proposal. Such modifications can be accomplished in a number of ways. Either through private consultation with legislators or through open legislative debate, the executive may become aware of significant criticisms of its proposals and respond to such criticism by agreement to amendments. Alternatively amendments may be forced upon the government through a voting process. Or the government may respond to legislative demands because the only other alternative would be to dissolve the legislature—a step that the government may not care to take.

Legislatures may be constraining the executive in this manner even in systems where government proposals always are approved by the legislature. Private discussions between the government and its supporters in the legislature may lead the government to modify its proposals before submission to the legislature in order to mollify party dissidents, even though party discipline could be imposed to pass the proposal in its original form. Anticipated opposition in the legislature may lead the government to postpone a potentially controversial proposal until the climate of opinion is more favourable, or it may lead it to phrase its proposals in such a way as to ameliorate anticipated objections. Thus all government proposals appear to pass the legislature unopposed and unamended simply because the government avoids introducing those things which may provoke legislative resistance, or because it has acceded to changes privately.

One observer of the Jordanian Parliament summarized the situation there in these terms:

> the executive . . . tries as hard as humanly possible to avoid open clashes with the legislature. Both the legislature and the executive realize they have a share in the maintenance of the status quo and in a stable political order and are aware of the dangers to both from an open clash. Objectionable items are often ironed out before they reach the floor. Key legislators are consulted, cajoled, etc. beforehand.[9]

This type of constraint is frequently ignored by students of legislators because it is difficult to nail down empirically. One can observe a proposal being rejected or amended on the floor and in public view, but it is difficult to observe a bureaucrat or a president tailoring proposals to meet anticipated opposition in the legislature or privately consulting with government-party MPs before submitting bills. None the less such a legislative constraint can be very significant in systems where executive leaders wish to maintain a legislature but do not care to accord it any substantial policy-making powers.

A legislature can be placed into one of three discrete categories, depending on the constraints at its disposal. Legislatures can be classified as possessing *strong policy-making power* if they can modify and reject executive proposals;

[9] K. A. Jaber, 'Role and Function of the Legislature of the Hashemite Kingdom of Jordan: An Appraisal', paper prepared for the Conference on Legislatures in Contemporary Society, Albany, New York, 1975, p. 17.

legislatures that have no capacity to reject policy proposals but can modify them can be said to possess *modest policy-making power*, while legislatures that can neither modify nor reject policy proposals have *little or no policy-making power*. These three categories constitute one of the two dimensions I will be using to classify legislatures.[10]

SUPPORT

My second dimension for classifying legislatures is the degree of support accruing to the institution. By support I mean a set of attitudes that look to the legislature as a valued and popular political institution. One reason for suggesting support as an additional dimension for distinguishing among legislatures is because it lends a certain degree of predictability to the policy-making dimension that we already have defined.

Taken by itself, the policy-making dimension indicates where a legislature presently is located relative to the other policy-making institutions in a political system, but it offers no guidance to where that legislature might be five or ten years later. Only a casual survey of world events will confirm that the importance and salience of the legislature can be subject to significant change. For example, the Congress of the Philippines was always lionized as one of the most powerful legislatures in the world right up until the time in 1972 when President Marcos suspended the institution, with hardly a murmur of domestic dissent to be heard. Although the Philippine Congress would have been classified with the American Congress as a legislature with strong policy-making power, a carefully constructed support dimension would have distinguished between the two legislatures and indicates that the former was more vulnerable to extra-constitutional attack than the latter.

While it is significant to know how important a legislature is

[10] This classification may strike some as being incomplete because the fourth possible combination—power to reject but not to modify—is missing. It is missing simply because it seems to me inconceivable that a legislature could have the power to reject proposed legislation but not have the power to modify it.

today, it is equally important to know how stable the legislature's position is and therefore how likely it is to continue in that position in the foreseeable future. Such data can affect the roles that the legislators adopt, the recruitment of legislators, the way they behave, and the way in which the legislature itself functions.

Manifest indicators of support. There are two ways to infer the level of support for a particular legislature. One way is to interpret the events that occur in a nation and the public statements of significant political actors as indicators of the presence or absence of support. Another method is to analyse the attitudes toward the legislature extant among mass and élite publics and to attempt to identify a latent structure of attitudes that can be labelled as supportive of the legislature, and, in contrast, an attitude structure that can be labelled as non-supportive. The latter method, of course, is more sophisticated, but the problems that are encountered in generating appropriate cross-national data are nearly insurmountable.[11] The event-oriented method is more rudimentary, but it still conveys a clear notion of what we mean by legislative support.

One indicator of support is the legislature's institutional continuity. We can ask whether or not coups or other extra-constitutional attacks upon the existence or integrity of the legislature occur in a country. For example, the legislative institution in Thailand was inaugurated in 1932. Since then there have been nine different constitutions, all ushered in by a *coup d'état* and each specifying a different format for the legislature. In its 180 years of constitutional history France has been through five republics and three empires, each involving an alteration in the role of the National Assembly. A

[11] The one notable exception to this generalization is the ongoing research being conducted by the Comparative Legislative Research Center at the University of Iowa. . . . By 1979 the Centre had succeeded in administering parallel questionnaires to mass publics, legislators, and élite publics in six countries: Kenya, South Korea, Turkey, Switzerland, Belgium, and Italy. A preliminary report of some of their findings may be found in G. Loewenberg and C. L. Kim, 'Representative Orientations of Legislators and Legislatures in Five Countries', paper prepared for the Annual Meeting of the American Political Science Association Chi., Ill., 1976.

list of countries in which the legislature has been either suspended or abolished sometime during the last decade would include among others, Greece, Malaysia, Thailand, the Philippines, Indonesia, Pakistan, Bangladesh, Chile, Uruguay, Uganda, Nigeria, and Afghanistan. In addition, legislatures in most of Latin America, in South Korea, in pre-liberation South Vietnam, and in much of Africa have been subjected to threats against their institutional survival.

We also might investigate the attitudes of government leaders toward the legislature. Do they continually launch verbal attacks against the legislature which question not only the wisdom of legislative actions but the right of the legislature to continue to function? When the Congress of Uruguay was dissolved by a *coup d'état* in 1973, the president of the Republic explained his actions in the following terms:

> Essentially the crisis is institutional. Uruguay requires profound institutional changes; and the parliamentary institution does not function, except for reasons of petty politics. It fails to pass bills which are necessary for the country and prevents the executive from governing. . . . Laws which were favorable to the country were not passed; those which do not coincide with national feelings were. In brief: Parliament did not permit us to govern; it placed itself outside the institutions.[12]

One of the leaders of the 1958 coup against the Thai legislature spoke in similar terms: 'How can representative government function if those who are elected to represent the people in the National Assembly forget the interest of the country as a whole and pursue only their selfish gains'.[13]

The theme of corruption touched upon in this last statement suggests a third indicator of a low level of support—popular distrust of the legislature coupled with charges of corruption and/or incompetency. Robert Stauffer discusses at length the very negative portrayals of the Philippine legislator that consistently appeared in the Manila press in the years

[12] C. A. Astiz, 'Role, Recruitment and Background of Brazilian Legislators and Congressional Staff Members', paper prepared for the World Congress of the International Political Science Association, Montreal, 1973, p. 3.

[13] F. C. Darling, 'Marshall Sarit and Absolutist Rule in Thailand', *Pacific Affairs*, 33 (1960), 356.

immediately prior to the Marcos coup. He quotes one journalist's criticism:

Over the years, Congress has fallen into disrepute. . . . The lawmaking body has become an object of scorn, hated and despised. To many Filipinos, Congress stands as a massive symbol of all that is dirty and evil in Philippine politics. To think of the legislature as an assemblage of learned men, many believe, is to be out of one's mind. For one, horseplay and shenanigans are standard fare in congressional deliberations. Absenteeism is prevalent, discipline is sadly lacking, and intellectual bankruptcy characterizes congressional discussions. To some, Congress is virtually a theater of the absurd.[14]

Attitudes like this, of course, are not directed exclusively toward those parliaments in developing political systems. French citizens have been described as 'rather indifferent to Parliament as an institution' and 'full of distrust for parliamentarians as a collective group'. In the early fall of 1958, at the nadir of the Fourth Republic, 88 per cent of the French public said 'there are too many political parties in Parliament', 75 per cent said 'parliamentary morality is inadequate', and 44 per cent said 'Parliament has too much power'. As France moved into the Fifth Republic, Parliament's policy-making power was diminished significantly, a change which seemed to be accompanied by a perceptible rise in support for the Parliament.[15]

Why people support the legislature. Assessing the level of support for the legislature by looking at attitudes toward the institution leads us to ask and attempt to answer the question of why people support a legislature.

One possible source of supportive attitudes is policy satisfaction. Members of a political system may support the legislature because they are pleased with the types of policies that the legislature produces. David Easton has labelled this concept 'specific support' and has asserted that it 'flows from the favorable attitudes and predispositions stimulated by

[14] R. Stauffer, 'Philippine Congress: Causes of Structural Change', *Sage Research Papers in the Social Sciences* (Beverley Hills, Calif., 1975), 36–7.

[15] S. C. Patterson, J. C. Wahlke, and G. R. Boynton, 'Dimension of Support for Legislative Systems', in A. Kornberg (ed.), *Legislatures in Comparative Perspective* (New York, 1973), 309.

outputs that are perceived by members to meet their demands as they arise or in anticipation'.[16]

This notion of support has been criticized on the grounds that it assumes that citizens have some degree of knowledge about public policies and their utility for them. This assumption, it has been argued, flies in the face of survey data from several nations that show quite conclusively that few voters have specific policy demands, positions, or expectations, few have the knowledge of political structures, processes, and actors that they would need if they had demands to communicate, and that in any event few citizens communicate with their representatives or for that matter have very much interest in the day-to-day functioning of their governmental system.

Because of these data, John Wahlke[17] has asserted that it is erroneous to conceive of support as deriving from demand-satisfying outputs. Although it seems clear that the supportive attitudes of informed élites may well emanate from policy satisfaction, when it comes to the attitudes of mass publics Wahlke is probably correct in urging the use of a concept of support that is unrelated to the policy-making activities of the government and therefore does not assume that the supportive citizen perceives himself as receiving policy rewards in return for his support.

Wahlke and his colleagues at the University of Iowa have advocated 'diffuse support' as such a concept. According to Easton, diffuse support

> consists of a reserve of support that enables a system to weather the many storms when outputs cannot be balanced off against inputs of demands. It is a kind of support that a system does not have to buy with more or less direct benefits for the obligations and responsibilities the member incurs. If we wish, the outputs here may be considered psychic or symbolic, and in this sense, they may offer the individual immediate benefits strong enough to stimulate a supportive response.[18]

[16] D. Easton, *Systems Analysis of Political Life* (New York, 1965), 273.

[17] J. Wahlke, 'Policy Demands and System Support: The Role of the Represented', *British Journal of Political Science*, 1 (1971), 271–90 [pp. 97–123 in this volume—Ed].

[18] Easton, *Systems Analysis*, p. 273.

As explicated in the several Iowa studies, the concept when applied to the legislature incorporates such attitudes as a willingness to comply with decisions made by the legislature even if one doesn't agree with those decisions,[19] as well as a prospective resistance to any attempts to dismantle the legislature or to reduce its powers significantly.

While the origins of such supportive attitudes have not been thoroughly investigated, certain inferences can be made. First of all, diffuse support for the legislature may well be a cultural phenomenon nested within a set of supportive attitudes toward all of the political institutions that make up a political system. As such, it may be considered a part of a more broadly allegiant political culture.

Second, diffuse support, over the long run, is related to specific support. Succesful policies, as we have seen, produce specific support; successive successful policies over an extended period of time will produce diffuse support. And, if a regime persists over time, that very fact alone can engender supportive attitudes among citizens. One study of West Germany has shown that the economic successes of the post-war government eventually created allegiant attitudes toward the German Bundestag even among those who did not support specific policies of the government.[20]

The use of diffuse support is not without problems of its own. For one thing, it appears that diffuse support often exhibits no real political consequences or correlates. For example, one study tested the hypothesis that people whose

[19] It should be noted that there have been questions raised about the validity of the compliance dimension as a measure of diffuse support for the legislature. Easton, 'Re-Assessment of the Concept of Political Support', *British Journal of Political Science*, 5 (1975), 435–57, and Mezey, 'Constituency Demands and Legislative Support: An Experiment', *Legislative Studies Quarterly*, 1 (1976), 101–28, have discussed several reasons why compliance with the law need not imply diffuse support for the legislature and even the Iowa researchers themselves have voiced some doubts—see Patterson and Boynton, 'Citizens, Leaders, and Legislators: Perspectives on Support for the American Legislature', *Sage Research Papers in the Social Sciences* (Beverley Hills, Calif., 1974).

[20] Boynton and Loewenberg, 'Development of Public Support for Parliament in Germany 1951–1959', *British Journal of Political Science*, 3 (1974), 169–89.

expectations and perceptions of legislators were congruent would have higher mean legislative support scores than those with incongruent responses. The analysis showed the predicted differences, but these were generally slight and statistically insignificant.[21] In another study an attempt was made to correlate several dimensions of diffuse support for elections with voting turnout. Again, for two of the three support dimensions—approval of the electoral process and the efficacy of elections—the correlation with voting turnout was either small or non-existent. A modest correlation was found between voting and a third dimension called 'voting duty'.[22]

One reason why diffuse support measures do not yield high correlations with related attitudes and behaviour is that diffuse support is too abstract a concept, too far removed from the behaviour and attitudes that the researchers are trying to explain. When the concept of diffuse support is used to study legislatures in developing political systems, an additional problem may arise.

Diffuse support almost by definition develops over time. In new nations legislatures are often new institutions; they will not have had the time to develop a reservoir of diffuse support. Thus measures of diffuse support for legislatures in these systems are of little use and can be quite misleading. In the abstract world of survey research people may indicate a willingness to maintain the legislature and state their distaste for the notion of doing away with the institution. However, when put to the test, these attitudes may yield to less positive views of the legislature based less on abstractions and more on perceptions of current activities by the legislature and its members, no matter how fuzzy or casual these perceptions may be.

At a minimum, if measures of diffuse support for elections cannot predict whether or not someone will vote, it seems extravagant to claim that measures of diffuse support for the legislature will predict how citizens will react when tanks roll

[21] S. C. Patterson, G. R. Boynton, and R. Hedlung, 'Perceptions and Expectations of the Legislature and Support for It', *American Journal of Sociology*, 75 (1969), 74–6.

[22] J. Dennis, 'Support for the Institution of Elections by the Mass Public', *American Political Science Review*, 64 (1970), 833.

toward the parliament building. Clearly what is required is a concept of support that relies on empirical indicators less abstract than those appropriate for measures of diffuse support, yet not so specific as to assume policy knowledge among mass publics. Also, it would be useful to have a support concept that is equally relevant to mass and elite attitudes toward the legislatures. One source of such a concept is the expectations that form the mental constructs, or models that people have about legislatures, and of which we have spoken previously.

Expectations and support. Expectations, as we have seen, are views about how a legislature should perform—the types of things that legislators should do and the types of functions that the institution should perform. Expectations are more diffuse than the policy-related information relevant to specific support. Thus people can 'expect' their legislator to represent them and feel that their expectations are being met even if they are not aware of how he votes on specific issues and of what the consequences of his actions are for their interests.[23]

But expectations are more concrete than the attitudes associated with diffuse support measures because there are empirical and experiential counterparts to expectations. That is, people constantly confront their expectations of the legislature with their perceptions of how the legislature and its members are operating. In contrast, diffuse-support concepts measure support in terms of people's reactions to hypothetical situations—for example, how they would respond to attempts to abolish the legislature, or whether they would be willing to disobey a law as long as they don't get caught. For many respondents in many countries, these are abstractions without an empirical anchor. People do not ordinarily contemplate the abolition of their political institutions or the breaking of laws. Survey items probing attitudes toward these acts are not likely to be predictive of how people will act and what they will

[23] The view that supportive attitudes might emanate from the interface between expectations and perceptions has been discussed by Easton, 'Concept of Political Support', and Mezey, 'Constituency Demands and Legislative Support'. See Mezey, 'Support for the Legislature' for a complete review of this question and others concerning support for legislative institutions.

think when members of parliament are imprisoned or when conditions drive them to consider civil disobedience.

How then are expectations related to support? To the extent that mass, attentive, and élite publics agree on an expectational model of the legislature, and to the extent that legislative behaviour is congruent with this model, the legislature will be supported. Lack of agreement, or dissensus, on what constitutes the appropriate legislative model will diminish the level of legislative support. Incongruency between an agreed-upon model and legislative behaviour also will diminish support levels.

When a public consensus exits on the appropriate model for a legislative institution, legislative behaviour is constrained to conform to that model. For example, if British leaders and British citizens alike believe that something approximating a representation model is most appropriate for the British Parliament, a strong pressure is created on MPs to construct their roles and behaviour accordingly. Few members will view themselves as active creators of policy; few will ignore their representational obligations and view themselves exclusively as legitimators of government policy decisions. A failure to construct legislative roles in this manner likely would result in a sharp decline in support for the Parliament.

Dissensus among the several publics within the political system creates a situation of ambiguity which may provide the legislator with some degree of behavioural latitude. However, it also may create pressures on legislators to choose between satisfying élite expectations, satisfying mass expectations, or seeking something in between. For example, in one-party systems legislators are frequently caught between the system maintenance model of party élites that urges them to mobilize support for often unpopular government programmes and the representation model of their constituents that urges them to oppose government programmes which they perceive as causing them hardships. In such a context it is likely that no matter what the legislator does, he will violate the expectations of significant segments of the public outside the legislature and thereby jeopardize the support accruing to the legislature.

Other situations may present fewer problems for the legislator. It is possible that the expectations of mass publics toward the legislature will be vague and dissensual, while the expectations of élites will be 'crystal clear'. In this situation legislators are very likely to tailor their behaviour to conform to the expectations of élites, thereby increasing their support from those precincts, while at the same time ignoring the ambiguous and conflictual signals emanating from other sectors of society. The Tanzanian MP might find some support for the representation model among some segments of his constituency, but the clear, forceful, and frequently stated system-maintenance expectations of the president of the country heavily militate in favour of conforming to his particular legislative model.

The Tanzanian illustration suggests that congruence between legislative behavior and élite expectations is more important for legislative support than congruence with mass expectations. Two reasons for this can be adduced. First, élite views tend to be more salient than mass expectations. Élites in the executive branch of government, among the economic leaders of the country, and within the military services tend to deal with legislatures and their members on a continuing basis and so will develop a clearly articulated set of expectations about how that institution should function and how its members should behave. They will make these expectations known and they will also be in a position to accurately assess the extent to which legislative behaviour conforms to their expectations.

For the mass public, in contrast, politics is not very salient, expectations tend to be rather diffuse, and perceptions of how political institutions are operating tend to be very vague. Thus, while legislative deviance from their expectations is not likely to go unnoticed by élites, mass expectations can be interpreted in different ways, thus making it difficult to distinguish congruent from incongruent behavior.

The second reason for the greater importance attributed to élite expectations is that élites are likely to have powerful sanctions at their disposal to encourage the conformance of legislative behaviour to their expectations and to discourage deviancy. The use of force, or even the threat that it might be used, is frequently an option. While public opinion may or may not applaud such actions, when legislatures are shut down the deed is seldom accomplished by the people. Rather it is the institutional élites resident in the executive branch and the military that send the legislators packing. Aside from force élites often have more attractive, positive inducements to offer legislators in return for conformance to élite expectations: money, patronage, and political influence are three obvious examples.

The point is that if support is to be taken as an indicator of an institution's capacity to survive, then the support of élites is more important to the legislature than the support of mass publics. This is not to imply that the electoral sanctions of mass publics are always inconsequential. In stable democratic political systems, where explicit executive coercion of the legislature is unlikely to occur, the electoral sanctions of mass publics may be as powerful as those at the disposal of élites. However, in these systems it is also likely that élite and mass expectations will be roughly congruent. But in those political systems where incongruence is most likely to occur and where the integrity of the legislature is least certain, the sanctions of the executive are a good deal stronger than the electoral sanctions of the masses.

What all of this suggests is that a continuum of legislative support situations exists. Legislatures located toward the high support end of the continuum will function in a way that does not do violence to the expectations of élites outside the legislature; also, they probably will be acting in approximate conformance to the expectations of mass publics. As one moves down the continuum toward the less supported end, legislative behaviour will begin to deviate perceptibly and significantly from élite expectations. The expectations of mass publics may be ambiguous, or they may themselves deviate from the expectations of élites, but the key variable leading to a low level of support is increasing incongruency between the way the legislature operates and the way in which non-legislative élites expect it to operate.

As I have suggested, there is at least one obvious problem with this explication of the support concept and that is the difficulty in measuring with any degree of precision the support situation of a legislature. What we would need to do that job would be comparable survey data probing the expectations of mass and élite publics toward legislatures as well as precise indicators of the extent to which legislative behaviour is congruent or incongruent with these expectations. For now and for the foreseeable future, such data are beyond our reach.

This is not cause for abandoning support as a dimension for classifying legislatures, however. Rather, we can return to the first method that we described for inferring levels of support: that is, looking at the events in a nation and seeking to estimate the extent to which the atmosphere surrounding the legislature is supportive. The imprecision and subjectivity of such an approach literally leaps from the page. One way of dealing with such imprecision is to use a very low level of measurement. About as low as you can get (if I accurately recall my course in reseach design) is a dichotomized variable. Legislatures are thus divided into two support categories, one labelled 'more supported legislatures' and the second labelled 'less supported legislatures'.

That dichotomized variable may be combined with my previously defined trichotomized division of legislatures according to their role in policy-making. Such a cross-tabulation produces the five categories shown in Table 8.1.

A TALE OF FIVE LEGISLATURES

In Table 8.1 selected legislatures are divided into five categories labelled active, vulnerable, reactive, marginal, and minimal. The placement of a particular legislature into a specific category depends on my evaluation of that legislature; others who are more expert about a legislature may decide that it should be placed somewhere else. To further illuminate the criteria that I have used in placing legislatures, I will give a capsule description of five legislatures that are prototypical of each category.

An active legislature: The US Congress. For nearly two hundred years, the US Congress has stood at the centre of the American policy-making process. Its capacity to reject, amend, or ignore policy proposals initiated by either the executive or its own members has been attested to and

TABLE 8.1. A Typology of Legislatures

Policy-making power	Less supported legislatures	More supported legislatures
Strong	Vulnerable legislatures (Philippines, Uruguay, Chile, Italy, France (Fourth Republic), France (Third Republic), Weimar Germany)	Active legislatures (US Congress and American state legislatures, Costa Rican Congress)
Modest	Marginal legislatures (Thailand, Pakistan, South Vietnam (pre-1975), S. Korea, Kenya, Uganda, Malaysia, Colombia, Peru, Brazil, Afghanistan, Iran, Ethiopia, Syria, Jordan, Zambia, Nigeria, Argentina, Bangladesh, Guatemala, Lebanon)	Reactive legislatures (United Kingdom, Canada, Australia, New Zealand, India, Israel, Mexico, Norway, Sweden, Denmark, Finland, W. Germany, Belgium, Netherlands, Switzerland, France (Fifth Republic), Austria, Ireland, Japan, Turkey)
Little or none		Minimal legislatures (Soviet Union, Poland, Yugoslavia, Tanzania, Singapore, Tunisia, Taiwan, Ivory Coast, Ghana (Nkrumah)

Note: These entries should be taken as illustrative rather than inclusive. The absence of a particular country from the table means that I haven't the faintest idea where it should go and that I am not including the country in the analysis. The absence of a sixth cell in the table (lower left corner) will be discussed at the end of this chapter.

detested by thirty-nine presidents. Even though a decline in the power and authority of the Congress has been announced on several different occasions, it remains today one of the few legislative institutions in the world able and capable of saying no to a popularly elected president and making it stick.

What evidence there is tends to suggest that the American people are supportive of the Congress. Summarizing the existing research on the subject, Roger Davidson[24] concludes that 'citizens hold senators and their representatives in high esteem and would be proud to have their children pursue such a career. When asked to describe the characteristics of a representative, respondents (whose replies were favourable by a 9 to 1 ratio) stress the qualities of service orientation, good personal character, capability, good education, and personality.' In regard to its legislative activities Davidson says that 'Congress is not usually evaluated directly, but rather through a prism of attitudes to more familiar political objects', such as the goodness or badness of the times, or estimates of how well the president is performing. However, there also seems to be some evidence that support for the Congress tends to increase when it is being perceived as acting quickly and efficiently on legislation.[25]

Although presidents and bureaucrats may chafe against the active policy-making role of the Congress, in comparative perspective they have shown little inclination to challenge the legitimacy of the legislature. Among modern presidents Richard Nixon seemed to go the furthest in the direction of challenging the Congress's constitutional prerogatives and we all know how he made out.

Vulnerable legislatures: The Congress of the Philippines (1946–72). During the first twenty-six years of its independence from the United States the Republic of the Philippines had one of the strongest legislatures in the developing world. Jean Grossholtz[26] writes that despite a strong presidency, the Congress 'often refused to pass administration bills or so weakened them with amendments as to destroy their aim. This has been the

[24] R. H. Davidson, 'Congress in the American Political System', in A. Kornberg and L. Musolf (edd.), *Legislatures in Developmental Perspective* (Durham, NC; 1970), 169.

[25] Ibid. 171–2.

[26] J. Grossholtz, *Philippines* (Boston, Mass., 1964), 117.

common fate of land reform measures.' Robert Stauffer[27] reports that when the president wanted things passed by the Congress he had to negotiate with the legislators: 'bargaining goes on constantly before and during a session of Congress between the President and the legislative leaders over what will be passed and what will have to be paid by the chief executive for congressional cooperation'. Although this bargaining resulted in mutual legislative–executive control, 'Congress imposed a recognized set of parameters on where and how public resources [were] to be allocated and [had] an important voice in any changes in established patterns'.[28]

As the reader will note, this description of the Philippine Congress was altered from the present to the past tense because in 1972 President Ferdinand Marcos decided that he no longer cared to negotiate with the legislators, suspended the constitution, imprisoned some legislative leaders, and sent the rest home. These events occurred with almost no public dissent; Stauffer[29] reports that the 'government's precautionary move of calling out an élite unit of the Philippine Constabulary to put down any demonstrations that might occur . . . was wasted effort; resistance to martial law was not to be occasioned by regret over the closing of Congress'. Stauffer suggests that it was commonplace in the Philippines to think of legislators as corrupt people bent on enriching themselves as part of their duties. Steven Franzich observes that 'the Philippine Congress is one of the most criticized institutions in Philippine society'.[30]

It is not clear that such behaviour on the part of legislators seriously conflicted with the expectations of mass publics, for whom such activity, in the view of some observers, constituted a cultural norm. Grossholtz says this about the Filipino political culture: 'Those who have power are expected to use it to promote their own interests and that of their family. There is no moral contempt for those who benefit from their power.

[27] R. Stauffer, 'Congress in the Philippine Political System', in Kornberg and Musolf (edd.), *Legislatures in Developmental Perspective*, p. 351.

[28] Ibid.

[29] Stauffer, 'Philippine Congress', p. 6.

[30] S. E. Franzich, 'Comparative Study of Legislative Roles and Behavior', Ph.D. Diss., University of Minnesota, 1971, p. 404.

It is as it should be, and a man would be a fool to ignore his opportunities'.[31]

But it does appear that legislators did violate the expectations of President Marcos and other Philippine élites. Stauffer[32] suggests that prior to the coup, the Philippine Congress was pursuing a representational model with traditional local élites as the focus of representation. This behaviour came to be increasingly incongruent with the models employed by the new technocratic élites in the cities, thus provoking the 1972 coup.

A reactive legislature: The British House of Commons. Every veteran of a western European politics course knows that British politics is dominated by the prime minister and his cabinet who, working through a disciplined majority party in Parliament, can regularly produce a majority vote in the House and pass its programmes. A defeat of the government by the House of Commons could be interpreted as a vote of no confidence and the government likely would dissolve Parliament and call for new elections. Bernard Crick writes that 'all important legislation is government legislation and, with very few exceptions, goes through without substantial amendment—outright defeat is politically inconceivable and withdrawal phenomenally rare'.[33]

While it is clear that the House of Commons does not have the effective power to say no to the government, it seems equally clear that the House does set certain parameters within which the government must act and thereby discourages the government from introducing legislation that will cause a row in Parliament. Dissent from government back-benchers particularly may convince the government to modify legislation before submission to the Parliament. One writer concludes a careful analysis of back-bench influence on government policy during the 1945–57 period with the following statement:

> The role of the government backbenchers in the decision-making process is a substantial one. Neither their constituents nor their

[31] Grossholtz, *Philippines*, p. 163.

[32] Stauffer, 'Philippine Congress', p. 50–5.

[33] B. Crick, 'Parliament in the British Political System', in Kornberg and Musolf (edd.), *Legislatures in Developmental Perspective*, pp. 51–2.

leaders can claim them as puppets who respond only to the pull of a string. The members of both parties were quite often responsible for serious policy changes. . . . Furthermore, backbench pressure on the leadership was not by any means limited to a small backbench cabal. On the contrary, it has been noted that in each party there was an impressively large number of members who were energetically in disagreements with government leaders over issues which were of great concern to them.[34]

Another analysis of the 1968–9 parliamentary session comes to a similar conclusion. While few Opposition and back-bench amendments were accepted by the Government many others were indirectly incorporated or accommodated by the Government into its legislation.[35]

The results of national opinion polls in Great Britain indicate that the Parliament is a highly supported institution. In one poll, 85 per cent of the respondents indicated that they thought that 'what goes on in the House of Commons is important'. However, the same polls indicate some discontent with individual MPs, particularly in regard to what many feel to be the MP's overly subservient role in regard to his party and the consequent distance this subservience creates between the members and his constituency.[36]

In my terminology these data indicate that legislators in Great Britain are shaping their behaviour to meet the expectations of party élites rather than the expectations of mass publics. The dominance of legislative behaviour by party élites is a common characteristic of the reactive legislature, and is even more pronounced in the one-party dominant political systems in this category. In these countries mass expectations are unlikely to be either salient or very clear, whereas the expectations of the party élites will be quite unmistakable.

This is not to suggest that reactive legislatures are the objects

[34] J. J. Lynskey, 'Role of the British Backbenchers in the Modification of Government Policy', *Western Political Quarterly*, 23 (1970), 347.

[35] V. Herman, 'Backbench and Opposition Amendments to Government Legislation', in D. Leonard and V. Herman (edd.), *Backbencher and Parliament* (London, 1972).

[36] Patterson, Wahlke, and Boynton, 'Dimension of Support for Legislative Systems', p. 308.

of mass alienation. There is no evidence at all that mass expectations have been frustrated to the extent of threatening the institutional stability of either the Parent of Parliaments, or of its several offspring throughout the Western Caucasian world.

A marginal legislature: The National Assembly of Pakistan (1962–9). The legislature created by the 1962 Pakistani Constitution was designed to be subordinate to the president, with no real power to reject government proposals. During the 1962–5 period, the Government introduced forty bills, of which thirty-nine were passed.[37] In addition, presidential ordinances promulgated while the legislature was not in session were routinely approved when the Assembly reconvened.[38] Finally the Assembly's budgetary power was constitutionally restricted to new items; it could neither consider nor vote on continuing expenditures.

However, the Assembly did exercise the power to amend legislation. According to Rashiduzzaman,[39] from 1962 to 1968 eleven major government proposals were 'extensively amended' by the Assembly. The Security Act of 1965, for example, was amended in the Assembly to require the government to communicate its grounds for detention within fifteen days, to produce detainees before a board that included a Supreme Court judge, and to empower the board to prevent a detention from exceeding two months.[40] Public debate within the legislature often created a climate of opinion that encouraged the government to act. Ahmad[41] reports that the Political Detenus Amendment Bill and the Political Parties Bill of 1962, though officially sponsored, 'were the direct outcome of the demand inside the House backed by popular support outside'.

Government acquiesence to legislative pressures was most likely to occur without a vote or in the privacy of committee rooms. Although such activity was not always visible, it none

[37] K. B. Sayeed, *Political System of Pakistan* (Lahore, 1967), 107.

[38] M. Ahmad, *Government and Politics in Pakistan* (Karachi, 1970), 218.

[39] M. Rashiduzzaman, 'National Assembly in Pakistan under the 1962 Constitution', *Pacific Affairs*, 42 (1969–70), 492.

[40] Ahmad, *Government and Politics in Pakistan*, p. 244.

[41] Ibid.

the less seems clear that even though the National Assembly could not reject government proposals outright, the legislature was capable of modifying such proposals and thereby participated in setting the parameters within which the government operated.

During the twenty-eight years of its independence Pakistan has been through two periods of martial law during which the Parliament was suspended. Such occurrences stem from conflict between the behaviour of legislators and élite expectations about the role the legislature should play. While government leaders perceived the legislature largely in integrative, system-maintenance terms, legislators looked at the legislature in representative terms. General Ayub Khan explained the reasons for the 1958 coup this way: 'The army could not remain unaffected by the conditions around it, nor was it conceivable that officers and men would not react to all the political chicanery, intrigue, corruption, and inefficiency manifested in every sphere of life'.[42]

Apparently the 1969 imposition of martial law was welcomed by several segments of the population. It has been suggested that the corruption of the Parliament and the Ayub regime generally, as well as the lack of responsiveness to demands for greater regional autonomy, directly contributed to the re-imposition of martial law. All of this indicates that the legislative institution in Pakistan has been incapable of fulfilling the expectation of either the political élites with whom it must work or the mass publics whom it ostensibly represents.[43]

The support that élites give to legislatures in this category can best be described as tentative and that is why we have called these legislatures marginal. The élites create these legislatures and allow them a restricted but perceptible policy-making role. They do so because their control over their political systems is non-hegemonous and thus an élite consensus concerning the legislature does not exist. This is attributable in large measure to the weakness or in some

[42] Ahmad, Government and Politics in Pakistan, p. 176.

[43] T. Maniruzzaman, 'Crises in Political Development and the Collapse of the Ayub Regime in Pakistan', *Journal of Developing Areas*, 5 (1971), 23–7; R. S. Wheeler, *Politics of Pakistan* (Ithaca, New York, 1970), 276 ff.

instances complete absence of political parties in marginal systems. The legislature exists because of these intra-*élite* cleavages; when these cleavages shift or are reduced, the legislature must be either changed or eliminated. Mass expectations may provide some transient support for this leadership faction or that, but they count for very little when the inevitable institutional alterations are made.

A minimal legislature: The Supreme Soviet (1917–). That the Supreme Soviet can neither reject nor amend policy proposals put before it by the government is beyond dispute. Also, it seems clear that the legislature does not constrain those who do make policy even through the more informal, parameter-setting process. Such a constraint depends at a minimum on either an ability to criticize publicly or a capacity to oppose privately in a manner sufficiently strenuous to increase intolerably the cost to the government of pushing the proposal through. There is certainly no capacity in the Supreme Soviet to oppose publicly. The capacity to oppose privately within the parliamentary commissions seems to exist on a limited basis but does not appear to be potent enough to discourage the government from doing what it wants to do.[44]

Support is difficult to assess in the Soviet Union. None the less it is reasonable to say that sixty years after the Revolution, the major elements of the Soviet political system, including the Supreme Soviet, are generally accepted political institutions, supported by most Soviet citizens. The Supreme Soviet is an instrument of the political élite in that country and so their support for the legislature is a given. If that support were not there, the institution would not be there at all.

This points to a distinction between the marginal legislature category and the minimal legislature category and also indicates the reason why there is no sixth category of less-supported legislatures with little or no policy-making power.

Marginal legislatures have, while they exist, the tentative support of non-legislative élites; minimal legislatures have a more permanent and continuing commitment from élites. If, by definition, this commitment involves only the most

[44] J. P. Vanneman, 'The Supreme Soviet of the USSR: Politics and the Legislative Process in the Soviet System', Ph.D. Diss., Pennsylvania State University, 1972, pp. 288–90, 300, 305–6, 310.

minimal policy-making role, then the expectations of non-legislative élites must be oriented toward either the representation or the system-maintenance model, or toward some hybrid of the two.

The modest policy-making role of the marginal legislature derives in part from significant élite cleavages; we assume that similar cleavages are either non-existent or have no legislative consequences in minimal systems, and thus élite consensus exists, at least to the extent of agreement that the legislature should have no policy-making role. An élite consensus strong enough to ban the legislature from any significant policy-making activities is strong enough to impose a different exceptional model upon legislators *and* exact conformance to that model. By this reasoning, a non-supported legislature with no policy-making role becomes a logical impossibility.

. . . I am under no illusions about these categories and the reader should have no illusions either. As we move through the substantive topics of legislative behaviour, there will be countless instances of intra-category variation. There will not always be differences among the categories; on certain comparative dimensions some categories of legislatures will look very much like others. In some instances, the categories will have nothing at all to do with observed inter-legislative variation.

These categories, rough as they may be, will provide us with a mechanism for bringing some degree of order to the disparate data that we have on legislatures and legislative behaviour all over the world. The categories will enable us to begin the arduous process of seeking out similarities and differences so that some day in the future we can honestly speak of a discipline of comparative legislative behaviour.

9

PARLIAMENT AND POLICY IN BRITAIN: THE HOUSE OF COMMONS AS A POLICY INFLUENCER

PHILIP NORTON

In seeking to locate the place of legislatures in the process of policy development, the most important classifications have been those provided by Nelson Polsby and Michael Mezey.[1] Writing in 1975, Polsby distinguished between 'arena' and 'transformative' legislatures. . . . In his book *Comparative Legislatures*, published in 1979, Mezey classified legislatures on the basis of support accruing to the institution and on the extent of policy-making power. . . .

On the basis of his two variables, Mezey was able to construct a six-box classification of legislatures, though only five of these were occupied. The House of Commons constituted an example of what he termed a 'reactive' legislature: that is, one that ranked among the more supported institutions but with modest policy-making power. Mezey quoted Bernard Crick to the effect that outright defeat of government was politically inconceivable; but cited other studies to show that pressure from back-bench MPs could induce a shift in government policy. In short, the House was seen neither as an arena or a transformative legislature. Rather, if one takes Polsby's classification as providing a continuum, it

Philip Norton, 'Parliament and Policy in Britain: The House of Commons as a Policy Influencer', *Teaching Politics*, 13/2 (1984), 198–202. Reprinted by permission of the publisher.

[1] N. Polsby, 'Legislatures', in F. I. Greenstein and N. Polsby (edd.), *Handbook of Political Science*, v (Reading, Mass., 1975) [pp. 129–48 in this volume—Ed.] and M. Mezey, *Comparative Legislatures* (Durham, NC, 1979) [pp. 149–76 in this volume—Ed.].

ranks somewhere in the middle, veering more towards an arena than a transformative assembly.

... [T]he House of Commons over the past century can be characterized as having been a reactive assembly. It has been a well-supported institution but its capacity to modify government measures has been extremely modest; so much so, that some writers could be forgiven for having assumed it had little or no policy-making power. However, recent events have changed the capacity of the House to influence policy. During the 1970s, the government suffered a number of defeats on the floor of the House. Viewed solely from the perspective of its ability and willingness to reject as well as modify government measures, the House moved more towards being a transformative legislature.[2] It became eligible for inclusion in Mezey's category of active legislatures. The problem with this is that the House of Commons would thus find itself in the same category as the US Congress. Despite the greater willingness of the House to reject government measures, its place in the policy cycle is not on a par with that of Congress. Hence the need for a new or reworked categorization.

The distinction Mezey draws in terms of support is useful. However, it would be useful to rework his classification based on policy-making. I would distinguish between legislatures which have a capacity, occasionally or regularly exercised, for policy-making, for policy-influencing, and for having little or no policy impact.

1. *Policy-making* legislatures are those which can not only modify or reject government measures but can themselves formulate and substitute a policy for that proposed by government;
2. *Policy-influencing* legislatures can modify or reject measures put forward by government but cannot substitute a policy of their own;
3. and legislatures with *little or no policy impact* can neither modify or reject measures, nor generate and substitute policies of their own.

[2] See J. E. Schwarz, 'Exploring a New Role in Policy Making: The British House of Commons in the 1970s', *American Political Science Review*, 74 (1980), 23–37.

'Policy' has been subject to different definitions. I would define it as a related set of proposals which compromise a recognizable whole, based ideally but not necessarily (in practice probably rarely) on conscious and tested assumptions as to costs, needs, end products, and implications. 'Policy-making' is the generation of that recognizable whole. Once 'made', policy can then be presented for discussion, modification, acceptance or rejection, application and evaluation. 'Policy influence' can be exerted at these later stages. It may take the form of formal modification or even rejection. It may work through a process of anticipated reaction: that is, the policy-makers may be influenced by expectations of whether or not a particular policy will gain approval. In such instances, the 'making' of policy is influenced by, but is not in the hands of, the legislature. In cases of little or no policy impact, a legislature has no appreciable influence upon policy-making nor upon the later stages of the policy cycle.

If we liken policy to a small (or not so small) jigsaw the picture becomes clearer. Policy-makers put the jigsaw together. They may do so in a clumsy and haphazard manner. They may produce a well-structured piece. Whichever, the responsibility for putting it together is theirs. A policy-making legislature can modify or reject that jigsaw, substituting one it has compiled itself. A policy-influencing legislature can reject the jigsaw or, more likely, reject or move about some of the pieces, but has not the capacity to reconstruct it or create a new jigsaw. A legislature with little or no policy impact looks upon and approves the jigsaw, with or without comment.

This classification of legislatures has two advantages. Firstly, it provides a useful framework for distinguishing between the US and UK legislatures. Congress is a policy-making legislature. That is, not only can it amend or reject executive policy, it can—and occasionally does—substitute a policy of its own. It has the leadership capable of formulating a policy as a substitute to that of the executive. In the House of Commons, the equivalent leadership is the executive. Though it has the capacity, recently exercised, to modify and even reject executive proposals, the House does not have the capacity to generate alternative policies. It is a policy influencer, not a policy maker.[3] Secondly, the distinction is useful in helping understand recent developments . . . To make sense of their impact upon the House of Commons it is helpful to draw the distinction between the making and the influencing of public policy. Without it, the changes of recent years may appear confused and shapeless. . . .

[3] One problem with this assertion arises in the context of private members' legislation. However, procedural and political constraints ensure that such legislation is not used as a major policy-making medium. The government controls the timetable of the House (any contentious or extensive private members' bills require government acquiescence as a minimum condition for getting through), there is a minimal amount of assistance available in drafting, and such bills cannot make a charge on the public revenue (except where incidental to achieving the purposes of the measure). Furthermore, bills introduced by private Members are often already 'made' by outside organizations which have attracted the sympathy of the sponsoring member.

PART IV

EXECUTIVE–LEGISLATIVE RELATIONS

INTRODUCTION

Though advances in the literature in recent years have enabled legislatures to be looked at and understood in a much broader context than that of relations with the executive, executive–legislative relations remain clearly important. Those relations have been much discussed, though subject to few pioneering studies.

One of the most significant problems in the study of executive–legislative relations has been that of generating concepts and identifying indicators that would permit comparative analysis. Attempts to generate concepts and to operationalize them remain very much in their infancy. One of the most interesting attempts to generate means of cross-national measurement was made in 1969 by Jean Blondel and his associates at the University of Essex, the results of their labours being published in *Government and Opposition* in 1970. Among the indicators they generated to permit assessment of legislatures was that of 'viscosity', that is the ability to resist a flow (or as they put in the Oxford English Dictionary, to resist a change in the arrangement of molecules). Though confining their analysis to five legislatures—all of which fall within Mezey's categorization of 'reactive' legislatures—the researchers none the less identify some variations in viscosity and conclude that 'it does seem possible to suggest that the importance of legislation and the various levels of "viscosity" which affect the legislative process, if examined comparatively, will help to circumscribe much more precisely the role of legislatures with respect to the function of "lawmaking" '. Though chronologically prior to another attempt by Blondel to generate criteria for assessing the strength of legislatures in relation to the executive,[1] drawing on constitutional powers as well as internal and external constraints, it none the less—as Mezey notes in his contribution to this volume—'gets closer to the problem'.

[1] J. Blondel, *Comparative Legislatures* (Englewood Cliffs, NJ, 1973).

Anthony King, in the lead article in the inaugural issue of *Legislative Studies Quarterly* (1976), has also made a major contribution to the study of executive–legislative relations, principally by questioning the utility of the term. Drawing on the experience of Britain, France, and West Germany, he demonstrates different modes of relationships (potentially, up to sixty in the case of West Germany) that exist in these parliamentary systems, relationships that are not only more numerous but also not necessarily coterminous with or subsumable under the two broad rubrics of 'executive' and 'legislature'. 'It seldom makes sense to speak of executive–legislative relations. Rather, there are in each political system a number of distinct political relationships, each with its own "membership" so to speak, and each with its own dynamics and structures of power. If we wish to understand the real world of politics better, it is these separate relationships that we should seek to identify and study.'

A further attempt to explicate and give some shape to the complexity of the position of legislatures in relation to executives and the making of public policy was made by Malcolm Shaw—like Blondel and King, a non-British-born academic—in seeking to assess the importance and strength of committees in legislatures. With the late John Lees, he edited a volume on committees in eight legislatures[2] and, in the concluding chapter, he sought to rank committee strength on the basis of the impact of party, constitutional arrangements (whether a presidential system, continental parliamentary system, or Westminster parliamentary system) and the stage at which bills were considered in committee (before or after plenary consideration). Though the material on a number of the legislatures is now dated—the Philippines legislature under consideration, for example, was that prior to the declaration of martial law in 1972, and the British House of Commons has introduced a wide-ranging system of departmentally related investigative select committees[3]—the analyt-

[2] J. D. Lees and M. Shaw (edd.), *Committees in Legislatures* (Oxford, 1979).

[3] See G. Drewry (ed.), *New Select Committees* (Oxford, 1985); N. Johnson, 'Departmental Select Committees', in M. Ryle and P. G. Richards (edd.), *Commons under Scrutiny* (London, 1988), 157–85.

ical framework offered constitutes a significant base for further research.

All three studies constitute important departures in a sea of traditional literature. Each concedes that it is essentially a pioneering work, but individually and collectively they provide a spur to further rigorous, empirical research that will help lift study of executive–legislative relations way beyond the level of description, anecdote, and country-bound perceptions.

10

LEGISLATIVE BEHAVIOUR: SOME STEPS TOWARDS A CROSS-NATIONAL MEASUREMENT

JEAN BLONDEL *et al.*

While the literature on the legislators' attitudes has become impressive in the course of the last decade, the study of legislative *behaviour* lags markedly behind. Even S. C. Patterson's *Legislative Behaviour* remains primarily concerned with the examination of legislator's attitudes.[1] One of the clearest examples of this trend is exemplified by roll-call analysis: studies of roll-calls have principally attempted to elucidate the ideology or specific attitudinal characteristics of members of legislatures; they have not been concerned with the outcomes of these roll-calls as such, inasmuch as they might have constituted an indication of the extent to which legislatures could and did affect the 'rule-making' process in a national community. This situation is not surprising: the measurement of decision outcomes, as affected by legislatures or by any other structures of government is still in its infancy: reliable indicators have not as yet been satisfactorily developed even in simpler communities, such as local communities; for a national community the task appears huge. Yet it is only if we start, however crudely, to measure outcomes and, in particular, the extent to which legislatures can modify these outcomes, that political scientists will be able to answer some of the

J. Blondel *et al.*, 'Legislative Behaviour: Some Steps towards a Cross-National Measurement', *Government and Opposition*, 5/1 (1970), 67–85. Reprinted by permission of the publisher. This chapter summarizes the conclusions of a joint research project undertaken in 1969 as part of a graduate seminar in comparative politics in the Department of Government of the University of Essex by Jean Blondel, P. Gillespie, V. Herman, P. Kaati, and R. Leonard, University of Essex.

[1] S. C. Patterson, *Legislative Behaviour* (New York, 1968).

major questions which are of concern to them. Specifically, as long as legislative behaviour is not studied, it will not be possible to discuss meaningfully the key problems which legislatures pose: does it make much, some or no difference for a country to have or not to have a legislature, other things being equal? Where two political systems are similar (e.g. in two 'liberal democracies'), does the 'weight' of legislative influence remain constant, irrespective of the structure of the legislature, the size of the majority, the origin of members, etc.

These problems are vast, and the present article can only partially explore a limited number of aspects. But although the empirical findings which are discussed here relate, as we shall see, to bills and bills only, as discussed in full house, and in five liberal democratic countries (the United Kingdom, France, Sweden, India, and Ireland), some general substantive and methodological questions have to be raised at the outset. Indeed, the findings must be regarded as merely a preliminary investigation into the methods which might be used in order to study legislative behaviour, while giving some indication of the nature and extent of the variations. As is well known, most liberal democracies are now composed of disciplined parties through which governmental policies are implemented with relatively little trouble: it is precisely because of this situation that the question of legislative influence both needs to be raised and is difficult to measure. The present article hopes simply to suggest where variations may occur and how they might be assessed.

LEGISLATURES AND THE POLITICAL SYSTEM

The study of government implies the study of a number of structures, one of which is the legislature. One of the drawbacks of behavioural analyses has been that they have concentrated too often almost exclusively on the politics of the people at large or on the background or attitudes of policy-makers. The reasons for such a situation are well known; it was indeed essential to move away from a legalistic examination of structures. But structures still need to be studied for theoretical and practical reasons, and they must be studied from a 'decision-making', not a legalistic point of view. As long as this is not done, political scientists will continue, in relation to legislatures (as well as other structures) to mix some of the most formal textbook legalism with somewhat impressionistic remarks about individual legislatures which scarcely lead to precise spatial or temporal comparisons.

However, an analysis of legislature behaviour on a cross-national basis implies that we have at our disposal a model which will enable us to map out the points at which any given legislature may be involved in the political process. As comparative analysis has now progressed sufficiently, it is possible to begin to elaborate such a model, even though it is likely to encompass much more than we can empirically begin to measure adequately—as will be seen from the data presented in the following sections. But, unless we outline the major points at which legislatures are involved in the political process, it will not be possible even to determine to what extent the data used here, or elsewhere, are indeed partial: for this reason alone, it appears necessary to attempt to summarize what are or may be the points of insertion of legislatures in the political process.

Legislatures (and legislators—the terms are used here indifferently and no attempt will be made to assess the extent to which legislators act in their private capacity, or as members of other organizations, or as members of the legislature) are involved in the political process (and contribute or may contribute to decisional outputs) at three analytically distinct levels.

First, they are part of the *input* machinery through which 'ideas' of various kinds are passed on to the decision-makers: these are of considerable importance in that they create a climate within which the executive may find itself constrained to 'initiate' legislation, such an initiation being in fact a response to the 'ideas' which have been generated through or by the legislators, within the legislature or outside it. These 'ideas' may be pitched at various levels of generality: they may concern trivial matters of purely local interest or they may be aiming at the most general policies. Legislative studies have sometimes been concerned with such inputs (in particular the context of the 'surgeries' or the mail received by politicians[2]) but they should be studied systematically: there is, for instance, impressionistic evidence to the effect that these individual activities of legislators at the detailed level may be the most universal way in which legislatures are involved significantly in the political process, as they are likely to take place even where the executive is authoritarian. The present study is not concerned with the measurement of this aspect of legislative involvement: the analysis of such inputs needs to progress substantially both theoretically and empirically before the beginnings of a cross-national analysis can be attempted.

Secondly, at the other extreme of the decision-making process, legislatures and legislators are concerned with the *supervision of the rule-implementation* aspect of governmental activity. Such supervision is also difficult to measure in general, although some aspects are commonly mentioned and have indeed been scrutinized, for instance in the context of the activities of legislative committees; but committees are only one of the means by which legislatures (or legislators) scrutinize the implementation of rules and this is likely to be true in inverse correlation with the liberal character of the regime: the more authoritarian the system, the more scrutiny, if it takes place at all, is likely to take place in private, by means of discussions between legislators, on the one hand, and ministers and civil servants, on the other. But such *private* scrutiny takes place also, and probably on a large scale, in liberal countries. The identification of the extent of scrutiny and the measurement of its influence are therefore probably tasks of the same magnitude as the identification and measurement of the 'ideas' brought forward by legislators. Indeed, these two aspects of legislative involvement are connected, as feedback is likely to occur between the scrutiny of existing policies and the development of new ideas.

Finally legislatures are involved in what might be loosely called the '*rule-making*' *process* of government. This is of course what studies of legislatures typically concentrate on and the findings of the present article are also concentrated on this

[2] See esp. R E. Dowse, 'MP and his Surgery', *Political Studies*, 11/4 (1963), 332–41.

level. But, even in this context alone, the involvement of legislatures needs to be considered in some detail. In the first place, and assuming that we term 'rule-making process' all those activities which aim at determining authoritatively the policies of the nation, the 'rules' in which the legislature may be involved are not coextensive with, but indeed larger than, 'legislation'. The constitutional and legal tradition with which political scientists remain associated, whether consciously or not, has led to the general assumption that in so far as they are concerned with rule-making, assemblies are concerned with bills and with bills only and to a second assumption, also generally made, that bills are among the most important 'rules' which affect a political community. Both these assertions may be empirically valid, at any rate in some countries and during definite periods, but they need to be tested. It is also well known that in many countries which do have legislatures, whether in the communist world or in parts of the developing world, bills constitute a small fraction of rule-making. As a result, an attempt to measure generally the part played by assemblies in the field of 'rule-making' has to take into account all the processes by which rules are made and policies implemented and to assess the relative 'weight' of bills, other types of legal rules (such as regulations, decrees, orders, etc.), and types of decisions which are not formalized into legal documents, for instance informal agreements, pressures, and inducements. An example of such pressures, if rather inconclusive, is that of the attempt made by the UK Government in 1969, through a series of melodramatic episodes, to achieve some modicum of trade-union reform. Legislatures may or may not be involved in all these types of activities: they may pass bills; they may, directly or indirectly, be concerned with regulations, orders, or other legal rules; they may (through debates and in other ways) be concerned with approving, rejecting, or delaying governmental actions which do not take the form of legal 'rules'.

Thus, in the context of rule-making, a comprehensive analysis of legislative behaviour should extend beyond legislation. But such a comprehensive study is still much beyond the scope of our tools of analysis as it raises two types of technical questions which are as yet unsolved. First, and assuming that the full extent of 'rule-making' (defined in the broad sense as above) was determined for a given country, we would need to have some instruments by which to find out whether, or rather to what extent, the extent of such 'rule-making' varies from country to country: where there is much state intervention, there is, or so one would infer, more 'rule-making'. But we have as yet no means of measuring the 'more or less' adequately. Second, we need to be able to weigh the relative part played by bills, other formal rules, and informal decisions in this total of 'rule-making' (particularly as long as it is easier to measure the part played by legislatures with respect to bills than with respect to other types of 'rule-making'). If a government succeeds in inducing various bodies to agree through informal pressures and only presses for legislation in relatively few cases, the rule-making process will be different than where bills are the way in which rules are made. Yet it is as difficult to measure the weight of informal pressures as it is to measure legislative inputs or the supervision of outputs: much is likely to happen behind the scenes, in committees, or even in private discussions and we need to develop better techniques of measurement before we can even begin to compare relative 'amounts'.

The present study is thus of necessity confined to what is in reality a partial aspect of the activity of legislatures, law-making, though it is the one which is most commonly referred to in textbooks. It follows from the previous discussion that, even though we might be able to weigh the role of legislatures in relation to bills, it is not possible to state (except somewhat indirectly, as we shall see) whether one given country devotes more of its 'rule-making' to bills than another. We can merely state whether the weight of bills, for instance in a given year, is greater in one country than in another: we might therefore infer indirectly that, if it appears that two countries are equally *dirigiste*, the one which uses bills less makes rather more use of other types of rule-making. But this is merely a tentative inference, which can be drawn only for countries which have achieved similar levels of socio–economic development and appear to have similar ideologies: it cannot therefore be used as a measure for general comparative studies.

Another problem needs to be solved, however, even if we are to limit the study to the comparative influence of legislatures on bills. Let us consider the cases of two countries, A and B, where bills appear to play a similar part. Let us suppose that in Country A the legislature amends or transforms about 50 per cent of the bills and that in Country B the legislature passes almost on the nod over 90 per cent of the legislation. Yet it should not be concluded that the weight of the legislature of Country A in relation to bills is greater than the weight of the legislature of Country B. The laws passed by the legislature of Country A may be less numerous; the distribution of trivial and important bills may be very different. It may be that the unamended bills are the important ones and that the legislature of Country A is only allowed by the government to amend those bills which are of little concern to the executive. Conclusions can therefore be drawn only if a preliminary step is taken by which bills are weighted for their importance on a cross-national basis. We shall therefore devote the next section to a tentative measurement of the importance of legislation before attempting to assess the weight of legislatures in relation to these bills. Given the methodological problems involved, it is understandable that, even on bills alone, the study of legislative behaviour should require further investigations before most of the major problems come to be fully covered.

THE MEASUREMENT OF THE IMPORTANCE OF LEGISLATION[3]

It is intuitively recognized that legislation varies markedly in importance and ordinary political language takes importance almost continuously into account.[4] Yet the criteria to be used to assess importance are not easy to identify and, consequently, to operationalize. Moreover, importance is also

[3] This section of the chapter draws heavily on P. Gillespie's research paper.

[4] The *Congressional Quarterly* e.g. makes its calculations of presidential 'success' in getting legislation through after having taken into account the importance of legislation.

intuitively associated with subject-matter and some would probably make subject-matter part of, or even coextensive with importance. It is therefore necessary to begin by describing some of the criteria and indicators of importance before examining how important legislation appears to have been in the countries studied.

Criteria designed to measure the importance of legislation. The measurement of importance of legislation is still crude, but two types of classificatory schemes appear to have considerable potential. One takes into account the apparent desired result of the policies. Lowi and Salisbury suggest[5] that one might classify policies according to whether they aim at 'redistributing' goods, at 'distributing' them or at 'regulating' activities. Regulatory policies have in turn been subdivided into those which regulate the state as a whole ('constitutional regulatory'), those which are regulatory at the level of ordinary activities of citizens, and those in which classes of people obtain legislation to regulate their own activities ('self-regulatory').

Such a classificatory scheme makes it possible to describe in broad terms the activities of legislatures and to compare legislatures over time or space irrespective of the particular field in which laws are being enacted. But it does not make it possible to rank these activities and therefore to obtain an impression of the overall importance of legislation in a given country, unless we were to postulate that, for instance, redistributive policies are always more important than, say, self-regulatory policies, an assumption which is probably widely held but needs to be tested.

The importance of individual bills should therefore be measured by the extent to which they appear to be designed to affect the community and constitute elements of departure from the current situation. Such a scheme was suggested by Polsby in relation to community policies and can be used for national legislation, at least in principle. Four criteria were suggested: (1) How many people were affected by the outcomes; (2) How many different kinds of community (in this case

[5] T. J. Lowi, 'American Business, Public Policy, Case-Studies and Political Theory', *World Politics*, 16/4 (1964), 677–715; R. H. Salisbury, 'Analysis of Public Policy: A Search for Theories and Roles', in A. Ranney (ed.), *Political Science and Public Policy* (Chi., Ill.: 1968), 158.

national) resources are distributed by the outcomes; (3) How large is the amount of resources distributed by the outcomes; (4) How drastically present community (in this case national) resource distributions are altered by the outcomes.[6] Polsby adds that decisions (which in the present case would mean legislation) can be ranked 'in principle . . . by making use of one or another or a combination of these criteria'.[7]

These criteria are difficult to operationalize, however, in the present state of the techniques which we have at our disposal. In this study, it did not appear possible even to begin to assign values to the 'different kinds of community resources distributed by the outcomes'. The index of importance of bills was therefore computed on the basis of values assigned to the three other criteria as well as to the length of pieces of legislation, as it appeared intuitively that the length of bills did bear some relationship with their importance. The combination of these criteria had to remain somewhat arbitrary, since there are no guidelines which would suggest that any one of these criteria contributed more than any other to the determination of the importance of a particular bill.

A maximum of 10 points was therefore attributed to each bill, two or three of which were allocated in respect of the three substantive criteria and of the extent to which a given bill was substantially longer or shorter than the average legislation. Very important bills were thus given 9 or 10 points, while unimportant bills scored no point or 1 point and bills of intermediate importance received between 2 and 8 points. Unquestionably, such a method will need to be refined as further studies of legislation are carried out and sample surveys of élite groups relating to particular pieces of legislation might help to suggest guidelines for the weighting of the different criteria suggested by Polsby. But it seemed possible to draw a number of conclusions based on the classification of bills covering a whole year of the activities of a legislature.

The importance of legislation in the United Kingdom, Ireland, Sweden, France, and India. For the purpose of this inquiry a sample of the bills was drawn from all the bills passed by the

[6] N. W. Polsby, *Community Power and Political Theory* (New Haven, Conn., 1963), 95–6.
[7] Ibid.

legislatures of each of the United Kingdom, Ireland, Sweden, France, and India (see Table 10.1).[8] A non-election year was chosen for each of the countries, as it might be assumed that election years would lead to a greater amount of short-term legislation designed to attract voters.

First, the raw index of legislative output shows that even countries which appear to have similar systems of government display marked differences in the total legislative output. These variations affect both the number of bills, the size of the average bill, and the total length of legislation. Total amount of legislation is not correlated with the population size of the country: indeed, it appears to be inversely correlated with population size, though such a conclusion would need to be confirmed for other countries: it is noticeable, however, that the only federal country in the group, India, had substantially fewer bills per inhabitant and fewer pages of legislation per inhabitant than all the other countries except France.

TABLE 10.1. Quantity of Legislative Output

	United Kingdom (1966–7)	Ireland (1965)	Sweden (1966)	France (1966)	India (1966)
Number of bills passed	98	34	285	147	51
Number of bills in sample	49	28	28	49	15
Average number of clauses	19	35	16	7	15
Average length in words	7,500	2,800	1,600	600	3,500
Total legislative output (in thousands of words)	730	95	456	88	178

[8] A proportion of the bills of each country was chosen, half in the UK, a third in France and India, one-tenth in Sweden; all Irish bills were analysed, except those carried over from the previous session and those which did not go through all their stages during the session under consideration.

Second, when bills were classified by their social aims (Table 10.2), they appeared to divide somewhat unevenly between the redistributive group and the others: there were no bills in this group in Ireland, and they constituted a small minority of the bills in the other countries, except in India, where, however, the sample of bills considered was small and variations due to sampling error could be large.

TABLE 10.2. Social Aims of Legislation (percentages)

	United Kingdom	Ireland	Sweden	France	India
Redistributive	4	0	11	8	20
Distributive	27	25	14	25	47
Constitutional regulatory	16	11	18	22	20
Regulatory	24	39	21	18	13
Self-regulatory	29	25	36	27	0
TOTAL	100	100	100	100	100

While redistributive bills are less numerous than other types of legislation, it could be expected that their weight in the total legislative output is larger. If each bill is scored for its importance (Table 10.3), the overall average and the average for each of the categories of bills is as follows:

TABLE 10.3. Importance of Legislation

	United Kingdom	Ireland	Sweden	France	India
Average importance	3.2	3.1	2.1	1.3	3.1
Redistributive	6.5	none	7.0	0.7	8.3
Distributive	4.1	3.4	2.0	0.8	1.0
Constitutional regulatory	3.3	2.3	1.2	1.8	0.1
Regulatory	3.0	3.2	2.0	0.7	6.8
Self-regulatory	1.9	2.5	1.2	2.0	none

Redistributive bills are indeed on average more important than other bills in three of the four countries where such bills were passed during the session studied, but they were among the least important bills which were passed in France. Moreover, distributive bills are also more important than bills of a regulatory character in a majority of countries, France and India being the two countries which do not confirm this trend. However, neither distributive bills nor even redistributive bills are so consistently and so markedly more important than regulatory bills as to suggest that there is a sharp cleavage in the apparent effect on the national community of bills of different types. When bills are examined individually in each country it appears that some of the regulatory bills, including some of the self-regulatory bills, were indeed important. While, except for the case of France, to which we are coming, redistributive bills are almost uniformly relatively important, bills of a regulatory nature range widely across the continuum of importance.

Patterns of legislative output and of distribution of bills according to their social aims vary appreciably between the five countries, but the one profound cleavage is that which distinguishes France from the other four polities. French bills are appreciably shorter than those of any other country; they are strikingly less important than those of the other countries; and France is the one country where the most important (or perhaps more accurately the least unimportant) bills are those of a regulatory kind. While bills score on average slightly over 3 points in the United Kingdom, Ireland, and India, and slightly over 2 in Sweden, they score only 1.3 points in France—which means that on length, on numbers of people affected by the outcomes, on amounts of resources distributed, *and* on the alteration of resource distribution, French bills tended to score low or very low. This was true even of the redistributive bills: in effect the redistribution which took place through legislation during the year only affected limited numbers of people and involved relatively few resources.

This is not the place to attempt to explain the relatively trivial nature of the bills which were presented to the French legislature during the year 1966, though this finding is, to say the least, consistent with the generally accepted view of the role of Parliament in the Gaullist phase of the Fifth Republic. But this situation indicates that the measurement of the role played by legislatures, even in liberal democratic countries, must take into account the average importance of the legislative outputs which these legislatures process during a given period; it also points to the direction which cross-national studies of legislatures are likely to take: by measuring the importance of the bills which go through a number of legislatures, it will become possible to rank these legislatures and thus to group them into similar categories from the point of view of their legislative output. As long as it is difficult to measure other forms of activities of legislatures (inputs, supervision of implementation of policies and other forms of rule-making), it is important to compare legislatures within each of the groups defined by a similar weight of legislative output.

THE ROLE OF LEGISLATURES IN RELATION TO LEGISLATION[9]

In the present study, the weight of legislatures in relation to legislation was considered through activities taking place in the whole house. Committee procedure varies widely from country to country and the precise impact of committees is difficult to measure; moreover, if committees were to be examined, individual pressures on ministers should also have been considered. In fact, as a preliminary assessment, it is more logical to attempt to measure the apparent influence of the legislature as a whole: the effect of pressures taking place in committees or elsewhere will be perceived through changes made to the legislation on the floor of the house. To take one example: if, for whatever reason, the government declares itself in favour of an amendment after a committee discussion, the effect will appear on the floor of the chamber, since the government will move the amendment. The same would apply to amendments suggested by individual members, whether they are defeated or passed in committee.

[9] This section of the chapter draws particularly on V. Herman's research paper.

What an analysis of activities (and outcomes) on the floor of the chamber will not reveal, however, is what might be termed the 'preventive' action of the legislature, but studies of committee activities would not help appreciably to identify or measure this role. We can see whether bills are modified; we cannot assess how many bills are *not* presented by the government because the government realizes (or, strictly, thinks) that these bills would not be passed, or would consume too much energy on its part. Clearly, this type of preventive role is important, and may indeed be the most important role of the chamber with respect to rule-making, though it might be difficult to determine whether it is the chamber as such or the pressure of various bodies taking place through the chamber which is the most important. To take two examples: the UK Government abandoned two important pieces of legislation in 1969: one related to trade-union reform, and it could be suggested that this was due to pressures exercised by various bodies, legislators being merely one of the elements; the other related to House of Lords reform, and it might be suggested that this was due primarily to the 'preventive' role of legislators. However, these are only two of the 'ideas' on legislation which the UK government did not pursue further: many ideas do not even reach the stage of a White Paper or a debate in the Chamber; they simply do not go further than the files of the minister.[10]

As could be expected, most of (and in two countries all of) the influence of legislatures in relation to legislation related to government bills. No private members' bill was passed in either Ireland or India and the numbers passed in the other three countries was small: their overall weight in the total legislative output ranged from nil to a maximum of 10 per cent in France, with the United Kingdom and Sweden scoring respectively 5 and 3 per cent.[11] The case of France should be

[10] The problem is very similar to that of 'non-decisions' which have begun to be studied in the field of community politics, esp. by Bachrach and Baratz. See e.g. P. Bachrach and M. S. Baratz, 'Two Faces of Power', *American Political Science Review*, 56/4 (1962), 947–52. See also P. Bachrach, 'Non-Decision Making and the Urban Racial Crisis', paper read at the 65th meeting of the American Political Science Association, New York, 1969.

[11] The number of private members' bills passed was 14 in the UK, 11 in Sweden, and 14 in France.

seen as confirming the trend which began to emerge in the previous section: the weight of private members' legislation was relatively large, but within a general situation in which the weight of legislation is relatively small. Thus the absolute importance of private members' legislation is greater in the United Kingdom than in France and it appears that some freedom was left to the French Parliament to make some laws on its own, but that these laws were of a trivial character.

Private members' bills are a measure of the power of *initiation* of the legislature: they are truly the converse of the *preventive* power of legislatures which we described earlier in this section and of which it is not possible, as yet, to find a satisfactory measurement. Between these two types of powers lies what might be termed the role of legislatures as a *reaction* to the intitiative of the government. But such a power of reaction can take various forms, which tend to be exercised jointly in practice, though they need to be distinguished analytically. First, and most obvious, is the power of the legislature to change the contents of the legislation with which it is confronted: at the limit, such a power of amendment merges with the power to alter the bill radically or indeed to kill it. However, since most legislatures, even in 'liberal democratic' countries, pass most of the bills which are presented by the executive and indeed scarcely alter these bills against the wishes of the government, other types of milder influence need to be taken into account. If one plots possible government–legislature relationships in relation to bills along a continuum ranging from total compliance to total freedom (Fig. 10.1), one encounters a number of steps which can be taken as indicative of various degrees of *viscosity*[12] in the legislative process. Where the legislature is very compliant, bills do not merely pass, they pass very easily and, in particular, the time spent or the number of speakers engaged in debate is very small. As the legislature become freer, the time spent increases and amendments are discussed and indeed passed. The origin, number, and fate of these amendments are all indicative of a number of steps in the viscosity of the process. First, one finds amendments presented

[12] In the sense of 'power of resisting a change in the arrangement of the molecules', *OED*.

by the opposition, but these are presented for propaganda purposes and the opposition knows that they will be rejected: this will have to be related to time spent and we shall see that the tabling of opposition amendments may well be a sign of lower viscosity than large amounts of time spent in debate. Second, and at the other end, amendments presented by the opposition—or perhaps by government 'supporters' linking with the opposition—will be passed by the legislature against the wishes of the government. Third, between these two positions, amendments may be passed with the consent of the government.

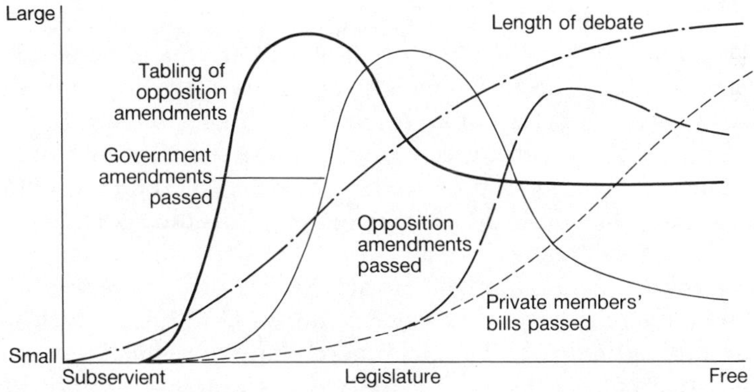

FIG. 10.1. Government–Legislature Relationships in Relation to Bills

As we shall see, this category is in fact very important: bills are indeed amended, but mainly at the overt request of the government, in the legislatures of 'liberal democratic' countries. Yet it is not possible to know without a detailed analysis of each particular case or at least of a sample of cases, whether the government did in a real sense initiate the amendment. It can be postulated that at least in a number of cases the government received a suggestion from outside and either genuinely liked it (in which case there is already a response to outside intervention) or felt neutral or even somewhat negative, but for general political reasons considered it appropriate to make a gesture. If government amendments are lumped together, it appears reasonable to locate them between the tabling of opposition amendments and the passage of opposition amendments on a continuum of legislative viscosity.

We therefore find four different steps of legislative influence between the two extreme positions of full compliance and total 'freedom', although it is likely that these four steps will overlap in real situations. A precise index of the viscosity of legislatures would take into account each of these four steps and combine them into a weighted index in relation to each bill, this being in turn weighted for each bill in relation to the importance of that bill. But the weighting of each of the steps of legislative influence is even more complex than the weighting of the criteria of importance: length of debates and the tabling of propaganda-type opposition amendments are related to the expectation which opponents of the government may have of being able to swing public opinion or to blackmail the government to make concessions in the future for fear of public opinion reactions. It is therefore not axiomatic that the gain of an amendment in the short run is evidence of greater overall influence than the persistent nagging of the government in debate. We will therefore not attempt here to weight the various indicators of 'viscosity' into a combined index and we will merely draw conclusions from the apparent distribution of the various practices across the countries studied.

Although each country scores very differently on most of these indices, the analysis of the pattern of distribution suggests that there are broad similarities between the United Kingdom and Ireland, and between Sweden and India, while France displays very peculiar characteristics (see Table 10.4).

In the United Kingdom and Ireland, the number of hours spent by the legislature in discussing each bill is relatively high, while the number of government amendments is also appreciably higher than elsewhere; but the number of opposition amendments tabled and the number of opposition amendments passed is either intermediate or relatively low. India and, though less so, Sweden, have the converse characteristics. Admittedly, the Swedish legislature scores low or very low on all the indicators, but it is on time spent and the number of government amendments passed that the difference is most marked. Thus for Sweden as for India, scores are better or good in relation to the number of opposition amendments tabled or passed than they are, at least relatively speaking, where the United Kingdom and Ireland score best, as if the behaviour of these two legislatures were characterized by different means of attempting to influence the executive. Finally, the French legislature differs from the other four chambers in that it spent relatively little time discussing bills, received relatively few opposition amendments, but passed a greater amount of both government and opposition amendments.

One can immediately see why it would be of considerable value to be able to weigh the different means by which

TABLE 10.4. Government Bills and Apparent Activities of Legislatures

	UK	Ireland	Sweden	France	India
Bills analysed (government only)	49	28	26	41	15
Average importance of bills (all bills)	3.2	3.1	2.1	1.3	3.1
Hours of debate per bill	7.1	5.2	0.4	1.5	2.8
Ratio Hours: per point of importance	2.2	1.7	0.2	1.1	0.9
Number of opposition amendments per bill	4.4	3.0	3.3	3.6	10.1
Number of government amendments passed per bill (includes those accepted by government)	14.5	7.9	0.8	6.0	2.8
Number of government amendments *x* per point	46.5	24.5	1.7	7.8	8.7
Number of opposition amendments passed per bill	0.18	0.20	0.10	0.49	0.31
Number of opposition amendments per point of importance	0.58	0.63	0.21	0.64	0.96

legislatures manifest their 'reactive' activities to governmental legislation; but one can also see that the orders of magnitude are so different that no simple weighting mechanism can be adopted. In particular, the number of amendments passed against the government's wishes is extremely small: even where it is largest—in France—the number of opposition amendments passed is slightly smaller than one for every two bills passed by the legislature. It is not clear whether the passage of such amendments is a sign of greater influence of the legislature or, more precisely, by what factor such amendments should be weighted before they are compared to the large numbers of government amendments which are passed in all the legislatures, even in Sweden where it is smallest. It is therefore on the basis of differences in patterns of distribution that some tentative hypotheses can be advanced.

First, while all these legislatures appear fairly compliant, this compliance would seem to be, on the surface, most marked in Sweden, and least marked in France, with India, Ireland, and the United Kingdom constituting intermediate cases. But the data presented here, as well as other types of information concerning executive–legislative relationships in Sweden and France suggest that the extent of legislative influence needs to be interpreted in a somewhat different manner. Let us first compare the cases of the United Kingdom and Ireland, on the one hand, with that of India. In the first two countries, as we noted, the weight of the legislature is felt essentially through fairly long debates and the passage of governmental amendments; the average importance of bills in the three countries is about the same. If it is postulated that the fact that the government suggests amendments indicates a willingness to make some concessions to the opposition, or to bow to the importance of the legislature, it would follow that, the more the government proposes amendments, the less there will be need for (or desire on the part of some of the more rebellious government supporters) to vote for opposition amendments; thus time spent in debate *added to* the passage of government amendments would correspond to the tabling of vast numbers of opposition amendments and the passage of some of them. Overall, the figures characterizing these legislatures seem to suggest that, of the three, the Indian legislature is the least powerful (with respect to government bills) and the UK Parliament the most powerful; it might be further hypothesized that the tabling of large numbers of opposition amendments is in fact more of an empty gesture than relatively long hours spent debating bills, as this latter characteristic would suggest that the government has at least to hear the case and to make some efforts to answer it.

Second, these conclusions, however, concern merely what happens once the bill has been presented to the legislature. Let us suppose that, prior to the bill having even been tabled, discussions have taken place within the caucus of the government party or between the various parties: it might therefore be that the apparent concessions are smaller, but that some concessions have taken place before. Where the discussions have taken place within the caucus of the government party, it is likely that the overt manifestations of legislative activity will emanate merely from the opposition: party supporters have been placated, *ex hypothesi*, and they will be fairly peaceful. Where discussions have taken place between the various parties, it is likely that there will be little manifestation of legislative activity, as everybody will have been placated, also *ex hypothesi*. In such situations, one would witness relatively short debates, few government amendments and only minimal manifestations of opposition power in the form of amendments passed. These situations appear to correspond broadly to the cases of India and Sweden, particularly in comparison with the United Kingdom and Ireland. The differences in the patterns of legislative activity exemplified by India and Sweden, on the one hand, and by the United Kingdom and Ireland, on the other, seem to suggest that in these last two countries, legislation is presented to the legislature at a somewhat earlier stage of 'preparation of minds' than in the former two, and certainly than in Sweden at least.[13]

Third, the case of France becomes easier to interpret if the concept of the preparation of minds is taken jointly with the

[13] The role of Royal Commissions in preparing the ground for legislation in Sweden is well known. These commissions seem to come closer to creating a common ground for legislation than their equivalents in the UK.

finding about the importance of legislation. If it is remembered that French legislation was on average less important than that of the other countries, it would seem to follow that French bills need not be debated at such length as bills in other legislatures. But it also appears that the French executive need not bother so much about the extent to which it sees its own draft of legislation passed; indeed the whole exercise becomes more of a gesture towards the legislature (to keep it occupied and, so to speak, out of mischief) than a genuine situation of conflict of influence in which the government has to concede points to the legislature. In fact, a weighted index of amendments passed as a result of opposition initiative scarcely leaves the French Parliament at an advantage compared to the UK and Irish Parliaments and the number of amendments passed appears related to their triviality. Thus the French legislature is relatively free, but within its domain—and this domain is a restricted one. This situation is surely repeated in a number of countries which might be deemed to be peripheral to the liberal democratic world. It clearly indicates that the measurement of the superiority of the status of the government in relation to the chamber is strongly correlated with the extent to which it can remain free not to present to the legislature more than a specified amount of important bills.

CONCLUSIONS

The study of the 'viscosity' which legislatures introduce in the rule-making process needs to be undertaken on a much broader front before some of the tentative generalizations which have been presented here come to be confirmed. Moreover, an examination of a larger number of countries will give a clearer picture of the range of the variations, even between 'liberal democratic' countries: it is not possible to state categorically that France is exceptional among the countries of the group until most European countries, at least, have beem examined in this way. However, it does seem possible to suggest that the importance of legislation and the various levels of 'viscosity' which affect the legislative process, if examined comparatively, will help to circumscribe much more precisely the role of legislatures with respect to the function of law-making. From this preliminary step, the study of legislatures will extend naturally to other forms of rule-making, as well as to the broader context of the selection of inputs and the supervision of policy-implementation. Whether the role of legislatures in relation to bills appears important or not, it should stimulate studies of legislative behaviour, since it should contribute, negatively or positively, to the solution of the nagging problem which faces modern political systems: are legislatures a significant part of the process of government?

11

MODES OF EXECUTIVE–LEGISLATIVE RELATIONS: GREAT BRITAIN, FRANCE, AND WEST GERMANY

ANTHONY KING

Political scientists often write about the relations between 'executives' and 'legislatures'. Politicians use the same language. We all speak of the decline in parliament's power over the cabinet or of new strains in the relations between congress and the president. The purpose of this paper is to suggest that in fact it is usually highly misleading to speak of 'executive–legislative relations' *tout court* and that, if we wish to understand the phenomena subsumed under this general heading, we need to identify and consider separately a number of quite distinct political relationships. We need, to put it another way, to 'think behind' the Montesquieu formula.[1]

The nature of the different relationships that the term 'executive–legislative relations' tends to mask can be expected

Anthony King, 'Modes of Executive–Legislative Relations: Great Britain, France, and West Germany', *Legislative Studies Quarterly*, 1/1 (1976), 11–34. Reprinted by permission of the author and the Comparative Legislative Research Center. The chapter is a revised version of a paper given at the annual meeting of the American Political Science Association, San Francisco, Sept. 1975, which in turn was a substantially revised version of a paper first given at the annual meeting of the Political Studies Association of the United Kingdom, Oxford, Mar. 1975. For their comments on successive drafts, the author is especially grateful to Jack Hayward, Gerhard Loewenberg, Lester Seligman, and Maurice Vile.

[1] For a general critique of the Montesquieu formula as a way of characterizing executive–legislative relations (and indeed as a way of characterizing executives and legislatures), see A. King, 'Executives', in F. I. Greenstein and N. W. Polsby (edd.), *Handbook of Political Science*, v (Reading, Mass., 1975).

to vary considerably from country to country. It would be very surprising if the important relationships in Great Britain were the same as those in the United States. The claim is not being made here that executive–legislative relations in different countries can be discussed in identical, or even similar, terms. On the contrary, our contention is that the use of the same term, executive–legislative relations, with regard to different countries has tended to conceal the important differences between them. What these important differences are will emerge as we proceed.

The treatment in a short chapter cannot be exhaustive. The aim here is rather to illustrate an approach. Our evidence is drawn for the moment from only three countries—Britain, France, and West Germany. Although the aim is mainly to suggest a way of approaching the study of executive–legislative relations, the paper will also contain a number of observations about the substance of these relations in the three countries studied.

BRITAIN: A CASE OF MAJORITY-PARTY GOVERNMENT IN A PARLIAMENTARY SYSTEM

Anyone glancing at the pages of the standard textbooks on the British system of government frequently comes across phrases such as the following: 'the power of Parliament', 'the impact of Parliament on the executive', 'the influence of Parliament over the administration', 'the Commons and the Executive' or 'how to strengthen the House of Commons in relation to the Government of the day'.[2] The implication is that there are two bodies, one called Parliament or the House of Commons, the other called variously the executive, the administration, or the government, and that the aim is to understand, often with a view to altering, the relationship between these two bodies. Of course the relationship between the two bodies is perceived to take a variety of forms. Thus, Richards refers to 'the challenge

[2] Page references could be given for these quotations, but it would be invidious to. The quotations have been chosen more or less at random. They tell one nothing about the quality of the rest of the writers' work.

to the executive by the whole House' and to 'the challenge to the executive by committees', and Crick refers, on another plane, to 'what the Commons do individually' and to 'what the Commons do collectively'. The two-body image, however, is very nearly constant.[3]

The question is: is this the most useful, and the most precise, way of conceiving of executive–legislative relations in Great Britain? Doubts about the two-body conception ought, one would have thought, to have arisen out of the fact that British politics are dominated by political parties and that it is quite cumbersome to fit political parties into this conception. Some writers on Parliament, indeed, do not really try. The index of one standard work[4] contains only three references to political parties in general, three to the Conservative party, and none to the Labour party. Another[5] contains no references to parties at all. One is reminded of the words of Hill and Whichelow.

> We have the curious situation that in a period when political parties have reached what may be a dominating position in Parliament, Parliament has continued to refuse to take official notice of them. Instead it has imposed something of a ban on the subject, a taboo even, a ritual refusal to mention a distasteful subject.[6]

Some writers on Parliament, by no means all, have for some reason followed Parliament's lead.

An alternative way of thinking about the relations between Parliament and the executive is perhaps suggested by the arrangement of the political parties in the Commons' Chamber itself. The Chamber, very schematically, is shown in Fig. 11.1. For simplicity's sake we ignore the minor parties, but they could quite easily be brought into the analysis. Even if we do

[3] P. G. Richards, *Backbenchers* (London, 1972), B. Crick, *Reform of Parliament* (London, 1964). The writings that constitute the most notable exception are Butt's. In *Power of Parliament* (London, 1969), Butt discusses the influence of government back-benchers quite separately from the influence of the opposition.

[4] G. Reid, *Politics of Financial Control: The Role of the House of Commons* (London, 1966).

[5] N. Johnson, *Parliament and Administration* (London, 1966).

[6] A. Hill and A. Whichelow, *What's Wrong with Parliament?* (Harmondsworth, 1964), 46.

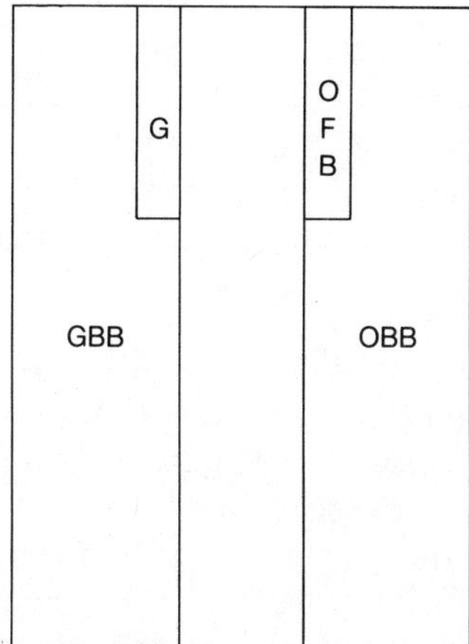

FIG. 11.1. The Chamber of the House of Commons

not bring them in, we still have four bodies to consider (G, GBB, OFB, OBB) instead of only two.[7]

The presence of the Government (G) in Parliament suggests straightaway that, if we wish to examine the influences brought to bear on the government by Parliament, we ought if possible to avoid using the term 'Parliament' since what we are interested in is not the whole of Parliament but Parliament (or the House of Commons) minus the government of the day. The presence of party groupings in the chamber further suggests that we should use as our units of analysis not Parliament as a whole or even Parliament minus the government but rather these party groupings and/or combinations of them. On this basis, there are, in logic, seven possibilities; the arrows in the diagram indicate possible lines of influence.

[7] Also for simplicity's sake, we ignore the relations between MPs and civil servants. In Britain these relations tend to be conducted on an individual basis and are mediated by the relevant minister. Things are of course very different in the US.

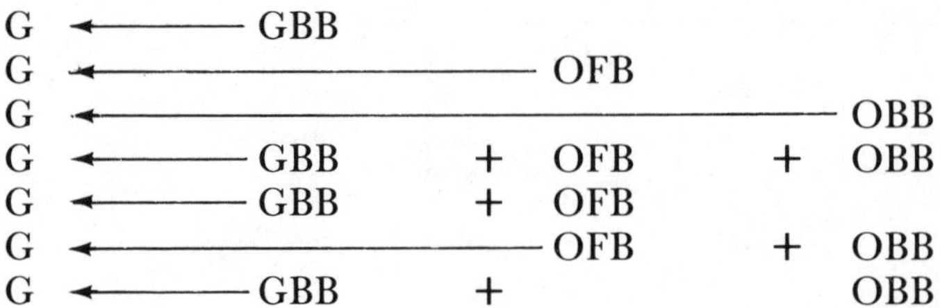

Of these seven possibilities, two—OFB alone and GBB + OFB—can probably be eliminated without further discussion, as being unlikely to arise, except very occasionally, in the real world. It is hard to imagine the leaders of the opposition (OFB) taking on the government entirely on their own, without at least some support from their own back-benchers. Likewise, it is a little hard to imagine the circumstances in which leaders of the opposition, without the support of at least some of their own followers, would combine with government back-benchers to attack the government.

Two other possibilities—OBB alone and GBB + OFB + OBB—can probably also be eliminated on somewhat different grounds. OBB alone can be eliminated because, although groups of opposition back-benchers do sometimes combine to attack and harass the government without the support of their own front bench (the 'Fourth Party' in the 1880s is the most famous historical example), this is not the sort of parliamentary pressure that governments are likely to feel that they have to pay much attention to. As soon as such pressure looks like becoming at all serious, the opposition front bench is bound to join in. GBB + OFB + OBB can be eliminated because, although governments not infrequently find themselves confronted with opposition both from the official opposition and from some or all of their own back-benchers (the cross-party opposition to the holding of a national count in the 1975 Common Market referendum being a recent case in point), governments almost certainly perceive GBB + OFB + OBB not as one source of pressure but as two, i.e. as a compound of GBB and OFB + OBB. The significance of this point will emerge later.

We are left, then, with the three remaining possibilities: GBB alone, OFB + OBB, and GBB + OBB. With regard to

Britain, it is these three relationships—between government and government back-benchers, between government and opposition (O), and between government and back-benchers of both parties—that are important and need to be studied. Each relationship is distinct. Each has its own dynamics. The first (G ← GBB), may be called the '*intra-party*' mode of executive–legislative relations, the second (G ← O) the '*opposition*' mode, and the third (G ← OBB) the '*non-party*' or '*private members*' mode. The reader should note that at least two of these modes, the intra-party and the opposition, are not modes only of executive–legislative relations. They are modes of political conflict more generally, the one relating to conflict within political parties, the other to conflict between them. The significance of this point, too, will emerge later.

Let us consider each of our three modes in turn.

The intra-party mode. We do not need to be persuaded that the intra-party mode exists in Britain—that there exists a relationship between governments and government back-benchers. Nor need we look far for examples of the influence that government back-benchers can have on governments. A reading of Butt's *The Power of Parliament* alone yields: the introduction of commercial television in the early 1950s, the drastic amending of the 1957 Rent Act, the dropping of the Macmillan Government's Shops Bill, the postponement of steel nationalization in 1965, the abandoning in 1969 of the bill that was to have been based on the industrial relations White Paper *In Place of Strife*.[8]

What gives government back-benchers influence? The answer lies in the needs that governments and government back-benchers have of each other and in the bargaining resources that they possess *vis-à-vis* each other. On the one hand, government back-benchers need from the government policies that they can approve of and that will help win the

[8] On the role of Conservative back-benchers in the campaign for commercial television see H. H. Wilson, *Pressure Group: Campaign for Commercial Television* (London, 1961). On the 1957 Rent Act, see M. J. Barnett, *Politics of Legislation: The Rent Act 1957* (London, 1969). On the postponement of steel nationalization in 1965, see D. E. Butler and A. King, *British General Election of 1966* (London, 1966), and W. Wyatt, *Turn Again, Westminster* (London, 1973). On *In Place of Strife*, see P. Jenkins, *Battle of Downing Street* (London, 1970).

next election. The government's resources *vis-à-vis* its own back-benchers include its superior sources of expertise and information, the fact of its day-to-day involvement in governing, and its authority, which rests partly on the role accorded to government in Britain's political culture (the government is expected 'to govern') and partly on the fact that the government's leaders are also the majority party's leaders. On the other hand, ministers have needs of government back-benchers. They need their moral support. They need them not to cause rows and to make hostile speeches that will attract publicity. They need, above all, their votes. In each case, ministers' needs of back-benchers constitute back-benchers' resources *vis-à-vis* ministers. Moral support can be denied, rows caused, hostile speeches made, votes (on occasion) withheld.

This is not the place to go into the details of the government–government back-bencher relationship. It is well known that government back-benchers' reluctance to exploit their greatest resource—their votes—greatly inhibits their exercise of influence.[9] It is also well known that, largely for this reason, their influence tends to be fairly limited (though less so in some situations than in others).[10] The point to be made here is that, from the government's point of view, this relationship—the intra-party relationship—is by far the most important of the three. Provided the government has a majority in the House of Commons, it can usually shrug off the opposition's attacks. Concerted attacks on the part of back-benchers of all parties are rare. But the government cannot always shrug off attacks from its own back-benchers. As far as the government is concerned, government back-benchers are the most important members in the House.

Several of the reasons why this should be so have already been mentioned: the government's needs of back-benchers,

[9] See R. J. Jackson, *Rebels and Whips* (London, 1968); A. King, 'Chief Whip's Clothes', in D. Leonard and V. Herman (edd.), *Backbencher and Parliament* (London, 1972).

[10] No one has as yet advanced a theory of the circumstances in which the influence of back-benchers can be expected to be at its maximum and minimum. Butt, however, provides a number of suggestions (*Power of Parliament*, chs. 6–10).

back-benchers' resources *vis-à-vis* the government. But there are three other reasons besides. The first is the simple fact, uniting both sides of the G/GBB relationship, of common party membership. Intra-party conflict may be tolerated, even taken for granted, but it is never welcomed. The aim with regard to the other party is to defeat it; the aim with regard to one's own party is to bring it round to one's own point of view. One discounts the disapproval of the other party; the disapproval of one's own is harder to bear. In a political party, as in a marriage, propinquity produces the need to seek accommodations and therefore to the possibility, indeed the probability, of mutual influence. One partner may be dominant; the other is likely to be listened to even so.

The second reason why government back-benchers are important is that they are seldom speaking only for themselves. Rebellious MPs more often than not have the backing of rebellious elements in the party outside of Parliament. Just as the government has needs of MPs, so also it has needs of the party outside—for money, for work in elections, for votes at the party conference. Intra-party battles are seldom fought out wholly within Parliament; they almost always have an extra-parliamentary dimension. Pressure outside can be translated into influence inside. The classic case was the aborted Industrial Relations Bill of 1969, when the Government knew that, in dealing with rebellious back-benchers, it was also dealing with the trade unions—and that it was dealing with the trade unions not least as the Labour party's chief supplier of funds. The case of the aborted Shops Bill of 1956–7 was similar.[11]

The third reason why government back-benchers matter to the government is that, on any given issue, the executive–legislative dichotomy is likely to be false to reality. Every view held by government back-benchers is likely to be held by some government ministers. Far from government back-benchers bringing pressure to bear on the government, some ministers are likely to sympathize with some back-benchers. On occasion they may even be in cahoots with them. Again the classic case was *In Place of Strife* in 1969, when it was well

[11] Ibid. 220–8.

known that at least one senior Cabinet minister, James Callaghan, was more in sympathy with the dissident back-benchers than with his Cabinet colleagues.[12] It is for these last two reasons that the intra-party mode is not solely an executive–legislative mode.

Indeed it may be best not to construe the intra-party mode as an executive–legislative mode at all but rather to see the relations between governments and government back-benchers as part of a larger intra-party relationship which manifests itself not only in Parliament but at, and across, all levels of the party, as shown in Fig. 11.2.

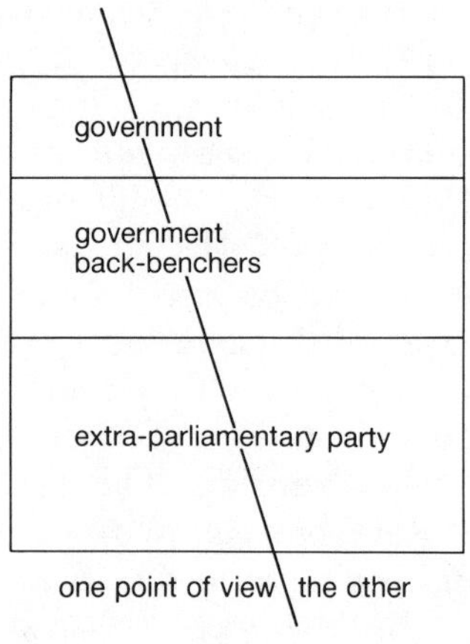

FIG. 11.2. Intra-Party Relationships

We have moved, it will be seen, some distance from talking about 'the impact of Parliament on the executive', that is, from the two-body image.

The opposition mode. The opposition mode is the one in which the larger part of party politics in Britain takes place: the set-piece debates in Parliament, the confrontations on television, the competition for votes in the constituencies. There is nothing Parliament-specific about this mode; the House of Commons is merely one of the arenas, not necessarily the most important, in which the party battle is fought out. It is up to the opposition (just as it is up to dissidents on the government

[12] Jenkins, *Downing Street*, ch. 5.

side) to decide how important the parliamentary battle should be allowed to loom in the larger scheme of things.[13]

The opposition mode is characterized by, indeed defined by, conflict. The politicians in the different parties—whether leaders or followers—are not members of the same party; they have few incentives to agree (and many not to); their aim is not accommodation but conquest. It follows that the extent of the influence of the party (or parties) out of office—i.e., of O on G—will be determined largely by needs and resources—by what each side needs from the other, by what resources each side can bring to bear in its relations with the other. If the intra-party mode can be likened to a marriage (however stormy at times), the opposition mode resembles a war game. There are rules which each side must observe, but both sides play to win.

In Britain, as is well known, the dice used in the game are loaded heavily in the government's favour. The opposition lacks all the things that government back-benchers lack—information, expertise, day-to-day involvement in governing, moral authority—and much else besides. The government fully expects the opposition to make hostile speeches. It does not need, or want, the opposition's moral support.[14] It does not need the opposition's votes. The opposition's votes become important to it only on the fairly rare occasions—usually during the committee stages of government bills—when dissident government back-benchers and the opposition join forces.[15] The government then finds itself having to operate in two modes at once: the intra-party and the

[13] There is an unexpected parallel here between this view and the views of extreme left-wingers about the non-centrality of Parliament's role in the struggle for socialism; see D. Coates, *Labour Party and the Struggle for Socialism* (Cambridge, 1975).

[14] This is usually true but it may not always be. The government may want, even need, the opposition's support *vis-à-vis* foreign governments or e.g. the different factions in Northern Ireland. Under these circumstances the dynamics of the opposition mode may change quite strikingly, to the opposition's advantage. See P. G. Richards, *Parliament and Foreign Affairs* (London, 1967), esp. pp. 158–68.

[15] See J. A. G. Griffith, *Parliamentary Scrutiny of Government Bills* (London, 1974), ch. 3; A. King, *British Members of Parliament: A Self-Portrait* (London, 1974), ch. 8.

opposition. One of the reasons government back-benchers have influence is precisely because governments do not like to find themselves in this position.

But most of the time oppositions can draw on only two resources in their relations with governments: good reasons, and time. They can try to persuade the government; or they can consume time in order either to delay measures for the sake of delaying them or to disrupt the government's parliamentary timetable. As an opposition spokesman has put it:

> One of the things people . . . tend to forget is that almost the only weapon an Opposition has is time. Almost the only thing one can do is to deny the Government a certain amount of time. If you can persuade the Government, fine. If not, time is all you have.[16]

Time, however, is a nuisance weapon, not a lethal one. The fact that time is 'all the Opposition has' is the measure of the opposition's weakness in the British system. The opposition has most influence when it speaks not with its own voice but with the voice of the people. But then the influence belongs not to the opposition but to the people—not to Parliament but to the electorate.

The non-party or private members' mode. Most relationships in British politics are party relationships, but not all are. In Parliament some decisions are made deliberately (not to say self-consciously) on a non-party basis. Some of these decisions are taken by means of free votes in the House of Commons.[17] Others are taken—or at any rate other attempts at exercising influence are made—by means of non-party committees of one sort or another. The role of these non-party committees is worth considering since much was made of them by parliamentary reformers in Britain in the 1960s. There now exists in the House of Commons a number of such committees, some specializing, some like the Expenditure Committee dealing with a variety of matters. They have to be called 'non-party' rather than 'all-party' committees because the members of all of them accept that, if they are to be permitted to continue to exist and to succeed, they must function in a non-party mode.

[16] King, *British Members of Parliament*, pp. 99.

[17] See P. G. Richards, *Parliament and Conscience* (London, 1970).

If they were to become caught up in partisan controversy, they would either be wound up or else the party whips would be put on, in which case they would lose their reason for existence.[18]

Those who participate in the work of non-party committees (usually select committees) change their perception of their own roles. They cease to see themselves as members of the Conservative party or the Labour party, concerned with scoring points off the other side, and come to see themselves simply as back-bench MPs concerned with investigating the quality of the performance of the executive (of whichever party), with protecting the rights of the citizen against the executive (of whichever party) and with asserting the prerogatives of back-bench MPs (irrespective of party). They come to see themselves rather as American Congressmen, for whom the executive–legislative dimension is sometimes more important than the partisan dimension. 'You can get the minister', said one back-bench MP with obvious relish, 'and grill him—grill him in all-party [i.e., a non-party] atmosphere'.[19] It obviously did not matter to this Member whether or not the minister was of his own party. He was functioning as a 'professional' back-bench MP.

The central fact about these committees, however, is that they have little influence, less even than the official opposition. The reasons are not difficult to find. Since the committees function on a non-party basis, and since most of the important questions in British public life are dealt with on a highly partisan basis, the committees do not deal, on the whole, with important questions.[20] Even when they do deal with important questions, they deal with them in ways that raise administrative, 'instrumental' issues rather than large political ones. The reports of the committees are usually muffled in

[18] See Richards, *Backbenchers*; King, *British Members of Parliament*, ch. 8.

[19] King, *British Members of Parliament*, p. 101.

[20] This general statement needs to be qualified of course. Select committees have studied such obviously important subjects as race relations and the conditions under which North Sea oil prospecting concessions were granted. The fact remains, however, that select committees are seldom where the political action is—and the political action usually includes most of the important questions facing the country, however these are defined by the observer.

tone. Even when they are not, the attention paid to them is no greater—and may be a good deal less—than their arguments deserve, because the committees are not politically influential. Governments do not have need of them. They have virtually no resources *vis-à-vis* governments. To be non-party most of the time in British politics is to be non-influential. The non-party mode—which is probably what most people have in mind when they speak of 'the impact of Parliament on the executive'—is thus also the least important mode. The more Parliament behaves like 'Parliament' the less influence it has. . . .

THE FIFTH FRENCH REPUBLIC: A CONSTITUTIONAL HYBRID

The approach illustrated in the case of Great Britain involves one in identifying politically significant sets of relationships and then in describing the political dynamics characteristic of each of these relationships taken separately. There is every reason to suppose, as we said at the outset, that the important relationships will vary from country to country. The value of the approach lies chiefly in its ability to sensitize the student to the relationships that matter most within any given country. The approach ought also, however, to alert us to similarities and differences—perhaps unexpected similarities and differences—among different countries. For this reason we turn now to look at executive–legislative relations in two other countries, France and West Germany. Our discussion of France will be briefer than in the case of Britain, partly because the general approach has already been spelt out and partly because there are few empirical (as distinct from quasi-juridical) studies available of executive–legislative relations in France.

The constitutional regime of the Fifth French Republic is a hybrid, exhibiting both pronouncedly presidential and pronouncedly parliamentary features. The power of the executive is enhanced by the setting out in the Constitution of a *domaine de la loi*, with matters not falling squarely within this domain being reserved for the government, by the direct election of the president, and by the enormous prestige with which General de Gaulle endowed the presidential office. But at the same time the survival of a French government continues to depend on its ability to secure a working majority in the National Assembly. There is no telling what would have happened if, for instance, Mitterrand instead of Giscard d'Estaing had been elected president in 1973. The institutions of the Fifth Republic might suddenly have looked remarkably like those of the Fourth.

Be that as it may, circumstances since 1958, and especially since 1962, have contrived to create a pattern of executive–legislative relations in France that bears a striking surface resemblance, at least, to the pattern to be found in Britain. The Governments of Debré and his successors have been sustained in office by majorities almost as solid as those that sustain British governments in office. The French legislature has, if anything, become even more subordinate to the executive than the British. We might therefore expect the dominant modes of executive–legislative relations in France to resemble those in Britain quite closely.

The intra-party mode. And up to a point they do. At least two of the modes found in Britain—the intra-party (G ← GBB) and the opposition (G ← O)—can be identified in France straightaway. Indeed one authority, Charlot, has drawn attention to an almost uncanny Anglo–French parallel:

> The essential contacts between the executive and the Legislature are made finally through the most important group in the majority [i.e., the Gaullists]. In the course of time a whole web of relations has been woven between the Gaullist groups and the government.
>
> Some men, carefully chosen, play a vital role in these relationships. First of all, the minister charged with managing the government's relations with Parliament, who attends the meetings of the executive committee and the meetings of the parliamentary group; he is a sort of French version of the British Chief Whip and has the same duties. His task is to avoid disputes, to anticipate and smooth out difficulties, to encourage compromise, to ensure discipline.[21]

Moreover, all the evidence suggests that, in so far as French ministers bother their heads about Parliament at all, the main

[21] J. Charlot, *Gaullist Phenomenon* (London, 1971), 150–1.

relationship that concerns them is, as in Britain, the government/government back-bencher relationship. The government may have a majority but it depends on that majority's votes and is bound therefore, to some degree at least, to defer to its opinions.[22]

The parallel must not, however, be pressed too far. If the most important mode politically in France as in Britain is the intra-party mode, the dynamics of the mode differ substantially as between the two countries. In the first place, although there has been a Gaullist or 'post-Gaullist' majority in the French National Assembly since 1958, it has not been a one-party majority; the Gaullist party proper has always had to rely on the parliamentary backing of one or two of the smaller *oui mais* or *non mais* parties.[23] And since 1973 the leader of these parties, Giscard d'Estaing, has been president of the Republic. We thus find an '*inter-party*' mode intruding into the intra-party mode. Moreover, even the Gaullist party proper is not quite a party in the European (and also the British) sense of the term. It is rather a loose confederation of conservative politicians united by electoral interest but often divided by constituency interest. Its instinct for electoral self-preservation leads it not to challenge the government to the point of overthrowing it or even of disputing its authority; but the divergent views, and often essentially local orientations, of its members force governments to devote some time and energy to party management. As Hayward wrote of Pompidou in 1970 'Pompidou must and does (covertly) concern himself much more with party matters than did de Gaulle because he cannot take for granted the cohesion and loyalty of what is a heterogeneous coalition.'[24]

Two other factors, in addition, produce something like a

[22] On the influence (admittedly limited) of French Government back-benchers on the Government, see J. E. S. Hayward, *One and Indivisible French Republic* (London, 1973), esp. pp. 69–70; P. M. Williams, *The French Parliament 1958–1967* (London, 1968), esp. p. 109; and the case study in N. Wahl, 'French Parliament: From Last Word to Afterthought', in E. Frank (ed.), *Lawmakers in a Changing World* (Englewood Cliffs, NJ, 1966), 54–7.

[23] J. E. S. Hayward, 'French Parliament under the Fifth Republic', *Parliamentary Affairs*, 22 (1969), 275–81.

[24] Id., 'War of the Republics: From Government by Assembly, through Presidential to Party Government?' *Political Studies*, 18 (1970), 541.

mutation of the British intra-party mode in the French political environment. One is the increasingly overt partisanship of the French administration. Whereas British civil servants are scrupulously neutral in their dealings with MPs of different parties (they are not even permitted to treat government ministers differently from other MPs), the French Civil Service under the Fifth Republic has increasingly become an organ of the Gaullist near-majority. As one Gaullist minister put it to Suleiman, a civil servant would be expected to address an opposition deputy as 'M. le Député' but a Gaullist deputy as 'M. le Député, cher ami'.[25] Civil servants are in a position to dispense favours to friendly deputies, withhold them from the enemy. There is no hard evidence on the point, but it would be surprising if Gaullist and near-Gaullist deputies were not aware that, were they to step too far out of line in the National Assembly, the administration's favours would probably be withdrawn.

The other factor differentiating France from Britain is the limited opportunities that French MPs have in Parliament itself for criticizing the government. The formal restrictions placed on Parliament by the Fifth Republic Constitution do not alter the regime's political basis fundamentally; a determinedly hostile parliamentary majority can still bring the government down. But they do have the effect of depriving deputies of the sorts of regular opportunities for bringing pressure to bear on the government that were a feature of the Fourth Republic and are still characteristic of Britain. In Britain, institutions such as parliamentary questions, adjournment debates, and the debates on the Consolidated Fund Bill positively encourage MPs of all parties, not just opposition MPs, to be openly critical of the government of the day. In France, by contrast, parliamentary criticism is, if not silenced, then at least muffled by the fact that Parliament meets for only six months of the year, by the fact that question time takes place only once a week and even then is held (in the National Assembly) at the least propitious time of the week, on Friday afternoons, and by the government's near-monopoly of parliamentary time. No wonder that, for these and other

[25] S. N. Suleiman, *Politics, Power and Bureaucracy in France: The Administrative Élite* (Princeton, NJ, 1974), 362.

reasons, many deputies and senators in France simply stay away.[26]

The opposition mode. If the intra-party mode is the dominant mode in France, however much its dynamics may differ from those of the comparable mode in Britain, this is partly because of the relative unimportance, even more in France than in Britain, of the parliamentary opposition. The opposition in France does not, of course, consist of a single party. It consists in early 1976 of at least three separate parties, two of them, the Communists and Socialists, uneasily allied for electoral purposes, but none of them prepared to submerge its separate identity for purposes of forming an effective opposition in Parliament. The opposition parties have shown signs of reviving recently, but in the 1960s they were 'demoralized by electoral defeat and internal division'.[27]

Even if, however, the opposition in France consisted of a single party, one with a good chance of itself forming the government in due course, its position would be weak. The lack of parliamentary opportunities for criticism that affects all French MPs affects the opposition no less. The Constitution and the rules of the two French Houses of Parliament secure the government against harassment and damaging votes on minor points. There is no equivalent in France of the opposition's 'supply days' in the British House of Commons, when Parliament is required to debate whatever subject the opposition chooses. In Britain, as we saw, the opposition has only two weapons: good reasons, and time. In France, it has only one: good reasons. As Williams remarked of the opposition parties in the sixties, 'they had no weapon but argument':

> The opposition parties had little political opportunity to persuade the majority, and little procedural opportunity to arouse public opinion against it through Parliament . . . The regular opposition

[26] Every writer on French politics comments on the prevalence of absenteeism under the Fifth Republic. See e.g. Williams, *French Parliament*, p. 110, and L. G. Noonan, *France: The Politics of Continuity in Change* (New York, 1970), 320. Noonan quotes a writer in *Le Monde* as saying of French deputies, 'Some arrive from the provinces Wednesday morning and go home Thursday night.'

[27] P. M. Williams, *French Parliament 1958–1967* (London, 1968), 112.

contributed little . . . [for] the new rules, which prevented Parliament being used as a forum for manœuvres to divide the majority, also enabled that majority to hamper its opponents in criticizing the government and appealing to the country as a skilful Opposition Front Bench can at Westminster.[28]

The non-party mode. To identify, as we can, a fairly distinct non-party mode of executive–legislative relations in Britain is to be led to ask whether the same, or a similar, mode can also be found in France. And in France, as in Britain, the answer largely, though by no means wholly, turns on MPs' behaviour on parliamentary committees. It is here that MPs would seem on the face of it to have the greatest opportunities for non- or even cross-party activity. Unfortunately, the decline in the importance of the standing committees in the French legislature has been matched by a decline in political scientists' interest in them. There exists no major study, in either English or French, of the workings of a parliamentary committee in the Fifth Republic.

It seems, however, that the non-party mode, not terribly important in Britain, is missing almost entirely in France. There are no parliamentary committees in France equivalent to the British House of Commons' select committees. French deputies and senators cross party lines in the legislature at least as frequently as British MPs do, but they are not in general encouraged to take a 'legislature vs. executive', 'us against them' view of the government of the day—whatever its, or their, political complexion. The reasons are probably straightforward. Formally, the National Assembly is limited to six standing committees (though subcommittees called 'working groups' can be established). Informally, French governments are presumably no more anxious than British governments have usually been to provide backbench members of parliament with a mechanism which, however little powerful, would be bound to be used to embarrass the government rather than anyone else; the history of the Third and Fourth Republics is a standing warning to governments of the Fifth. It would be interesting to know, however, how far in the six standing committees and in other forums that may

[28] Ibid. 109, 110, 112.

exist French MPs do adopt self-consciously non-partisan roles and whether there is any pressure in France for the creation of British-style non-party committees. Of course the absence of such committees may not even be noticed in France. If so, it is all the more surprising that they have been so much noticed in Britain.[29]

Other modes? The question arises: if at least two of the three modes to be found in Britain can also be identified in France, are there modes in France that are not to be found in Britain? The answer is probably no. French deputies have a wider range of contacts with members of the administration than do British MPs but, as Suleiman[30] and others have pointed out, they have these contacts mainly not as deputies but as mayors or holders of other local offices. The relationship is thus not primarily an executive–legislative relationship. Indeed the deputy's status as an MP is usually at most tangential to it.

To the extent, however, that the main Gaullist party in France has been, is now, or were to become in future, dependent on non-Gaullist political forces, then of course the relationship between the Gaullists and these other forces would constitute a distinct, politically important relationship, and therefore, in our terms, a distinct mode. It would be important—indeed it already is—to investigate the dynamics of the relationship in the early days of the new republic between the Gaullists and their allies and the rather different relationship that has existed since about the mid-sixties between the Gaullists and the Independent Republicans.[31] But such a distinct inter-party mode has not yet emerged as a stable feature of Fifth Republic life, and it is to other countries on the Continent that we must turn if we wish to locate flourishing instances of it.

[29] Since the above was written, Prof. Hayward has pointed out to the writer that the French under the Fifth Republic do still have equivalents of *ad hoc* select committees, examples being the committees that inquired into ORTF (the French state radio and state organization) and the activities of the petroleum companies. Moreover, committee *rapporteurs* often adopt self-consciously non-partisan stands. It seems, then, that a non-party mode is to be found in France, even if it does not appear to be as fully developed as in Great Britain.

[30] Suleiman, *Administrative Élite*, pp. 365–6.

[31] Hayward, 'French Parliament'.

WEST GERMANY: A CASE OF COALITION GOVERNMENT IN A PARLIAMENTARY SYSTEM

When we looked at executive–legislative relations in Great Britain, we quickly became dissatisfied with the 'two-body image'. We identified not two bodies that mattered, the executive and the legislature, but four, the government, government back-benchers, the opposition front bench and opposition back-benchers. And we noted that, if we wanted to focus on the legislature's influence on the executive, we needed to examine not one relationship (executive ← legislature) but seven. Fortunately, four of the possibilities that were present in logic could reasonably be disregarded in practice, and we were left with only three politically significant executive–legislative relationships.

We also became dissatisfied with the two-body image, readers will recall, for a different reason: namely, that when we came to examine each of the three politically significant executive–legislative relationships we found that the two most important ones—that between the government and government back-benchers (G ← GBB) and that between the government and the opposition (G ← O)—could not usefully be described as involving relationships between 'the executive' and 'the legislature'. The only one of the three that could be so described—that between the government and both government and opposition back-benchers, in their roles as back-benchers—was also, of the three, the least important. For all of these reasons, it is hardly too strong to say, with regard to Britain, that there is no such thing as 'the relationship between the executive and the legislature'. The language simply does not fit the facts.

When we come to look at West Germany, however, the position is subtly different. In the cases of Britain and France, it as convenient, and did not distort reality too much, to take as one of our units of analysis 'the government', ignoring the different roles and differences of opinion that of course exist within any British or French cabinet. But in the case of Germany, to speak of 'the government' *tout simple* is misleading. Since the formation of the Federal Republic, governments in Germany have typically not been one-party governments but coalitions of at least two parties. We have therefore to take into account the separate identities of the dominant and subordinate parties in the coalition (DPC and SPC) and also of their separate parliamentary followings (DPBB and SPBB). It is worth remarking in passing, too, that, whereas in Britain and France civil servants are, in the strict sense, servants of the party in power, having little direct contact with the opposition or even with government back-benchers, in Germany officials participate actively in the deliberations of parliamentary committees. A complete description of executive–legislative relations in Germany would have to take into account this participation.

West Germany differs from Britain and France in another important way. In our discussion of Britain, we emphasized the fact that most MPs see themselves, most of the time, not primarily as MPs, irrespective of party, but as Labour MPs or Conservative MPs or whatever. The partisan role is more important than the parliamentarian role. At least since the beginning of the Fifth Republic, the same has largely been true of France. Deputies sit in the National Assembly to support the Government or to attack it, not to club together, as deputies, to take part in it.[32] In Germany, by contrast, as many writers have pointed out, the idea that the chief function of MPs is to support or attack the Government in a partisan fashion coexists uneasily with the quite different, more traditional idea that the job of the MPs is to represent the people and to act as a check on government. 'Traditionally', as Johnson puts it 'Government and Parliament have kept each other at arm's length.'[33]

The continuing strength of this more traditional conception of the role of the MPs in Germany has two closely connected consequences. The first is that members of the Bundestag take seriously their work as members of parliamentary committees and approach it in a non-party or, more precisely, a cross-party frame of mind. Members of committees are prepared to

[32] This statement is broadly true, though a certain amount of cross-party activity is engaged in on parliamentary committees in France (Hayward, *The One and Indivisible*, pp. 69–70; cf. O. H. Woshinsky, *French Deputy* (Lexington, Mass., 1973)).

[33] N. Johnson, *Government in the Federal Republic of Germany* (Oxford, 1973).

examine details of bills on their merits and to make concessions on a cross-party basis. The second is that, in marked contrast to the position in Britain, where a party's ministers are also its parliamentary leaders, there exists in Germany a 'complete separation between the organization of cabinet and of parlimentary party leadership, despite the development of government by a parliamentary majority'.[34] The chancellor and the leader of the majority party's parliamentary faction, in other words, are not the same person. They have different jobs, and the latter is unlikely to see himself simply as the servant of the former. This element of organizational discontinuity complicates the relations between leaders and followers in all of the parliamentary parties (though especially in the government parties) and reinforces the disposition that German MPs would have in any case to regard themselves as, to some degree, members of the Bundestag first and members of their party second.[35]

With regard to Germany, then, we need to increase the number of our units of analysis, and to bear in mind the 'cultural' factor just described. We now have six units of analysis instead of the four that served for Britain:

DPC = ministers of the dominant party in the coalition
SPC = ministers of the subordinate party in the coalition
DPBB = dominant-party back-benchers
SPBB = subordinate-party back-benchers
OFB = opposition front bench
OBB = opposition back-benchers

[34] G. Loewenberg, *Parliament in the German Political System* (1st edn., Ithaca, New York, 1966), 217. The contrast between Britain and Germany in this respect is not quite as marked as it was. On the Conservative side in Britain, there are signs that the back-bench 1922 committee, and in particular its chairman, are gradually acquiring greater authority and autonomy. On the Labour side, the positions of leader of the party and chairman of the Parliamentary Labour Party, which used not only to be occupied by the same person, but to be, constitutionally, the same position, have since 1964 been separated. Although the process has only just begun, one can imagine the internal structures of the British parliamentary parties coming more closely to resemble their German counterparts.

[35] The American reader perhaps needs to be reminded that the contrast being made here is with Great Britain and France and not with the US. As compared with the US Congress, members of the German Bundestag are of course highly partisan.

Even before they have done the arithmetic, readers will be uneasily aware that the number of possible combinations of influence in this situation must, in logic, be very large. In fact, if we allowed that every possible combination of influence could play upon the dominant-party ministers (DPC) and the subordinate-party ministers (SPC), the two taken separately, the number of possible combinations would be sixty. If, in addition, we allowed that every possible combination of influence could also play upon the dominant-party and subordinate-party ministers taken together (i.e. upon the government as a whole), the number would increase from sixty to seventy-five. We have come a long way from the seven possible combinations of Britain.

Fortunately, the number of actual, or probable, political alignments in West Germany is a good deal smaller than seventy-five. There are in fact probably no more than seven that need to be considered:

1.			DPC	←→	SPC		
2.		OFB	+OBB	→	DPC		
3.		OFB	+OBB	→	SPC		
4.		OFB	+OBB	→	DPC	+SPC	(i.e. G)
5.			DPBB	→	DPC		
6.			SPBB	→	SPC		
7.	OBB	+DPBB	+SPBB	→	DPC	+SPC	(i.e. G)

Furthermore, close inspection of the seven suggests that they can be grouped under four headings: an '*inter-party*' mode, consisting of (1), (2), and (3); the usual '*opposition*' mode (4); the same '*intra-party*' mode that we found in Britain and France, (5) and (6), but this time involving two parties instead of only one; and finally a new mode that we have not encountered in either of the other countries, a '*cross-party*' mode, (7).[36] Given our discussion, a fairly brief consideration of each should suffice.

The inter-party mode. This mode is undoubtedly the most

[36] Simply from a description of the parties to the relationship, it could be inferred that this mode should be given a 'non-party' rather than a 'cross-party' label. In Germany, as in Britain, one needs to know not merely who the parties to the relationship are but how they relate to each other.

important of the four in West Germany in general political terms. Inter-party bargaining determines which parties will combine to form the government. It is important in determining which government offices will go to representatives of which parties. If no one party has an overall majority in the Bundestag, inter-party bargaining could lead to the fall of one government and its replacement by another. The relations between the parties in the coalition, moreover, are bound to have an effect on government policy. If, for example, the subordinate-party ministers (SPC) decided that their association with the dominant party was no longer to their electoral advantage and that it might be worth their while to leave the governing coalition, the dominant-party ministers (DPC), if they feared the breakup of the coalition, would be almost certain to consider making concessions to the subordinate party in policy terms. Even in less extreme cases, the coalition parties' electoral fortunes and the public standings of their ministers are bound to affect their mutual relations.

We need not dwell on the inter-party mode here, however, because it is more confusing than helpful to analyse this mode in executive–legislative terms. To be sure, the party leaders who take part in inter-party bargaining are mainly members of the Bundestag; and it is votes in the Bundestag that determine the composition of the government (or, more precisely, who is elected chancellor). But the process of inter-party bargaining is not a parliamentary process or an executive–legislative process, and the influence that the various bargainers have depends not on their positions in parliament but on their positions in the party. Certainly it is not at all meaningful in this context to speak of 'the legislature' or 'the executive'.[37]

The opposition mode. The opposition party or parties in Germany have exactly the same difficulties in bringing

[37] That said, it must be added that, of course, it may matter a great deal whether the participants in an intra-party decision-making process are or are not MPs. MPs, in Germany or anywhere else, are likely to view the world differently from non-MPs. One remembers the two old sayings: 'where you stand depends on where you sit' and 'two deputies, one of whom is a revolutionary, have more in common than two revolutionaries, one of whom is a deputy'. Moreover, one determinant of someone's influence as a party member is likely to be whether or not he or she is also an MP.

influence to bear on the government as do the opposition parties in Britain and France. The government does not need their votes; it fully expects their voices to be raised against it. As in Britain, when the opposition does have influence, it has it not because of its own political strength but because the government calculates that the views being expressed by the opposition are views that are also widely held among the electorate.

But there are two other factors that partially differentiate the West German opposition mode from the British or the French. The first has already been mentioned—the tendency for the opposition parties to be allowed to play a fuller part in the proceedings of parliamentary committees than their opposite numbers in Britain and France—and will be referred to again below. The second is the relatively small importance attached to the set-piece parliamentary debate in Germany. The Bundestag meets in plenary session much less often than the parliaments of most other countries, and members of the Bundestag appear not to take plenary sessions very seriously.[38] It is a moot point whether the relative unimportance of full-scale debates in the Bundestag increases or diminishes the influence of the parliamentary opposition; but it may possibly be a necessary concomitant of the large part that the opposition parties play in the work of the parliamentary committees. It may not be entirely an accident that the highly oppositional style of debates on the floor of the British House of Commons is matched by a highly oppositional style in those committees upstairs in Britain that deal with legislation. If the pleas of Hennis[39] and others for an uprating in the importance of the Bundestag's plenary sessions were heeded, an unintended consequence might be increased partisanship in the

[38] On the relative infrequency of Bundestag plenary sessions, see table 39 in Loewenberg, *Parliament in the German Political System*, p. 404. In the period 1953–7 e.g., the Bundestag met for 425 hours on average per year. The British House of Commons, in about the same period 1954–8, met for an average of 1,280 hours each year. On the role of debates in the Bundestag generally, see K. Sontheimer, *Government and Politics of West Germany* (London, 1972), 127–34.

[39] W. Hennis, 'Reform of the Bundestag', in G. Loewenberg (ed.), *Modern Parliaments: Change or Decline* (Chi., Ill., 1971).

Bundestag's legislative committees—the upshot of which would probably be a diminution in the opposition's influence overall.

The intra-party mode. The intra-party mode is as important in West Germany as in Great Britain and France. The governing parties in Germany need the support of their own supporters if they are to secure the passage of their measures in parliament. The chancellor himself could be deposed if enough dissidents in his own party combined with members of the other parties to secure a majority for his successor. Members of the German Bundestag thus have in their hands the same two-edged swords that British MPs have in theirs. On the one hand, government back-benchers in either country can inflict great damage on the government of the day, perhaps even destroy it. On the other, any damage that back-benchers inflict on their own government they also inflict on their party and themselves. Not surprisingly, therefore, in West Germany, as in Britain, the wars fought between ministers and Government back-benchers are almost invariably limited wars, with the ultimate weapons not used.

Indeed the resemblances between the dynamics of the intra-party modes in the two countries far outweigh their differences. Party leaders and followers in the two countries have the same needs of one another, and the same resources *vis-à-vis* each other. They are united by the fact of a common party membership. Dissidents on the back benches owe much of what influence they have in both countries to the support of party allies outside Parliament and inside the government. A catalogue of instances of successful back-bench pressure, such as that given above for Britain, could easily be supplied for Germany. Safran, for example, describes how the Adenauer Government was forced to abandon its 1959 Health Insurance Bill.[40] Loewenberg in his chapter on 'Lawmaking' describes how the 1956 Volunteers Bill, in particular, was heavily amended in committee, largely as the result of the activity of CDU/CSU back-benchers.[41]

[40] W. Safran, *Veto-Group Politics: The Case of Health Insurance Reform in West Germany* (San Francisco, 1967).

[41] Loewenberg, *Parliament in the German Political System.*

Only two qualifications need to be entered to this account of Anglo–German similarities—and both may be of declining importance. The first is that CDU/CSU back-benchers in the 1950s and 1960s had influence partly because it was often not difficult for them to form cross-party alliances with members of other parties, including the SPD. By contrast, alliances between Conservative and Labour back-benchers in Britain, although by no means unknown, have always been fairly rare. Secondly, the influence of German back-benchers may have been enhanced by the fact, already mentioned, of the formal separation between the government and the parliamentary leadership of the majority party. It would be surprising if this degree of institutional independence did not lead, to some degree, to a parallel independence of view. This formal separation does not exist, of course, in Britain.

Before we assume, however, that these features are permanent, and will always have the effect of making German back-benchers more powerful than their British opposite numbers, we should remember that in the 1950s and 1960s West German politics were, to a high degree, consensus politics. The political parties did not differ over much that was important to any of them; it was even possible for the two major ones to form a Grand Coalition. Hence the cross-party alliances in Bundestag committees. Hence also, one might surmise, the 'luxury' of a divided majority-party leadership. Were German politics ever to become more polarized—were, for example, the Social Democrats to seek to introduce more radical reforms than they have hitherto—there might occur a rapid closing, both horizontally and vertically, of all the major parties' ranks.

The cross-party mode. The major points that arise under this heading have already been made. To an extent remarkable in a parliamentary system with only a limited number of major political parties, the committees of the West German Bundestag function in a genuinely 'legislative' style. The committees themselves specialize. So do their members. Not all committee chairmen are members of the majority party. Cross-voting is common. The results are as Safran describes them: 'The very frequent sessions of the committees and the mutual recognition of expertness contribute to an *esprit de corps* which makes possible an objective examination of the paragraphs and technical details of legislative proposals.'[42] Occasionally, as in the case of the Volunteers Bill, a committee's *esprit de corps* is so great that it can unite to condemn the Government for legislative incompetence.[43] The bemused foreign political scientist, used to the highly partisan character of the proceedings in legislative committees in Britain (and in other countries with similar parliamentary systems), is reduced to asking, again, whether the cross-partisan atmosphere of the West German committees could survive a prolonged period of heightened inter-party tension.

In the meantime, there can still occur in Germany the sort of direct confrontation between the executive and the legislature that makes sense of the Montesquieu formula and allows one to speak of 'executive–legislative relations' without the qualifications insisted upon in this paper. As Braunthal says of the Bundestag debates over the Transportation Finance and Highway Relief Bills in the 1950s:

> In this legislative tug of war concerning two basically non-political bills, tensions and emotions mounted precipitously between the executive and legislative branches. The classic parliamentary principle of a fusion of powers between these branches was inoperative at times, and was replaced momentarily by the United States principle of a separation of powers.[44]

But, even in West Germany, as Braunthal implies, such instances are rare.

CONCLUSION

The central argument of this paper is simple and can be restated briefly. There are in the real world institutions called 'executives' and 'legislatures', and it is tempting to speak of the 'relations' between them. It is tempting, but much more often than not misleading. It seldom makes sense to speak of executive–legislative relations. Rather, there are in each

[42] Safran, *Veto-Group Politics*, pp. 169–70.

[43] See Loewenberg, *Parliament in the German Political System*, p. 340.

[44] G. Braunthal, *West German Legislative Process* (Ithaca, New York, 1972), 234.

political system a number of distinct political relationships, each with its own 'membership', so to speak, and each with its own dynamics and structure of power. If we wish to understand the real world of politics better, it is these separate relationships that we should seek to identify and study. The traditional separation-of-powers language is not only unhelpful most of the time; it is a positive hindrance to understanding. It blurs distinctions that ought not to be blurred and distracts attention from important political phenomena.

The analysis presented in this paper needs, of course, to be made more rigorous and to be extended. In particular, the present paper has considered neither a political system in which minority governments are the norm, nor a system with a true separation-of-powers constitution. Other modes of executive–legislative relations will undoubtedly be found in such systems. They deserve to be identified, and explored.

12

COMMITTEES IN LEGISLATURES

MALCOLM SHAW

COMMITTEE IMPORTANCE

I have fallen into a pattern of mentioning the eight countries [United States, Italy, West Germany, Philippines (pre-1972), Canada, Britain, India, Japan] in an order that seems to reflect the relative importance of their systems of official committees. In arriving at this rank order, I have taken into account the evidence contained in the country chapters and such additional evidence as could be found. These data seemed to point to the rank order of committee importance set out in Table 12.1.

TABLE 12.1. Relative Importance of Committee Systems in Eight Legislatures

Country	Legislature or Lower House	Rank order
United States	Congress	1
Italy	Parliament	2
West Germany	Bundestag	3
Philippines	Congress	4
Canada	House of Commons	5
Britain	House of Commons	6
India	Lok Sabha	7
Japan	Diet	8

Note: In cases in which the lower House is markedly more important than the upper House, only the former is listed. In the other cases the name of the legislature is given.

Malcolm Shaw, 'Committees in Legislatures', from 'Conclusions' in John D. Lees and Malcolm Shaw (edd.), *Committees in Legislatures* (Oxford; Martin Robertson, 1979). Reprinted by permission of Basil Blackwell.

The first thing that needs to be established in relation to this rank order is what is meant by 'importance'. In the present context the matter of importance can be looked at from two vantage points—that of a particular governmental system and that of the eight systems collectively. The two focuses are interrelated in that the importance of committees within a country's governmental system determines that country's position in the rank order. What is specifically meant by importance is the ability of the official committees in the legislature to influence or determine the outputs of the legislature and the polity. This characterization is close to a definition by Edelman and Zelniker[1] of 'strength' in a legislature: 'Parliamentary strength or weakness we consider as an institution's command of political resources for the purpose of influencing public policy.'

Such a basis for assessing importance lays stress on what Packenham has called the 'decisional' functions of legislatures, and this bias in the present analysis is acknowledged. While such 'non-decisional' functions as legitimation and recruitment are important, it can be argued that putting one's stamp on the substance of outputs is particularly important. In specifying 'outputs', the intention is to go beyond legislating to policy-related control in all its aspects. This broadened perspective makes it possible to take into account any shift from an emphasis on legislating to an emphasis on oversight, which many writers have discerned in legislatures. It is relevant to note Neustadt's discussion of 'committee clearance' in the US Congress:

> In recent years we find numerous statutory provisions . . . which require that an agency report particular administrative actions in advance to a committee, or, stronger still, which require that an agency 'come into agreement' with committee personnel before action is taken or, strongest of all, which require that an agency respect committee veto [*sic*] in a fixed time-period after the fact.[2]

[1] M. Edelman and S. Zelniker, 'Information Utilisation in the Knesset: The Question of Legislative Autonomy', paper presented at the 9th World Congress of the International Political Science Association, 1973, p. 2.

[2] R. E. Neustadt, 'Politicians and Bureaucrats', in D. B. Truman (ed.), *Congress and America's Future* (Englewood Cliffs, NJ, 1965), 105–6.

When committees effect 'clearance' in these ways, they are influencing governmental outputs.

Jewell and Patterson have attested to the particular importance for committees of the legislative and oversight functions. 'The two most important functions of legislative committees in the larger political system', they have said,[3] 'are the making of decisions with regard to legislation and the authorization and oversight of administrative actions.' Accordingly, the higher in the rank order one goes, the more marked the tendency for the committees to put their imprint on the substantive outputs of government. This is achieved, in large measure, by (1) exercising discretion in regard to legislation and (2) overseeing executive actions in such a way that it affects what is done (or not done). Committees in the lower reaches of the rank order, on the other hand, are more likely to perform such non-decisional functions as deliberation, representation, legitimation, recruitment, socialization, training, and mobilization. It must be emphasized that these orientations are not exclusive. Strong committees perform non-decisional as well as decisional functions, while weaker committees 'perform' decisional functions. The point is that in their performance of decisional functions, the weaker committees exercise little independent discretion compared with that exercised by the stronger committees. This circumstance has the effect of making the non-decisional functions the real functions performed in the weaker committee systems, while in the strong systems both roads are travelled.

It must be admitted that the basis for establishing the rank order is imprecise. No survey or statistical exercise could determine in a definitive way a set of relationships that subsume so many variables and contexts. We are to some extent comparing soup and nuts. In addition to the general shortcomings, a number of specific difficulties are evident. First, some committees within a given committee system are more important than others. Thus, an estimate of the general importance of a system masks the degree of importance of particular components. Second, assessments depend on when

[3] M. E. Jewell and S. C. Patterson, *Legislative Process in the United States* (2nd edn., New York, 1973), 219.

they were made. If, to take a case in point, the appraisals had been made five years earlier, Britain would rank above Canada in the rank order rather than the other way around. Third, the gaps between different points on the scale are in reality less uniform than the simple listing connotes. In this respect, therefore, the rank order is a crude one.

Notwithstanding these problems, the establishment of a rank order is a useful preliminary to the discussions in the remaining sections of this chapter. These sections are devoted to exploring a range of contextual variables. It is hoped that the rank order will provide an overall perspective and thus assist the reader as various characteristics of the eight committee systems are taken up. More important, it is hoped that the reasons for particular rankings will become evident as the analysis proceeds.

Before proceeding to the contextual variables, it will be useful to examine the sequence in which countries appear in the rank order. The pattern has a ring of familiarity. In various earlier connections a distinction was made between committee arrangements in Commonwealth parliaments, where British traditions are strong, and those in which American or Continental traditions are strong. We found a reluctance in the Commonwealth parliaments to devolve authority from the plenary level to committees. This propensity was found to be reflected in various procedures, notably in an unwillingness (except recently in Canada) to create a comprehensive structure of permanent and specialized committees. By contrast, in the American–Continental legislatures we found a marked commitment to devolution, notably in the form of permanent and specialized committees.

These orientations are reflected in the rank order. The Commonwealth parliaments are grouped in the lower half of the order, while the other legislatures, except for Japan, are found in the top half. Moreover, the order is broadly consistent with published assessments of the relative strengths of committee systems. These assessments invariably rate the committee system of the American Congress as very powerful, or 'the most powerful one in the world', assert that committee systems in Continental parliaments are likewise strong, and cite Commonwealth committees as being relatively weak or restricted.[4] It is useful to find that a specialized empirical investigation confirms the conventional wisdom of more broadly based studies.

At the same time a specialized enquiry enables one to put flesh on the bones, to add definition to the general picture, and perhaps to uncover a few aberrations. Why, for example, are the precise placements on the scale thought to be appropriate? Japan has a formal commitment to devolution and a parliament strongly influenced by the United States. Why, then, is the Diet at the bottom of the order? Why is Italy ahead of West Germany, and why is the Philippines in the top half? How is it that Canada has created permanent and specialized committees without notably increasing the decisional efficacy of its committee system? Various idiosyncratic factors must obviously be taken into account.

THE FACTOR OF PARTY

The impact of political parties on the working of committees in legislatures is clearly a matter of crucial importance. As a factor that conditions committee behaviour, party is probably more important than any other single conditioning influence that can be isolated. Factors other than party are also vitally important, as we shall see, but looking across the board at the eight systems it would not seem much of an exaggeration to say that committees in legislatures are as they are largely because the party systems are as they are. In fact, the relationship between party characteristics and committee behaviour is sufficiently strong to enable us to link certain party characteristics with certain styles of committee behaviour. Since our sample of committee systems is small, we cannot be more than suggestive about these relationships, but the evidence is persuasive.

[4] See K. C. Wheare, *Legislatures* (1963; Oxford, 2nd edn. 1968), 57–8; M. Ameller, *Parliament* (2nd edn., London, 1966), 163–5; J. Blondel, *Comparative Legislatures* (Englewood Cliffs, NJ, 1973) 67; G. Nelson, 'Assessing the Congressional Committee System: Contributions from a Comparative Perspective', *Annals of the American Academy of Political and Social Science*, 411 (1974), 123, 131.

There is a widely utilized arrangement in legislatures that might be said to constitute official recognition of the importance of the link between parties and committees. However different the eight committee systems may be in other respects, in one respect they are the same: members are assigned to committees in proportion to party strengths in the chamber. . . . This is required by the Constitution in Italy; elsewhere, it is required by standing orders. The intention is to ensure that each committee replicates party divisions in the chamber and gives the majority party (if there is one) a majority on each committee. . . .

Another widespread practice is that the parties determine the composition of their committee delegations. The formal designation of committee members may be made by the chamber, the presiding officer, or a selection committee, but the real choices are usually made by party groups. Moreover, when committee substitutions are permitted, the substitutes are normally designated by parties. As far as committee chairmanships are concerned, again they are usually, though not invariably, held by members of the dominant party in the chamber. Studies[5] that deal with more of the world's legislatures than we do have suggested that the aforementioned arrangements are also usual elsewhere.

While the parties in the present study have various committee-related characteristics in common, they also possess a number of more fundamental characteristics that vary from one polity to another. These variations may be identified as to whether there are one, two, or more than two major parties; whether the parties tend to be cohesive or non-cohesive; whether one of the parties is continuously dominant in national politics; whether the cabinet is of the one-party or coalition type; and whether the leading parties are ideologically close or distant. In Table 12.2 these characteristics are assigned to the various national party systems. The intention is to explore whether any patterns emerge when the characteristics are linked to the rank order of committee strength.

The first thing that needs to be said is that reality is less

[5] e.g. S. L. Shakdher, 'The System of Parliamentary Committees', *Constitutional and Parliamentary Information*, 93 (1973), 47.

TABLE 12.2. Party Characteristics and Rank Order of Committee Strength

Country	Number of major parties	Cohesive or non-cohesive	Competitive or dominant-competitive	One-party or coalition cabinets	Ideologically close or distant	Rank order
United States	2	Noncohesive	Competitive	One-party	Close	1
Italy	More than 2	Cohesive	Competitive	Coalition	Distant	2
West Germany	2	Cohesive	Competitive	Coalition	Moderately distant	3
Philippines	2	Noncohesive	Competitive	One-party	Close	4
Canada	2	Cohesive	Dominant-competitive	One-party	Close	5
Britain	2	Cohesive	Competitive	One-party	Moderately distant	6
India	1	Cohesive	Dominant-competitive	One-party	Distant	7
Japan	More than 2	Cohesive	Dominant-competitive	One-party	Distant	8

categoric than the table suggests. For example, in the matter of the number of major parties, the Free Democrats in West Germany are more than a minor party but less than a major party; nevertheless, the strong tendency is toward two-partyism. The position is similar in Canada, except that there are two important minor parties. It is difficult to classify India and Japan in terms of the number of major parties. In the Lok Sabha and the Diet (in 1973) one finds a single major party confronted by a range of less important parties. The disparity is so pronounced in the Lok Sabha that it seems right to designate only one party as major. In the Diet the disparity is less pronounced, and the boundary into multi-partyism would seem, arguably, to have been crossed.

There are also anomalies in the matter of cohesion. For present purposes 'cohesion' and its surrogate 'discipline' are taken to refer to party unity in parliamentary voting. Yet parties that are cohesive in this respect may exhibit disarray in others. We have categorized the India party system as cohesive, but this ignores the fact that it is not uncommon for members of the Lok Sabha to defect from one party to another! In terms of voting and in other ways, Japanese parties are the most cohesive in the present study; yet the same parties tend to be divided into formal, organized factions under factional leaders. In general, Italian parties are cohesive, but as a matter of degree this is less true of the Christian Democrats than the Communists.

Turning to the next category, a competitive party system is one in which major parties alternate in office. A dominant-competitive system is one in which competition for national office occurs, but a dominant party is the predictable winner. We call the American system competitive despite the fact that the Democrats have had majorities in both houses of Congress for all but four years since 1932; our justification is that Republicans have won four of the eleven presidential elections since that date. While Liberal dominance is strong in Canada, there were minority governments from 1962–8 and after 1972. While the Philippine party system is (1971) fundamentally competitive, there is more authoritarianism and corruption than in any of the other countries.

Assessments of ideological distance are necessarily crude.

The most important distinction is between those legislatures in which there is a wide ideological chasm between the governing party and its principal adversary and those legislatures in which the two sides are relatively close ideologically. In the former category one finds three parties that are perpetually in opposition—Communist parties in Italy and India and the Japan Socialist party—confronting parties that are perpetually in office. In the latter category one finds, at its extremity, the Philippine Nacionalista and Liberal parties, which Jackson says are 'virtually identical'. Turning, finally, to the matter of cabinet coalitions, one should distinguish between a situation (Italy) in which several parties have a major say and a situation (West Germany) in which typically there is a dominant partner and a minor partner.

Having made suitable qualifications, we are now in a position to explore such patterns as are suggested by the data in Table 12.2. The most important point is that particular types of party arrangements tend to be found in countries that have strong committee systems, while other types of party arrangements prevail in countries with weaker committee systems. In this connection let us consider the committee systems at the top and bottom of the rank order.

Where the committees are strongest—in the United States and Italy—one finds the lowest level of party control over the committees. What is meant by this is that *no single party* can exercise effective control. The key explanatory factor in the American case is the marked lack of cohesion in the Democratic and Republican parties. While either the Democratic or Republican party has a majority on each committee at any given time, there is a conspicuous absence of effective party direction. This means that each committee member has a great deal of independence. In Italy it is not lack of cohesion that provides the main explanation. As has been noted, each Italian party is in fact relatively cohesive. Rather, the main explanatory factor is the multi-party situation. The fact that no Italian party ever has a majority of members on the committees means that single-party control is not possible. Thus, we can postulate that lack of party control—whether resulting from non-cohesion or multi-partyism—tends to be associated with strong committees. Put another way, where single-party control of committees is absent, the circumstances are right for the development of a strong committee system.

Moving down to the four countries in the lower half of the rank order, we find that in these cases there are, again, common party characteristics. Although it is not immediately clear from the table, these characteristics differ from those in the United States and Italy. The four in the lower half have in fact two important features in common. On each committee in Canada, Britain, India, and Japan one party has a majority of the members and is cohesive. This combination of circumstances facilitates single-party control of the committees. Paradoxically, this situation is compatible with contexts in which there are one (India), two (Canada and Britain), and more than two (Japan) major parties. In general, it can be postulated that control by a single, cohesive party tends to be associated with weak committees. Put another way, a cohesive party with a majority on all the committees can normally get its way unless non-party conditioners of unusual importance are present.

As for West German committees, which are in-between the top and bottom groups, one finds some 'in-between' party characteristics. Whereas the West German parties are cohesive, there is not usually a one-party majority on committees in the Bundestag. At the same time a West German party is usually close to having such a majority. As for the other in-between system—that in the Philippines—the position is not clear-cut.

Evidence outside the present study lends support to the aforementioned generalizations about party control. For example, prior to 1973 the Chilean Congress provided an example of a situation similar to that in Italy. Chile had a multiparty system with no party having a majority of seats in the permanent, specialized committees. . . . Similarly, the Knesset in Israel has committee and party characteristics like those in Italy and pre-1973 Chile. . . . The Swedish Riksdag provides another example of a multi-party legislature with an 'important' committee system, within which 'Sweden's famous politics of compromise occur'.[6]

[6] Nelson, 'Congressional Committee System', p. 128.

The basic relationship that has been established would seem to be:

Single-party control	=	weak committees.
Absence of party control	=	strong committees.

In fact, these blunt depictions overlook a number of more subtle aspects of the relationship between parties and committees. For example, it is interesting to find that three of our legislatures have dominant parties and also weak committees. We have already suggested that if *any* cohesive party has majorities on committees, the committees may be expected to be weak. A further refinement suggests itself: if the *same* cohesive party maintains a dominant position in national politics persistently over time, then the committees may become exceptionally weak. A possible explanation of this is that governing parties (e.g. in India and Japan) which have no expectation of becoming opposition parties are less sensitive to the 'rights' of committee minorities than parties which expect to become minorities themselves from time to time. If, to carry this still further, the dominant party has institutionalized factions that thrash out policies prior to the committee stage and if the party rigidly coheres behind those policies in committee, then committees may become rubber-stamp bodies. The last is of course the position in Japan.

In two of our eight countries—Italy and West Germany—the cabinets consist of party coalitions. This is likewise the case in three other political systems to which we have referred—Israel, pre-1973 Chile, and pre-1958 France. In all five instances committees in the legislature are (or were) strong. Moreover, those coalition cabinets with the most instability—in pre-1958 France and Italy—have (or had) the strongest committee systems among the five. There is clearly a relationship between executive weakness and committee strength.

In the matter of the ideological distance between parties, the relationship between this factor and the rank order of committee strength is not clear-cut. On the one hand, there is a pronounced tendency for weak committees to be found where party distance is substantial. It would seem logical that when ideological distance is considerable, the possibilities for committee bargaining and committee cohesion (as opposed to party cohesion) are limited. Japan provides the clearest case where this is so. On the other hand, it is often the case that a softening of party divisions occurs in committees at a time when it may not be occurring at the plenary level. This process appears to be particularly evident in Italy where the ideologically disparate Christian Democrats and Communists are the principal adversaries in committees that are second in the rank order.

So far no mention has been made of the party committees that, to use Johnson's word, 'shadow' the official committees in many legislatures. A systematic examination of party committees is beyond the scope of the present study, but their working is so often linked to that of the official committees that they cannot be ignored. The structural relationship between official and party committees can be defined in terms of four models, based on whether the respective systems include a range of committees that are specialized in fields of public policy. First, there are situations in which both committee systems are specialized in this sense, as in West Germany. Second, there are situations in which the official committees are specialized and the party committees are nonspecialized, as in the United States. Third, there are situations in which the official committees are non-specialized and the party committees are specialized, as in Britain. Fourth, there could be situations, of which there are no examples in the present study, in which both the official and party committees are non-specialized.

One can imagine the various modes of interaction that might prevail in each of these situations. For present purposes we can only be suggestive and note that the essential difference between official and party committees is that the former are microcosms of the whole House while the latter are normally restricted to members of one of the parties in the House. It is conceivable that the party committees could be more important than the official committees. Kashyap says that 'the most important committees' in the Indian Parliament 'are the committees of the ruling party', which are specialized according to ministerial jurisdictions. Despite their importance, these committees, according to Kashyap, are 'largely informal' and 'rudimentary', and not all of them are active. In Japan extra-parliamentary party bodies are clearly more important than either the official committees or the party committees (*Kokutai*) in the Diet. In Britain party committees provide useful forums for two-way communication between ministers and back-benchers with special interests, but the impact of such committees on the official committees appears to be sporadic and indirect. Party committees, such as they are, in the American Congress are very much overshadowed by the official committees. In fact, party leaders in Congress often take their advice on policy questions from party specialists on the official committees.

A particularly interesting and distinctive style of interaction between official and party committees occurs in West Germany. In the Bundestag the two committee systems—both of which are specialized on policy lines—constitute parallel structures that interact with an unusual degree of symmetry and empathy.[7] Party committees for the three main parties meet on Monday. Party executives and plenary party caucuses meet on Tuesday. The Bundestag and its committees meet on Wednesday, Thursday, and Friday. Having met in their respective party groups to determine policies and tactics, members converge in the official committees to join issue, and genuine give-and-take on substantive points occurs. A striking feature about the party committees is that they do more thorough work than their counterparts in the other seven legislatures. In preparing their recommendations on bills and other matters, they form subcommittees, receive written testimony, meet with civil servants, ministers, and spokesmen for interest groups, and are aided by small staffs. Apel[8] has in fact argued that party committees in the Bundestag have become too powerful.

It is clear that a wide variety of scenarios exist in various political systems in terms of the interactions that occur among

[7] See G. Loewenberg, *Parliament in the German Political System* (1966; 2nd edn., Ithaca, New York, 1967), ch. 4; H. Apel, 'Policy-Making in the Bundestag Parties: The Role of the Working Groups and Working Circles', *International Journal of Politics*, 1 (1971–2), 339–52.

[8] Ibid.

official committees, party committees, party caucuses, legislative party leaders, party groups outside the legislature, and executive departments. Examinations of various aspects of these interactions in a range of countries would provide a useful basis for future research.

CONSTITUTIONAL FACTORS

Constitutions may be said to affect committee behaviour in two ways. At a general level, constitutions set out broad principles of government, explicitly or implicitly. The working of political structures is influenced, more or less, by such principles, an example being the separation of powers. At a more specific level, constitutions occasionally include committee-specific requirements that are to be observed in the day-to-day implementation of the principles.

The most instructive principles to focus on are ones that broadly characterize whole systems of government. Specifically, it is useful to look at our political systems in terms of whether they are 'parliamentary' or 'presidential'. It must of course be acknowledged that these categories are far from clear-cut and that within each category there are variations that sometimes result in qualified designations. It would seem, for instance, that the political system of India falls broadly within the parliamentary (Westminster) classification for analytical purposes, but Kashyap maintains that 'such significant departures have been made in adapting the system to Indian conditions that it can no more be called a parliamentary system of the British type'. Despite such difficulties, our eight committee systems will be examined in the context of the parliamentary and presidential 'models', not least because the countries of origin of both traditions are included in our study.

In practice, it will be useful to make a two-way breakdown on the parliamentary side, thus producing a trichotomy. The categories of constitutional systems now become (1) parliamentary (Westminster), (2) parliamentary (Continental), and (3) presidential. Another way of looking at this trichotomy is to indicate whether the model derives from Westminster,

Paris, or Washington. In this connection each model had its origin in particular historical events—the constitutional conflicts in England in the seventeenth century, the French Revolution, and the founding of the United States. In terms of the relationship between legislature and executive, the models can be further delineated as follows: constitutional systems based on the Westminster model presuppose that political executives will operate within the legislature and lead it; constitutional systems based on the Washington model presuppose that political executives will be separated from the legislature; constitutional systems based on the Paris model presuppose a range of 'parallel' executive–legislative relationships tending to fall at various points between 'fusion' and 'separation'.

In Table 12.3 the eight political systems are allocated to the three categories. While seven of the allocations seem reasonably clear-cut, an explanation is necessary in the case of Japan. It will be recalled that earlier in this chapter a distinction was made between committee arrangements in which British traditions are strong and those in which American and continental traditions are strong. At that time it was suggested that Japan belongs on the American–Continental side, the main considerations being committee structure and purpose. Now, we are looking at whole constitutional systems rather than committee systems, and from this constitutional point of view Japan owes more to Westminster than to Paris. To complicate matters, there was an important American input into the framing of the Japanese Constitution, but this was not basic enough to give Japan a presidential system. Therefore, it seems right to classify Japan with the three Commonwealth countries in Table 12.3.

The pattern that emerges is strikingly uniform. The top half of the rank order consists of countries that either have presidential constitutions or parliamentary constitutions of the continental type. By contrast, the four countries that constitute the bottom half of the rank order all have parliamentary constitutions of the Westminster type. The uniform nature of the pattern is even more striking when one adds the factor of party control. The countries in which there is no single, cohesive party with a majority of seats on

TABLE 12.3. Constitutional System, Extent of Party Control, and Rank Order of Committee Strength

Country	Presidential system	Parliamentary system (Continental)	Parliamentary system (Westminster)	Party control	Rank order
United States	x			Absence of party control	1
Italy		x		Absence of party control	2
West Germany		x		Absence of party control	3
Philippines	x			Absence of party control	4
Canada			x	Single-party control	5
Britain			x	Single-party control	6
India			x	Single-party control	7
Japan			x	Single-party control	8

committees are the four in the top half of the rank order. Conversely, the countries in which there is a single-party control of committees are the four in the bottom half of the rank order. Conversely, the countries in which there is single-party control of committees are the four in the bottom half of the rank order.

Thus the basic constitutional relationships would seem to be:

Presidential system	= strong committees.
Parliamentary system (Continental)	= strong committees.
Parliamentary system (Westminster)	= weak committees.

The combined constitutional and party relationships would seem to be:

Presidential system	+ absence of party control	= strong committees
Parliamentary system (Continental)	+ absence of party control	= strong committees
Parliamentary system (Westminster)	= single-party control	= weak committees

How does one account for these patterns? Inevitably, the separation of the executive from the legislature in presidential systems must be stressed. Where the separation of powers exists, the legislature is by definition intended to be strong and independent. It can be argued that a legislature cannot have this strength without having strong committees serving as a 'counter-bureaucracy'. It follows that the country with the strongest committees—the United States—has a presidential system, a deep commitment to the separation of powers, and (viewed cross-nationally) a formidable counter-bureaucracy in its generously staffed committees and subcommittees. In the other presidential system the president of the Philippines is in a more dominant position than his American counterpart, and this circumstance constricts the capacity of the Philippine Congress to be stronger and more independent than it is. Yet, as Jackson points out, while the Philippines has a weak Congress, it also has a strong committee system.

Turning to Continental parliaments, a number of them owe

much to the French tradition of a strong legislative assembly, to the great committees of the Convention during the French Revolution, and to the powerful committees of the Fourth Republic. Such influences have led to the development of parliaments that keep their distance from the executive and work through strong, specialized committees. This spirit is certainly present in the governing arrangements of Italy and West Germany.

Italy is unique among our eight countries in having a full and direct commitment in the Constitution to a system of committees in the legislature. . . . The fact that key committee practices in Italy are given constitutional legitimacy has undoubtedly been an important factor in the development of the second strongest committee system in our study. The pertinent provisions of the Constitution require that every bill must be examined by a committee *before* the House debates it; that the composition of committees must be proportional to party strength; that committees of investigation may be established when desired; and that committees may enact legislation without consideration by the parent chambers, except in a few specified fields. The last-mentioned proviso is unique to Italy in our study. The significance of this procedure is evident when one considers, as mentioned earlier, that 75 per cent of the laws passed by the Italian Parliament are enacted in committee, without even nominal consideration on the floor of either chamber. It should be added, however, that the most controversial legislation is normally debated on the floor. Nevertheless, the enactment power gives Italian committees a weapon in their armories not available even to American committees.

The only other country in the present study in which there are significant constitutional references to committees is West Germany. (In the remaining five countries with written constitutions there is either no mention or very tangential mention, e.g. in connection with joint action by the two houses.) The West German Basic Law specifies that there shall be committees on foreign affairs and defence, thus more or less committing the Bundestag to a specialized committee system. In addition the Basic Law authorizes the Bundestag to appoint committees of investigation and authorizes the

Bundestag and its committees to require the presence of ministers. This explicitness in West Germany, as in Italy, is not unrelated to the fact that their constitutions were adopted within a year of each other in the shadow of a recent history of despotism that occupying powers were anxious to replace with democracy. Significantly, there is in Article 20 of the Basic Law, according to Johnson, 'in broad terms . . . a commitment to the separation of powers'.

Parliamentary systems based on the Westminster model provide the third and final category. Here, in terms of legislative–executive relations, the separation of powers is absent, the tendency being for political executives to operate within the legislature and to lead it. The typical consequence has been strong executives and relatively weak legislatures and committees. Walkland has characterized the position in Britain in the following terms:

> It has been a feature of the British system of parliamentary government in this century that the House of Commons has not discharged its main functions through a strong committee system. . . . The tight political relationship of Parliament and the executive largely accounts for this relatively sketchy committee structure, while the subordination of parliamentary organization to the requirements of government has determined the major characteristics of those committees that have operated. The need for political control of the assembly to be as complete as possible has disinclined the executive toward wide experimentation with committees.

In Canada the position has been even more favourable to the executive. As Rush says:

> Canadian Governments have from time to time treated the Commons with a degree of contempt that no British Government would dare to exhibit. Canada has been subject to something approaching 'prime ministerial government' for most if not all of its history since Confederation. It follows that the legislature in Canada has always been more subordinate to the executive than in Britain.

As in Britain, a consequence has been weak committees. A fuller committee structure than Britain's has long existed in Canada, but prior to 1968 it was much under-used. Following the creation in that year of a full panoply of permanent and specialized committees, they were more fully and systematically utilized, but with no appreciable diminution of executive dominance of their proceedings.

In India and Japan the same 'norm' of executive dominance prevails. In India, according to Kashyap, 'The Council of Ministers, with the Prime Minister at its head, controls both Government and legislature.' More specifically, through its party majority the Government controls such *ad hoc* committees on legislation as are formed. In addition, although a non-party spirit exists in financial committees in the Lok Sabha, they, too, appear to have limited influence. . . . As for the Diet, its weakness on both the plenary and committee levels has been mentioned in several earlier connections. While the Japanese Constitution provides that the Diet 'shall be the highest organ of state power and the sole law-making organ of the State', the reality, according to Baerwald, is that few Japanese would appear to take the Diet seriously.

Although in terms of constitutional systems, party control, and committee strength the pattern is remarkably uniform, there is an interesting lack of uniformity in relation to a further factor. This factor is the degree of permanence and specialization of committees. Earlier it was suggested that when a legislature creates a permanent committee system, with committees specialized on policy lines, it tends to be committing itself to a substantial degree of devolution and to the development of specialized expertise among members. Not surprisingly, the committee systems in the upper half of the rank order are all of the permanent, specialized type. However, a notable variation is seen in the lower half of the rank order where two of the committee systems are of the permanent, specialized type and two are not. Thus, it would seem that where one finds a parliamentary system of the Westminster type combined with single-party control of committees, the committees tend to be weak whether they are predominantly of the permanent, specialized type, as in Canada and Japan, or whether they consist of a mixture of *ad hoc* and permanent committees, with *ad hoc* committees playing a major role, as in Britain and India.

The finding is particularly useful in connection with the long-standing argument in Britain concerning the desirability of incorporating permanent, specialized committees into the House of Commons. Because the finding derives from an eight-nation study, it meets the objection by Nelson[9] to 'bifocal' inferences that relate solely to America and Britain. The general point is that Canadian and Japanese experience, particularly the latter, illustrates that a comprehensive system of specialized committees can coexist with strong executive and party control of the legislature. This evidence supports a view expressed two decades ago by Wheare[10] 'There can be no doubt whatever if a system of specialized standing committees were set up in Britain and were composed in proportion to the party strengths in the House, the government would control the committees, just as it controls the House.' That British governments have been less confident about this than Wheare is suggested by Walkland's account of the 'troubled history of the carefully chosen specialist committees that operated in the 1966–70 Parliament and attracted Government hostility and obstruction out of keeping with their importance'.

DEVELOPMENTAL FACTORS

I should now like to introduce the dimension of time into this analysis, which brings us to the concept of political development. I shall take up two themes that are stressed in discussions of political development: capacity and differentiation. The question of capacity arises, according to Almond and Powell,[11] because of 'some significant change in the magnitude and content of the flow of inputs into the political system'. This results in political development, which, according to Kornberg and Musolf, 'can be regarded as an increased capacity of a political system to accommodate the essential demands upon it', or, put another way, 'an increased capacity for problem-solving'. The means of achieving more capacity is to increase differentiation, and this is typically brought about

[9] Nelson, 'Congressional Committee System', pp. 126–7.

[10] K. C. Wheare, *Government by Committee* (Oxford, 1955), 157.

[11] G. A. Almond and G. B. Powell jun., *Comparative Politics: A Developmental Approach* (Boston, Mass., 1966), 34.

through a multiplication of political structures. As Cutright[12] has said, 'a politically developed nation has more complex and specialized national political institutions than a less politically developed nation'. The end result is 'to increase the effectiveness and efficiency of the performance of the political system'.[13] Pye[14] has said that developed systems 'not only do more things than others but also do them faster and with much greater thoroughness. There is thus a trend toward professionalization of government.'

A concept related to development is 'institutionalization'. Kornberg[15] has called institutionalization 'a surrogate and an analogue' for development. In fact, there is notable lack of agreement on definitions for both terms. For present purposes Polsby's discussion of the 'institutionalization' of the US House of Representatives is of interest. According to Polsby,[16] an institutionalized political organization is one that is (1) differentiated from its environment, (2) relatively complex, and (3) inclined to use universalistic and automatic rather than particularistic and discretionary criteria for conducting its internal business. Polsby applies these criteria to the House of Representatives, where he finds they are historically relevant.

It will be useful to devote some attention to the institutionalization (or development) of the American House of Representatives—in particular of its committee system, which, not surprisingly, is the most institutionalized system among the eight. During the very early years—the 1790s—the orientation of the House was strongly plenary. Polsby calls this 'the no-committee, Hamiltonian era, in which little or no internal differentiation within the institution was visible'. Yet even then there were four standing committees working alongside *ad hoc* committees. During the next decade more standing committees were created, but they were not heavily

[12] P. Cutright, 'National Political Development: Measurement and Analysis', *American Sociological Review*, 28 (1963), 255.

[13] Almond and Powell, *Comparative Politics*, p. 105.

[14] L. W. Pye, *Aspects of Political Development* (Boston, Mass., 1966), 46.

[15] A. Kornberg, 'Introduction', in id. (ed.), *Legislatures in Comparative Perspective* (New York, 1973), 2.

[16] N. W. Polsby, 'Institutionalisation of the US House of Representatives', *American Political Science Review*, 62 (1968), 145.

relied on; bills that should have gone to them sometimes were sent to *ad hoc* committees. By 1814 the committee system had become the dominant force in the House; five new committees were created to oversee executive expenditure; and the president's influence in the appointment of committee members was reduced.

By 1850 the number of standing committees in the House of Representatives had increased to thirty-six. The House was now fully committed to conducting its business through a comprehensive system of permanent, specialized committees. By the turn of the present century there were fifty-eight such committees. Later on, their number was reduced, but this did not mean less complexity and specialization. It meant *more* of it because the reduction in the number of standing committees coincided with a growth in the number of subcommittees. By 1945 there were 106 subcommittees in the House; by 1969 there were 145. Thus, there has been a steady development throughout the history of the House toward increased structural complexity. Meanwhile, coinciding with this tendency was a movement toward increased committee autonomy. After a brief period of strong influence by the president in committee matters, there followed one hundred years during which the congressional parties, and particularly the speaker, managed from time to time to exercise substantial control over the committees. Then, following the revolt against Speaker Cannon in 1910–11 the committees become more autonomous. Polsby[17] has described the present-day, 'decentralized' situation:

> committees have won solid institutionalized independence from party leaders both inside and outside Congress. Their jurisdictions are fixed in the rules; their composition is largely determined and their leadership entirely determined by the automatic operation of seniority. Their work is increasingly technical and specialized, and the way in which they organize internally . . . is entirely at their own discretion. Committees nowadays have developed an independent sovereignty of their own, subject only to very infrequent reversals and modifications of their powers by House party leaders.

The American position has been detailed in order to illustrate how the legislature at the top of the rank order has

[17] Ibid. 156.

progressed in accordance with the aforementioned scenario for development. To round out the picture, it should be mentioned that the staffs of Congress, of members, and of committees have grown as committee differentiation and autonomy have. . . .

But what of the other seven legislatures? Does American experience have any relevance to the history of legislatures elsewhere? Does the scenario fit? In general, it can be said that tendencies noted in the case of the American Congress have also occurred to some extent elsewhere. But while this is so, there have been major variations on the principal developmental themes and some contradictions. Once again one sees the usefulness of applying grand designs devised mainly in the United States to a range of alien contexts.

Before turning to particular countries, a general point needs to be made. It is well known that considerable 'development' has been occurring throughout governmental systems for a long time. Industrialization, urbanization, the extension of the suffrage, and the creation of political parties have contributed to an enlargement of the concerns of governments and a consequent need to expand capacity through differentiation. The resulting structural complexity became mainly evident in the executive, but legislatures also responded in varying degrees. In Western Europe, as in the United States, pressures on legislators were not only an adjunct to pressures on executives but also a consequence of new representational imperatives. While committees had long existed in legislatures, it became evident in the nineteenth century that enlarged agendas could not be got through unless the use of committees was extended. At first *ad hoc* committees and, later, permanent committees were created in order to increase the time available to the legislature. In some instances this early division of labour 'constituted at least a pale imitation of bureaucratic organization'.[18] These tendencies have continued during the present century.

Italy acquired a parliamentary system in 1876. *Ad hoc* committees were thereafter utilized in the Italian Parliament, appointments to the committees being made on a relatively

[18] G. Loewenberg (ed.), *Modern Parliaments: Change or Decline?* (Chi., Ill., 1971), 7.

random basis. The development of a multi-party system led to the adoption of proportionate party representation in 1922, but the immediate onset of Fascism meant the end of parliamentary life in Italy for a generation. This experience resulted in a preoccupation with establishing strong representative institutions—with permanent, specialized committees playing an important part. The need for structural differentiation in Parliament became acute because of requirements that statutes be enacted in relation to matters which in other democracies are left to the executive. The solution was extreme devolution, i.e. the plenary stage was eliminated in relation to most legislation, and the committees became enacting bodies.

Thus, the Italian Parliament has clearly increased its capacity and complexity in some respects, but there are signs of political underdevelopment in others, if the criteria mentioned earlier are applied. Although the committees are formally authorized to create subcommittees, D'Onofrio informs us that 'no consistent subcommittee structure has developed'. An important reason for this is that, due to the large number of parties involved, it would be impossible to achieve equitable party representation on subcommittees. In fact, D'Onofrio asserts, 'there is no significant committee autonomy', due to party cohesiveness. On the matter of staffing, the position is rudimentary; one overworked clerk is assigned to each committee. Finally, D'Onofrio advises us that functions other than law-making 'have not been fully developed as yet' in the committees. Loewenberg[19] mentions parliamentary discontinuity in Italy and the resulting high turnover of members as factors that have 'impaired the process of institutionalization in terms of the establishment of organizational boundaries and the development of parliamentary rules and substructures'.

Loewenberg was referring to Germany as well as Italy when he made the foregoing statement. Germany progressed from *ad hoc* committees in the Imperial Reichstag to permanent, specialized committees in the Weimar Republic to authoritarianism and, finally, to a resumption of the Weimar committee

[19] Id., 'The Institutionalisation of Parliament and Public Orientations to the Political System', in Kornberg (ed.), *Legislatures*, 146.

pattern in 1949. The German example raises a number of important questions, with three aspects of committee development being of particular interest. First, there has been a marked reduction in the number of days devoted to plenary meetings. During the first decade of this century the Reichstag customarily met an average of one hundred days annually, whereas from 1961–5 the comparable figure was forty-nine days. Second, the related devolution has been bifocal. Whereas in the United States and Italy new capacity has mainly been found in official committees, in West Germany an arrangement involving both official and party committees has developed. The party working groups and the official committees interact in a distinctive sequential pattern. Third, the West German example illustrates that 'development' in legislatures involves much more than a simple multiplication of official committees. The number of official committees in the Bundestag declined from thirty-nine in 1949 to nineteen in 1970, while the importance of committees—taking official and party committees together—was increasing. This occurred, moreover, in the absence of the development of a compensating subcommittee structure. Loewenberg[20] has suggested that the reduction occurred because the government was finding the large number of committees unmanageable and because problems of co-ordination arose. In the matter of staffing, the more important committees in the Bundestag are more adequately serviced than their counterparts in most of our other legislatures, and party committees also enjoy some staff assistance.

[O]ne of the criteria for choosing countries for the present study was the stage of political development. In fact, all eight of our countries have achieved a high level of political development. Yet in two cases—the Philippines and India—the stage reached in terms of political development is incongruent with the stage reached in economic and social development, and we chose to look at committees in these countries in order to examine the working of committees under conditions of developmental incongruity. Significantly, both the Philippines and India have experienced major

[20] Loewenberg (ed.), *Modern Parliaments*, p. 9.

political changes since the chapters on these countries were written. . . .

It will be possible to deal only very briefly with India, Canada, and Japan. While India is developed politically, there are more signs of underdevelopment in the Lok Sabha than in the Philippine Congress. The fact that Westminster provided the model for India while Washington provided the model for the Philippines is undoubtedly important in this connection. The strong plenary orientation, the absence of a system of specialized committees, the high turnover of members, and the large number of members (more than 50 per cent) who have no committee assignments are factors that illustrate why the Lok Sabha is the least differentiated legislature in this study. Yet the financial and other committees have 'developed' since they were created. As Kashyap says, 'They have since [1950] grown beyond recognition.'

Canada provides a classic instance of an increasing utilization of committees over time. Between 1867 and 1906 there was no systematic arrangement of permanent, specialized committees in the Canadian House of Commons. Between 1906 and 1968 such a system existed, but it was very much under-used. Since 1968 a new, rationalized system of permanent, specialized committees was created, and it is fully utilized. These developments toward increased devolution and differentiation coincided with a need for increased capacity that resulted from longer parliamentary sessions and agendas.

As for the Japanese Diet, much has already been said about its committee system. What appears to be illustrated in this case is that one can have a marked degree of formal structural complexity in the form of permanent, specialized committees and large committee staffs without achieving effective differentiation of the legislature from its external environment.

One legislature remains to be discussed in relation to political development: the British Parliament. This is by a margin of nearly five centuries the longest-established legislature in the present study. Yet, paradoxically, the British House of Commons has less devolution, less committee capacity, and less differentiation from its external environment than a number of the other legislatures in this study.

Nevertheless, Loewenberg[21] has said that the House of Commons, like the American Congress, is 'highly institutionalized', pointing out that the Commons met an average of 154 days annually between 1900 and 1966, with a standard deviation, through war and peace, of only 14. The House of Commons has certainly developed elaborate, universal, and automatic procedures that have provided a model for many other legislatures. Yet in the matter of official committees, Walkland has characterized the end product of seven centuries of 'development' as a 'relatively sketchy committee structure'.

The British example suggests that some fundamental thinking needs to be done about 'institutionalization' and 'development' as these terms apply to legislatures. Huntington[22] has delineated four measures of the level of institutionalization of a political unit, and these criteria have been repeated by others. Yet when applied to the 'highly institutionalized' House of Commons, not all the criteria are relevant. One criterion is adaptability. Has the House of Commons proven to be adaptable? Yes, according to Hanson:

> The adaptability of British parliamentary institutions is . . . astounding. That a deliberative body originating from the medieval royal council should have successively served the purposes of the fifteenth century feudal baronage, the sixteenth century monarchy, the seventeenth century 'gentry,' the eighteenth century aristocracy, the nineteenth century plutocracy and the 'mass democracy' of our present age, is one of the world's political wonders.[23]

A second criterion mentioned by Huntington is structural complexity, by which he means 'multiplication of organizational subunits, hierarchically and functionally, and differentiation of separate types of organizational subunits'. In this matter it can be said that a moderate amount of institutionalization has occurred in the House of Commons. There are

[21] Loewenberg, 'Institutionalisation of Parliament', in A. Kornberg (ed.), *Legislatures in Comparative Perspective* (New York: McKay, 1973), pp. 144–5.

[22] S. P. Huntington, *Political Order in Changing Societies* (New Haven, 1968), 18–22.

[23] A. H. Hanson, 'The Purpose of Parliament', *Parliamentary Affairs*, 17 (1964), 279.

more official committees, party committees, other groupings of members, and supporting staff than there used to be. But in regard specifically to official committees, until recently the House and the Government have been reluctant to multiply them. Huntington's third criterion is coherence. By this he means that there must be 'substantial consensus on the functional boundaries of the group'. The House of Commons gets high marks for this.

The fourth criterion is autonomy. Are the official committees of the Commons autonomous in relation to other social groupings? Walkland and others agree: No. Walkland makes it clear that the executive has controlled the development of these committees, has used them for its own purposes, has been reluctant to give them much authority, and has been reinforced in this by strong party cohesion. Further reinforcement has resulted from a conviction on the part of many members that the plenary House and party committees should provide the main arenas in which the government should justify its policies. The amateur tradition in the House and a reluctance by members to specialize are additional explanatory factors. Walkland made the position clear when discussing committees on legislation: 'Standing committees are so tightly structured into the organization of the House of Commons as a whole as to reduce their autonomy almost to vanishing point. . . . There is no marked differentiation between the [standing] committees and the parent House.' . . .

The structural and procedural constraints that plenary chambers impose on their committees cover a very wide range of matters. Thus, standing orders specify whether committees are to have circumscribed or broad responsibilities within their fields; how members are to be appointed and whether substitutions will be permitted; whether committee meetings are to be private or open to the public; committee finance; whether the attendance of ministers, civil servants, and other persons may be requested or required; whether a summary or verbatim record of committee proceedings is kept; whether committees have large or small staffs; whether subcommittees can be formally established; when and where committees may meet; whether committees may concern themselves with 'policy'; and whether committees deal with legislation before or after there has been a debate on the floor of the chamber. Often committees themselves have some say in such matters, but not usually to an extent that would justify calling them procedurally autonomous.

The last of the aforementioned procedural variables is sufficiently important to warrant further consideration. In five of the legislatures in the present study, committees consider bills before they are dealt with on the floor. This procedure is followed in the United States, Italy, West Germany, the Philippines, and Japan. In the remaining countries—Britain, Canada, and India—bills are debated on the floor before they are referred to committees. This line-up is a familiar one. The committee-before-floor countries constitute the top half of the rank order plus Japan, while the committee-after-floor countries are in the lower half of the rank order.

Thus, there is a clear relationship between the timing of committee consideration of legislation and the strength of committees. Moreover, linkages can also be effected with constitutional and party variables. Addition of the 'timing' factor to the arrangements depicted in Table 12.3 produces the following relationships:

Presidential system	+	absence of party control	+	committee before floor	=	strong committees
Parliamentary system (Continental)	+	absence of party control	+	committee before floor	=	strong committees
Parliamentary system (Westminster)	+	single-party control	+	committee after floor	=	weak committee

These patterns fit in regard to seven of the eight legislatures. In the case of Japan there is one deviant element, namely the timing of floor consideration.

It is not surprising that strong committees are associated with the pre-plenary consideration of bills. If a committee can consider a bill before it is taken up on the floor, the chances of the committee influencing or determining the outcome tends to be greater than when the lines of battle have been predetermined in plenary meetings. In general, where a strong commitment to utilize committees exists, the committees get the bills first. Where a legislature has been reluctant to make such a commitment, the consequent plenary bias is reflected in its procedures. As Barber[24] has said, control over 'sequences in the decision process' is a 'power resource'.

[24] J. D. Barber, *Power in Committees: An Experiment in the Governmental Process* (Chi., Ill., 1966), 66.

PART V

LEGISLATURES AND THE QUESTION OF REFORM

INTRODUCTION

The issue of reform is a perennial one. Bryce's dictum of decline has given added impetus to schemes of reform in the twentieth century. Various writers have laboured over schemes of ambitious or detailed reform, others giving up in despair. So too have various official bodies set up to investigate reform within their own political systems.

A legislature cannot be analysed independently of the political system of which it forms a part. Equally, there is little reason why it should be viewed *exclusively* within the context of that system. What happens in one legislature may provide guidance as to what is possible elsewhere, allowance being made for differences in political systems and culture. Students of legislatures, like official committees, have too often fallen into the trap of complacent insularity.

Recent decades have been notable for the extent to which schemes of reform, not least those advanced by parliamentary bodies, have drawn on experience overseas. This has been noteworthy in the case of a number of Commonwealth countries, including the United Kingdom.

Pressure for parliamentary reform in Britain built up in the 1960s, with Bernard Crick in the van. His *The Reform of Parliament*, published in 1964 (following a Fabian pamphlet on the subject published in 1959), provided not only a broad reform menu that was drawn on extensively in the latter half of the 1960s but also a contribution to the cause of reform elsewhere. His memorable delineation of the concept of parliamentary control has been drawn on widely by political scientists and legislators elsewhere and has served to influence the language of debate on legislatures. His delineation of that concept, and his 'principles of constitutional interpretation' providing guidelines for parliamentary reform in Britain, are reproduced in this section. The period of parliamentary reform in Britain for at least ten years following publication of

The Reform of Parliament may be described as essentially Crickian.

Crick emphasized the imperative of a reformed committee system, with permanent committees of 'advice, scrutiny and investigation' being at the heart of his proposals for change. Such committees were experimented with in the latter half of the 1960s and early 1970s, but failed to live up to the expectations of their more optimistic proponents; by 1970, even Crick himself was—in his own words—'blowing hot and cold' about them.

Recognition that such committees were failing to have a significant impact upon the relationship between Parliament and the executive led to pressure for more radical change. A Select Committee on Procedure was appointed in 1976 to consider the issue again and, in 1978, it issued its wide-ranging report. Central to its proposals was the creation of a near-comprehensive set of investigative select committees, appointed with wide terms of reference to monitor and investigate the activities of the various Departments of government. The central part of the report, proposing such committees, is reproduced in this section.

The recommendations of the committee were considered too radical by the then Labour Leader of the House of Commons, Michael Foot, but he was forced by an impatient House of Commons to concede a debate on the Committee's report. The general election of 1979 then intervened. Most members of the incoming Conservative Cabinet were ill-disposed towards the Committee's proposals, but pressure from a reforming Leader of the House (Norman St John-Stevas) and a determined and largely united House overcame their objections. The result was the creation in 1979 of fourteen departmentally related select committees: essentially the twelve recommended by the Procedure Committee (except for trade and industry being combined and employment established as a separate committee) plus committees for Scotland and Wales. (That on Scottish affairs was not reappointed in 1987). Though the performance of these committees has been mixed,[1] they have proved major improve-

[1] See G. Drewry (ed.), *New Select Committees* (Oxford, 1985).

ments on what went before—with the potential to realize a support mobilization role, as noted by Beer—and have provided also a major focus of enquiry by parliamentary committees from other countries appointed to consider reform.

Among such committees have been the Canadian Special Committee on Reform, which issued its main report in 1985, and the New Zealand Royal Commission on the Electoral System, which reported in December 1986. Both were concerned (the New Zealand Commission especially so) to consider, and improve, the relationship between the legislature and the people as well as between the legislature and the executive.

In its recommendations, the New Zealand Royal Commission advocated a system of proportional representation for parliamentary elections. Such a recommendation was beyond the remit of the Canadian Committee. Both, however, were concerned to improve parliamentary scrutiny of government and both considered that the best means of achieving that was through a series of investigative committees, akin to the British (which the members of both bodies studied). Both, though, looked to wider change in order to provide conditions conducive to the effective workings of such committees.

In the case of the Canadian Committee, it advocated a change in the convention governing the position of the government in the event of a parliamentary defeat, recognizing that such a change required an attitudinal change on the part of ministers, party leaders, and back-benchers. In advancing this argument, it drew on British experience of the 1970s, when a change of attitude on the part of many MPs made possible the structural changes of 1979.[2] Members of the committee acknowledged that the Canadian House could not emulate precisely what had happened in Britain, but they recognized the lessons to be drawn from that experience.

With the New Zealand Royal Commission, the most important change recommended in order to achieve more effective committees was an enlargement in the size of the

[2] See P. Norton, 'The Norton View' in D. Judge (ed.), *The Politics of Parliamentary Reform* (London: Heinemann, 1983), 54–69.

unicameral Parliament. It was recognized that an enlargement would have other benefits (potentially better calibre ministers) but the need to generate powerful select committees was the principal motivation for the recommendation. Coupled with electoral reform, and a package of other constitutional changes (including a referendum on a four-year, as opposed to the existing three-year, parliamentary term), the Commission sought to create an enhanced role for Parliament ensuring that it was a scrutineer of government, operating—with popular support—through open committees of investigation. Bernard Crick would approve.

The reports of all three committees—British, Canadian, and New Zealand—are evidence of a more outward-looking and energetic approach to reform, evincing a willingness by legislators to draw on experience abroad in order to further understanding of their own political systems. It is an approach which has been influenced by some scholars but which most students of legislatures have probably yet to emulate.

13

THE REFORM OF PARLIAMENT

BERNARD CRICK

THE CONCEPT OF CONTROL

Politics, not law, must explain the concept and practice of Parliamentary control of the executive. In modern conditions any such control can only be something that does not threaten the day-to-day political control of Parliament by the executive. The hope for any worthwhile function of control by Parliament would be grim indeed if it depended on the ultimate deterrent of the vote: the undoubted constitutional right of Parliament to vote against the Queen's ministers and the convention by which they would then resign. But control, on both sides, is indeed political. Governments respond to proceedings in Parliment if the publicity given to them is likely to affect public confidence in the government, or even if the weakness with which the government puts up its case, even in purely Parliamentary terms, begins to affect the morale of its own supporters (though it takes a very long succession of bleak days for the government in the House before the country begins to be affected).

The only meanings of parliamentary control worth considering, and worth the House spending much of its time on, are those which do *not* threaten the parliamentary defeat of a government, but which help to keep it responsive to the underlying currents and the more important drifts of public opinion. All others are purely antiquarian shufflings. It is wholly legitimate for any modern government to do what it needs to guard against parliamentary defeat; but it is not legitimate for it to hinder Parliament, particularly the opposition, from reaching the public ear as effectively as it

Bernard Crick, from *The Reform of Parliament* (London: Weidenfeld and Nicolson, 1964), 76–8, 192–203. Reprinted by permission of the publisher.

can. Governments must govern in the expectation that they can serve out their statutory period of office, that they can plan—if they choose—at least that far ahead, but that everything they do may be exposed to the light of day and that everything they say may be challenged in circumstances designed to make criticism as authoritative, informed, and as public as possible.

Thus, the phrase 'parliamentary control', and talk about the 'decline of parliamentary control', should not mislead anyone into asking for a situation in which governments can have their legislation changed or defeated, or their life terminated (except in the most desperate emergency when normal politics will in any case break down, as in Chamberlain's 'defeat' in 1940). Control means *influence*, not direct power; *advice*, not command; *criticism*, not obstruction; *scrutiny*, not initiation; and *publicity*, not secrecy. Here is a very realistic sense of parliamentary control which *does* affect any government. The government will make decisions, whether by existing powers or by bringing in new legislation, in the knowledge that these decisions, sooner or later, will find their way to debate on the floor of one of the Houses of Parliament. The type of scrutiny they will get will obviously affect, in purely political terms, the type of actions undertaken. And the Civil Service will administer with the knowledge that it too may be called upon to justify perhaps even the most minute actions.

Governments are virile and adult; they are beyond the strict parental control of Parliament. But they are likely to be deeply influenced by well put home truths from the family, if only (or above all) because this may be some sort of clue to their public reputation; and also because, after all, they have to share the same overcrowded house. Defeating the government or having the whips withdrawn represent, like calling in the police, the breakdown, not the assertion, of normal control.

Governments deserve praise in so far as they expose themselves, willingly and helpfully, to influence, advice, criticism, scrutiny, and publicity; and they deserve blame in so far as they try to hide from unpleasant discussions and to keep their reasons and actions secret. Parliaments deserve praise or blame as to whether or not they can develop institutions whose control is powerful in terms of general elections and not of governmental instability. This 'praise' and 'blame' is not moralistic: it is prudential. A government subject to such controls is not likely to get too far out of touch with public opinion; it may not, even in Bagehot's sense, attempt to 'teach' public opinion, but it will not destroy it. So parliamentary control is not the stop switch, it is the tuning, the tone, and the amplifier of a system of communication which tells governments what the electorate want (rightly or wrongly) and what they will stand for (rightly or wrongly), and tells the electorate what is possible within the resources available (however much opinions will vary on what is possible). . . .

The purposes of this chapter should now be clear: to show the true function of Parliament in relation to British government (basically that of informing the electorate); to sound yet another alarm that it is being badly fulfilled and that public confidence will decline if remedies are not found, and to suggest the broad areas of possible action. It is not intended to be so presumptuous as to offer a detailed scheme for parliamentary reform. All it is proper, possible, and needful to do is to set out the broad areas of need and the possibilities of action. If this seems evasive, I can only reply that I am not much taken by paper schemes by outsiders, and that the method of this book may prove a welcome rebuttal to the usual view that people have of an academic's approach to politics. For I have sought to examine in detail and suggest only in general. Whatever happens, there will not be any sudden and great tearing up of Erskine May and beginning again on rational Benthamite principles. But there may be a concerted effort to stretch every existing procedure and institution of Parliament in the direction of reform, and to drop a few bits of business by the wayside.[1] I am very serious in thinking that there had better be some such effort, for there is ample evidence from the history of our times, and general

[1] I find the tone and temper of *Change or Decay: Parliament and Government in our Industrial Society*, by a group of Conservative MPs (London: Conservative Political Centre, 1963), admirable on this point. They quote Bagehot as a legend: 'The very means which best helped you yesterday, may very likely be those which most impede you tomorrow.'

grounds in political and social theory for believing that the strongest-seeming free systems of government can crumble from within if the masses cease to understand or care how they are governed, and begin to think that attempts to control or influence government are 'all a farce and a racket anyway.'

So I propose to set out certain general principles of constitutional interpretation and state the kind of consequences that should follow from recognizing them realistically:

1. Parliament serves to inform the electorate not to overthrow governments. Therefore, too much time is spent on ritualistic forms of debates and divisions on legislation which is going to be passed anyway. Too little time is spent on scrutiny of the administration. Too much stress is laid by both government and opposition on voting and not enough on 'publicizing' (both by means of investigations and general debates—but more of the latter will only serve any purpose if there are more of the former). Too little use is made of committees of inquiry in Parliament and of MPs as members of outside advisory committees to the government. Then if these things were remedial, Parliament could save time for both floor and committee by encouraging more, not less, delegated legislation.

2. Governments must govern, but strong government needs strong opposition. Therefore, the procedures of Parliament need rethinking to fit the concept of 'equal access to the electorate' by the parties, and this for the whole life of a Parliament, not merely during the statutory campaign, since in a real sense *Parliament is a continuous election campaign* (but one which needs to be more fairly conducted). This concept is a more relevant key to parliamentary procedure than concepts of ministerial discretion and governmental secrecy, but it should complement, not threaten, the normal government control of the House to put its business through. The facilities available to the opposition and back-bench members in general should be greatly increased, particularly the expansion of the Library into a Parliamentary workshop of research and investigation employing many trained research workers who could serve committees. There should thus be the deliberate creation of a 'counter-bureaucracy' to Whitehall, part complementary and part to break new ground, to obtain information for Parliament.

Failing all this, the opposition needs to shed the influence of the modern 'executive mind' and see itself again as an *opposition* whose primary duty is to *oppose*, not to preen and muzzle itself by too much conceit of being an 'alternative government'.

3. *Government must plan and must control finances both in broad terms and in detail.* Therefore, governments should continue to consult more (and more openly) with people representative of those whose willing co-operation is needed in planning (certainly including, though not exclusively, MPs themselves). But there is little hope or sense in Parliament reasserting 'the power of the purse', as if financial control could ever be divorced from political control. The government must take political responsibility for financial policy above all else. There is room, however, for great improvement in financial procedure, by putting the Finance Bill 'upstairs', both to save parliamentary time and to obtain closer and more informed scrutiny. Possibly the work of the Select Committee on Estimates could better be divided up among new specialized standing committees of advice, scrutiny, and inquiry.

4. *Members of Parliament are elected to serve their country, their party and their constituency, not themselves.* Therefore, the part-time MP should be discouraged. The job is too big for part-time service. Part of the present weakness of Parliament arises from the small numbers available for morning committee work. The small hard core of dedicated and hard-working MPs are exploited by the larger number of gentlemen amateurs. The leaders and whips should at least ensure better attendance in the mornings. If people are worried about *professional* politicians (though this is usually a silly animus against politics itself) or are worried, more realistically, about the 'representativeness' of the House, then it should be pointed out that representativeness may well be a function of a member's previous full-time occupation rather than of his present part-time job (plainly there are some MPs who rely on their position to get *new* and part-time jobs when they come to Westminster). In any case, there might be a remedy if the parties and constituencies tried to encourage some people to serve in Parliament and then return to their business or profession. But MPs need greater working facilities and larger salaries

before they can all be expected to work full-time. One man, one vote; one MP, one secretary; and one MP and secretary, a private double office.[2] Salaries should be increased together with a pension scheme, both tied to some quite high grade in the Civil Service to avoid recurrent disputes. But the more important principle in relation to salaries should be that all facilities, from postage to travel, which are a normal part of any professional man's office, should be provided free out of public funds.

5. *Controls on any government are all ultimately political.* Therefore, it is ultimately vain to seek impartial adjudication of the exercise of ministerial discretion. So is the quest for an ombudsman to make an impartial investigation of maladministration. At best such devices should be regarded as complementary to an increase in parliamentary scrutiny. But governments, by the same token, need not fear the direct power of specialized committees, since party lines will hold, and ultimate political power is found only in the electorate (or, more subtly, in the self-control exercised by both government and opposition when they remind themselves, and are reminded, of how the electorate is likely to react: expectations are as important as experience). So, once again, all forms of 'control' as influence which can reach the ears of the electorate need strengthening.

6. *No government can in fact be responsible or be held responsible for every error or act of maladministration.* Therefore, we should recognize the obvious that ministers will not resign, nor ought they to, except occasionally when they are personally culpable. Then there would be no threat to 'ministerial responsibility' from almost any degree of parliamentary scrutiny and inquiry which stops short of sheer obstruction or endangering national security. Control of the administration should be seen as a joint task between ministers and committees of MPs. 'Ministerial responsibility' is, in fact, now a purely legal concept which defines who it is can use certain powers and to whom

[2] And an individual telephone and proper modern office equipment, and a typing pool for all those November days when Miss Fortune is indisposed and for those spring budget days when her boss is churning it out faster than Miss Chance can manage it—it is ludicrous that these elementary things need to be mentioned.

questions on them must be put; but the concept is misused as a kind of knock-down argument against any examination of a minister's use of his powers. The real meaning of the concept is simply political, indeed all ministers are collectively responsible to the electorate more than to Parliament. So ministerial or collective responsibility should never be invoked to refuse any form of parliamentary scrutiny and inquiry which does not threaten political control of Parliament. That proceedings in Parliament indirectly and ultimately threaten the government's control of the electorate *should be* no argument against them, for Parliament should be a device (and easily could be) to ensure something like equality of access to the public between government and opposition.

7. Technical and expert advice is more and more necessary to modern government but is more and more open to opinion and interpretation. Therefore, such advice should be given (with as few exceptions as possible), openly, and the presumption should be for, not against, its coming through committees of Parliament. This would seem a protection for the government as well as for the public. There are very few fields of applied knowledge where experts will not differ, on matters of priority if not on principle. Certainly, the government must alone make the final decision and carry the responsibility; but decisions are likely to be more wise and rational if the issues have been openly canvassed. Everyone suspects, for instance, that the real area of defence secrets—whose discussion would endanger the safety of the State—is far smaller than any recent government has allowed, even on the bleakest view of international relations and the lowest estimate of the efficiency of foreign intelligence services; a large part of what Professor Edward Shils called *The Torment of Secrecy* is that so many of the secrets are not secret. At the very least Parliament, by developing the Library of the House of Commons into a great research library, should offer alternative expert advice even if unasked. MPs will specialize more than they have done, but they will rarely be experts: they need regular access both to outside experts and to trained research workers (who would be employed by the Library) and more experience in knowing how to use them.

8. Life is short, party politics is party politics, and the House of

Commons will always be too busy to look at everything that needs attention. Therefore, the House of Lords should be transformed into a small second chamber of about a hundred—let us call them—counsellors of Parliament. They would be salaried people appointed in virtue of political, legal, and administrative experience, and appointed not necessarily for life but perhaps as part of a career in some profession or some branches of the public service. It should have no political power but considerable authority for its tasks of scrutinizing legislation and debating general issues as at present, especially those bills and issues of a less politically contentious nature; it should be prepared for the additional tasks, especially if the Commons is slow to change its ways, of reviewing administrative cases, surveying the whole field of delegated legislation, generally scrutinizing the conduct of administration, investigating grievances and conducting such public inquiries as the House of Commons may require it to do. There is a sense in which a reformed second chamber could fill many of the gaps which lead one to advocate more work in and by committees in the House of Commons—so, if necessary, a 'Chamber of Committees' or a 'House of Scrutiny'.

9. Time and tide wait for no man and much of politics is the art of being present at the right time. Therefore, the time-span of the parliamentary session should be increased, though without necessarily increasing the number of days the whole House sits. From the end of July to the third week of October Britain is without a Parliament. There would be a great gain for the public interest and probably for the efficiency of government if the House only rose for a month in the summer, but spread its sitting days far more thinly over the rest of the year, even (as others have suggested) adjourning on Wednesdays to give time for research, reading, political and public business, and general digestion of Monday and Tuesday and preparation for Thursday and Friday. Both ministers and back-bench MPs would be less frantically over-busy, as they often are, and the public would see more of them. There would seem no general objection to some committees seeking to continue their work during periods of recess.

10. British government and politics is British government and politics. Therefore, it is misleading (and usually deliberately so) to suggest that greater use of committees of advice, scrutiny, and investigation would lead to their controlling the policy of the executive, as happens in the United States and in the France of the Third and Fourth Republics. *No* procedural changes in Parliament whatever could rewrite British social history which has created the two party system in its highly disciplined form. The constitutional arrangements of these other systems of government are entirely different, indeed they have (or had) written, fundamental constitutions which encourage deliberate divisions of power and formal checks and balances, unlike the British 'sovereignty of Parliament' (or complete executive power limited only by political considerations). Even further than this: such systems are as they are largely because they do not have parties as disciplined and political divisions so relatively clear-cut as in Britain.

All this points, in and out of every other consideration, to the need for a reformed committee system. Let us try to be more specific. There is a minimum position and a maximum position. The minimum position is simply that the nineteenth-century use of select committees should be revived, both to discuss future policy and to investigate particular topics or grievances. The maximum position is that standing committees on legislation should become specialized to definite areas and should be given general powers to discuss matters in these areas, and to scrutinize and investigate the work of departments concerned (even this maximum position rejects firmly, once again, any suggestion that they should share executive authority with the minister).

Something between them is more likely to be reached and more likely to work well. The existing standing committees should be left with their existing work of considering bills in the committee stage (though there is room to argue that more bills should go to a standing committee, that is less to 'Committee of the Whole', and even, as Sir Edward Campion argued, that reconstituted standing committees could well consider the report stage of most bills). They should not be confused with what I will now call cumbersomely, for the sake of clarity, standing committees of advice, scrutiny, and investigation. The House, we have suggested, spends too much time in any case considering the preordained passage of legislation; and any scheme of reform must avoid any threat or even suspicion of a threat to the passage of Government legislation.

I use the word 'standing' committees of advice, scrutiny, and investigation simply to differentiate them from the traditional idea that select committees are *ad hoc* committees. But in fact, as we have seen, there are certain select committees which are perennial—those of estimates, accounts, and the nationalized industries, for instance.

The kind of new committee that is needed should be set up for the whole life of a Parliament to give its members time to specialize and see things through. The basic power these committees should have would be to discuss matters and have their deliberations published—as in the normal *Hansard* for standing committees. But then they could have general power to send for persons and papers and to instigate inquiries within their field of competence; they would thus do much or all of the work for which some would wish to invent—a fantasy of despair in Parliament—a British ombudsman. If they work well on these grounds one would expect them to become used more and more by ministers, both as sounding boards for future legislation, and as partners in investigating the efficiency of sections of the administration. And, finally, their specialized knowledge and growing familiarity with expert opinion could make them far more useful than the present committee to perform the work of scrutinizing the annual estimates. This work could be shared round the specialized committees to ensure a far closure scrutiny of estimates than is at present possible. They would also take over the work of the present scrutiny committee on delegated legislation. . . .

Britain today suffers under the burden of three native curses: that of amateurism, that of 'inner circle' secrecy, and that of snobbery. All three serve to debase both the quality of political life and the energy of economic activity. The unreformed Parliament is more than a symbol of these things; it helps to perpetuate them by the most effective of all forces in politics and society—example. If Parliament were reformed, the whole climate of expectations could change, much of the sweet fog we muddle through might lift. Continued decline may be our lot, decline not merely in external influence but in any internal sense, both individually and together, that there are things worth doing in Britain. But if renewal in industry, learning, and the arts, if it comes at all, comes in such a way that it bypasses Parliament, then this could mean the rule of the expert and the bureaucrat alone—a condition far more frightening than that 'mere politics' of which at least ensures the existence of that which is the greatest of all things, freedom (or, more precisely, the ability to enjoy freedom). Politics is the great civilizer, the activity which mediates between the expert and the public, between declining classes and rising, indeed between all competing interests, whether of mind or matter, which compose society—competing so long as resources remain limited and demands (or imagination) infinite. Parliament is the forum of politics in Britain and any neglect of it means danger for freedom and for all those qualities of spontaneity, adaptability, and invention upon which depend both the very survival of States and their worthiness to survive at all.

14

FIRST REPORT FROM THE SELECT COMMITTEE ON PROCEDURE 1977–8

THE BRITISH HOUSE OF COMMONS

1.5. We agree that the relationship between executive and legislature is the crucial feature of the functioning of our institutions of government, and we are conscious of the widespread concern in the country about the present nature of that relationship. The essence of the problem is that the balance of advantage between Parliament and government in the day-to-day working of the Constitution is now weighted in favour of the government to a degree which arouses widespread anxiety and is inimical to the proper working of our parliamentary democracy.

1.6. We believe that a new balance must be struck, not by changes of a fundamental or revolutionary character in the formal powers of the institutions concerned, but by changes in practice of an evolutionary kind, following naturally from present practices. We have approached our task not in the hope of making the job of government more comfortable, the weapons of opposition more formidable, or the life of the backbencher more bearable, but with the aim of enabling the House as a whole to exercise effective control and stewardship over ministers and the expanding bureaucracy of the modern state for which they are answerable, and to make the decisions of Parliament and government more responsive to the wishes of the electorate. We believe that the proposals set out in this report could go a long way towards achieving that aim.

1.7. Although we have not sought to define the role of Parliament in the Constitution in rigid terms, there appear to

British House of Commons, *First Report from the Select Committee on Procedure Session 1977–8*, HC 588 (London: Her Majesty's Stationery Office, 1978), paras. 1.5–1.12, 5.7–5.25. Reprinted with permission.

us to be certain major tasks which the electorate expect their representatives to perform. These tasks overlap at many points, but fall into four main categories: legislation, the scrutiny of the activities of the executive, the control of finance, and the redress of grievance. This report is particularly concerned with the first two tasks, and with the changes in procedure and practice necessary to achieve their more effective performance. . . .

COMMITTEES: SOME GENERAL OBSERVATIONS

1.8. Much of this report is concerned, directly or indirectly, with the use made by the House of committees to undertake on its behalf a variety of tasks concerned with primary and secondary legislation, with the scrutiny of government activities, and with the control of government expenditure. Although the overwhelming weight of evidence has favoured the development and rationalization of the committee system of the House, we are aware that some members continue to have misgivings about the effects of the present extent of committee work—let alone an expanded committee system—on the working and character of the House. Expression was given to these views by the present Leader of the House, Mr Michael Foot, when he gave evidence to us. We are conscious of the dangers involved in attempting to make wholesale changes in procedure and practice without due regard to the effects which new practices, however desirable in themselves, may have on activities which the House now performs very well. In making our recommendations we have therefore taken great care to weigh the advantages of a rational and effective committee system against the need to retain the Chamber as the focus of the political and legislative work of Parliament, and to protect, and if possible, enhance, the opportunities of the individual member to influence the decisions of the House.

1.9. Members are already quite heavily burdened with service on committees, and that burden has markedly increased since the Second World War and, more particularly, since the early 1960s. During that period there has been a substantial expansion of work, first in legislative standing committees, then in investigative select committees and, more recently, in standing committees on statutory instruments and other matters. Although an analysis of the Select Committee and Standing Committee Returns reveals how unevenly the burden is shared, it is clear that the majority of back-bench members are now required to attend such committees much more frequently than in the past and many members are very heavily committed indeed. Moreover, each new committee meeting involves extra preparatory work as well as the need to attend. Any proposals concerning the number of committees, and their workload, must therefore take realistic account of the size of the pool of members available and willing to serve.

1.10. The present committee system has for the most part developed in response to the need to relieve the pressure of business on the floor of the House or in response to new obligations or to demands for the House to perform new functions involving detailed investigation which are unsuited to a large assembly. The system which we have inherited is unplanned and unstructured. Consideration of the details of private bills and public bills, of the *vires* (and more recently the merits) of delegated legislation, and of the political or legal importance of European Community legislation, has progressively moved from the House into committee, as has the scrutiny of public accounts, public expenditure, and selected areas of policy and administration, and the consideration of matters of concern to particular geographical areas such as Scotland, Wales, or Northern Ireland. The arrangements made for handling these matters have varied markedly according to the nature of the business involved, the degree of political importance attached to it, the extent to which the House as a whole has wished to retain control over it, and the political situation at the time when the arrangements were first made. Subsequent changes made in these arrangements have been in response to similar pressures and have been governed by similar considerations. Some of the results have been less than satisfactory. In particular, in too many fields, apart from primary legislation, the House has handed to committees the responsibility of investigating or debating matters, without providing adequate means by which the conclusions of those committees' deliberations can be brought to bear directly on the work of the House itself. This applies not only to investigative committees, but also to many of the debating committees established in recent years. This situation makes members reluctant to serve on committees whose work appears irrelevant to, or at least distant from, the decisions made in the House; it also lends credence to the views of some members,[1] that committees are seeking and obtaining information which rightly should be given to the House as a whole. We reject this view, and believe that the House as a whole can acquire much of the information it requires on the initiative of the committees directly responsible. Nevertheless, we believe that whatever other changes are introduced, more formal, practical and immediate links are needed between the work of committees of all kinds and that of the House which has appointed them.

1.11. In considering the use of committees in relation to different categories of business we have not been seeking merely to respond to the demands of those members and academics who believe that committees are desirable parliamentary institutions *per se* or that work in committees is inherently preferable to work in the Chamber. Rather we have examined the use of committees in relation to different categories of public business, and have made recommendations concerning their future use, with the aim of ensuring: first, that the business is suitable to be handled in committees; second, that the type of committee is appropriate to the nature of the business to be undertaken; third, that the work in committee makes a constructive contribution to the work of the House; fourth, that service in committees does not impose an unnecessarily heavy burden on members; and fifth, that members are not compelled to serve on committees if they believe that their contribution to the work of Parliament can be made more effectively in other ways. We endorse the view of the Leader of the House when he said in evidence that 'all back-benchers do not perform their functions in the same way. They perform it in roughly 600 different ways',[2] and agree that that freedom should be preserved. Our proposals, taken

[1] Official Report, 12 Jan. 1978, cols. 1853–1878, *passim*.
[2] Q223.

as a whole, should not lead to any significant overall increase in committee membership.

1.12. Committees are not, however, an end in themselves, but are a means to secure greater surveillance of the executive by Parliament. Surveillance will not be substantially improved unless other reforms also take place, such as the provision of more supporting staff for select committees and the provision by departments of better financial and statistical information. . . .

SCRUTINY COMMITTEES

5.7. The development of more effective means of scrutinizing the expenditure, administration, and policy of government departments, and of more adequate procedures for informing the House about the work of departments, and for calling ministers and civil servants to account for their actions, has been a recurring theme of proposals for parliamentary reform throughout this century. As long ago as 1918 the Haldane Report on the Machinery of Government referred to the possibility of improving the efficiency of the public service 'if steps were taken to secure the continuous and well-informed interest of a Parliamentary body in the execution by each department of the policy which Parliament has laid down'. Similar proposals have been made, from a variety of sources, and with increasing insistence, since that date. It is clear to us that there is now a strong desire, inside as well as outside the House, for the introduction of a new select committee structure to achieve these aims. . . .

5.14. Despite the considerable growth of the select committee system since 1964 and the changes which have taken place in their powers, the facilities available to them and their methods of work, the development of the system has been piecemeal and has resulted in a decidedly patchy coverage of the activities of government departments and agencies, and of the major areas of public policy and administration. While some departments, such as the Overseas Development Ministry or the Ministry of Defence, are subject to continuous and detailed scrutiny, other major departments have received scant or at least insufficient attention. Similarly, while one committee, such as the Select Committee on Nationalized Industries, may give detailed attention to certain of the responsibilities of a department such as transport, other responsibilities of the same department may not undergo scrutiny for considerable periods. Alternatively, a single department may find itself subject to investigation by two or more select committees at once, sometimes on closely related matters.

5.15. The Clerk of Committees drew attention to these problems, and suggested that they were 'reasons for arguing that the main weight of select committee investigation should be more evenly borne throughout the public service'. We accept this view. The House should no longer rest content with an incomplete and unsystematic scrutiny of the activities of the executive merely as a result of historical accident or sporadic pressures, and it is equally desirable for the different branches of the public service to be subject to an even and regular incidence of select committee investigation into their activities and to have a clear understanding of the division of responsibilities between the committees which conduct it. We therefore favour a reorganization of the select committee structure to provide the House with the means of scrutinizing the activities of the public service on a continuing and systematic basis.

DEMARCATION BETWEEN COMMITTEES

5.16. The unsystematic character of the present committee system has arisen largely because the House has at no point taken a clear decision about the form of specialisation to be adopted. During the 1960s much of the argument about proposals for establishing new select committees centred on the question of whether they should be 'departmental' committees or 'subject' committees, the former type concentrating on the activities of a particular government department, the latter (sometimes also called a 'functional' committee) examining a subject not directly tied to the responsibilities of any one department. Although this distinction has provoked considerable academic discussion over the years, it has mattered very little because in practice committees have decided for themselves how to operate and have interpreted their orders of reference with considerable latitude. As the Chairman of the Select Committee on Education and Science in 1968 to 1970 pointed out, that committee was intended to be a 'departmental' committee, but 'a Select Committee is in charge of its own proceedings and we acted as a subject committee'.

5.17. Nevertheless, the absence of demarcation has left a legacy of committees with widely differing orders of reference. So long as the majority of committees were only intended to undertake specific inquiries these differences and the resulting possibility either of overlap or of gaps in coverage could be accepted. If, however, select committees are to be envisaged as providing a means of scrutinizing all government activities on behalf of the House—a development favoured by the great majority of those who have given evidence to us—the form of specialization, and hence the demarcation between committees, take on greater significance.

5.18. We have concluded that the committee structure should in future be based primarily on the subject areas within the responsibility of individual government departments, or groups of departments. We have taken this view partly because we believe that one of the main responsibilities of the committees should be to continue and develop the work of the Expenditure Committee and its subcommittees in examining the expenditure and administration of the civil and public service—work which must be related to the existing departmental structure—and partly because any division of government activities into subject areas will in any case, with certain exceptions, reflect the division of responsibilities between government departments.

5.19. We recognize that the boundaries drawn between the responsibilities of the various government departments are to some extent artificial, and reflect administrative convenience or expediency as well as natural subject boundaries. As a consequence, they are liable to change, sometimes with alarming frequency. We recognize also that some common functions are spread amongst departments as a result of deliberate policy. This is particularly true in the fields of science, research, and development where, after brief experiments in the 1960s with co-ordinating ministries, governments of all complexions have decided to leave scientific and technical research in the hands of individual ministries with only vestigial co-ordinating functions remaining at the centre. Similarly, control of the nationalized industries has traditionally been vested in the relevant sponsoring departments, and has not been allocated to a single central government ministry. In contrast, some common services—such as those relating to land, property, buildings and furnishings, or to printing—have been centralized under a single department although they affect all departments of state. Any system of committees based on the responsibilities of government departments is bound to reflect this sometimes artificial grouping of subjects. We therefore accept that this principle must be tempered by some element of flexibility in the boundaries between committees and by adequate provision for co-operation between them.

5.20. We have therefore concluded that the terms of reference of the new committees should be widely drawn and that provision should be made for liaison and co-operation between them to allow joint inquiries and consultation, where committees share an interest. In addition, certain specialized functions performed on behalf of the House, such as the technical scrutiny of statutory instruments and the assessment of the legal and political importance of European Community legislation, should continue to be performed by committees specializing on a functional, rather than a departmentally related, basis.

A NEW PATTERN OF SELECT COMMITTEES

. . .

5.22 In the light of experience, we recommend that the Expenditure Committee and certain other existing committees should be replaced by a system of new, independent, select committees, each charged with the examination of all aspects of expenditure, administration, and policy in a field of administration within the responsibilities of a single government department or two or more related departments.

Between them the new committees would cover the activities of all departments of the UK Government, and of all nationalized industries and other quasi-autonomous governmental organizations within the responsibilities of the department or departments concerned. The committees would inherit the responsibilities of the subcommittees of the Expenditure Committee in respect of expenditure, and would be charged with the duty of examining the policy objectives underlying departmental estimates and the extent to which the expenditure incurred had achieved those objectives. . . .

5.23. Although we hope that the new committees will concentrate much of their attention on the consideration of estimates and other expenditure projections, we see no advantage in attempting to limit their activities in other directions. For the reasons explained above we would not wish to impose limitations which might come to be regarded as restricting the freedom of the new committees to examine matters for which the relevant departments have a leading but not exclusive, responsibility. Moreover, in addition to the functions inherited from the Expenditure Committee, and from other committees which they would replace, the new committees would also be permitted, but not required, to perform a range of other functions within their fields of responsibility, and might be instructed by the House from time to time to carry out specific tasks on its behalf. For this reason the orders of reference should be widely drawn. The committees should be free to consider any matters relevant to their field of interest. . . .

5.24. There is room for argument about the best division of responsibilities between the new committees, and about the number and size of committees to be appointed and we have received numerous proposals for the appointment of committees covering specific areas of government activity. We believe, however, that the division of responsibilities set out below represents a reasonable balance, and accordingly recommend that twelve new committees be appointed [see Table 14.1].

5.25. We recognize that changes in the division of responsibilities recommended above may be necessary in the light of experience or as a result of changes in the responsibilities of

TABLE 14.1. Division of Responsibilities between Twelve New Committees

Name of Committee	Government Departments and responsibilities covered
1. Agriculture	Ministry of Agriculture, Fisheries, and Food
2. Defence	Ministry of Defence
3. Education, Science, and Arts	Department of Education and Science
4. Energy	Department of Energy
5. Environment	Department of the Environment
6. Foreign Affairs	Foreign and Commonwealth Office Ministry of Overseas Development
7. Home Affairs	Home Office Lord Chancellor's Department Law Officers' Department
8. Industry and Employment	Department of Industry
9. Social Services	Department of Health and Social Security
10. Trade and Consumer Affairs	Department of Trade Department of Prices and Consumer Protection
11. Transport	Department of Transport
12. Treasury	Treasury Civil Service Department Parliamentary Commissioner for Administration

government departments. It will be noted that no reference is made in the responsibilities listed to Welsh, Scottish, or Northern Ireland affairs. We have intentionally excluded specific reference to these responsibilities in view of the uncertainty about the future form of government for Wales, Scotland, and Northern Ireland. We recognize that the appointment of separate committees for these areas may need to be further considered in the light of future constitutional developments. We recommend in the meantime that the new committees proposed above should be empowered to cover matters relating to Wales, Scotland, and Northern Ireland, and the activities of government departments in those areas, in addition to the responsibilities of the English or UK departments listed above. . . .

15

THIRD REPORT FROM THE SPECIAL COMMITTEE ON REFORM: THE McGRATH COMMITTEE

THE CANADIAN HOUSE OF COMMONS

In our First and Second Reports we made recommendations to enhance the role of the private member with regard to both committees and the general operation of the House of Commons. We realize, however, that these recommendations and those in this report will have little effect if traditional party discipline in the House continues. If their role is to become more meaningful, private members need to be able to assert a degree of independence without prejudice to the loyalty they owe to their parties.

Party discipline is related to certain misconceptions about our system of constitutional government. We therefore thought it wise to review the confidence convention. . . .

We have reached the conclusion that what is called for to resolve the issue is a change in attitudes rather than changes in the rules and procedures of the House. *Attitudinal changes are required on the part of governments, the leadership of parties, and private members themselves.*

The confidence of the House of Commons in the governing party lies at the heart of what we have come to know as responsible government. This form of government requires that the cabinet be responsible for its actions to an elected legislature. It implies necessarily that there be a policy-making body of ministers bound to provide unanimous advice to the Sovereign; that the public service be under the control

Canadian House of Commons, *Third Report from the Special Committee on Reform of the House of Commons: The McGrath Committee* (Ottawa: The Queen's Printer for Canada, 1985), 5–10. Reprinted with permission.

of political leaders responsible to the legislature; and that both the executive and the legislature be responsible to the people.

Ministerial responsibility, along with the fusion of the executive and legislative branches, are distinguishing features of responsible government. The rules relating to these features are not set down in the Constitution. They are governed by convention, precedent, and common sense. There is no single definition of ministerial responsibility; there are, in fact, three parts to the doctrine.

First there is the responsibility of a minister to the Queen or the Governor-General; this is often overlooked, but it is basic to our constitutional order. Governments are not elected but appointed, and ministers serve not for a term, but until they die, resign, or are dismissed.

Second, there is the individual responsibility of a minister to the House. This revolves around the questions of when a minister should offer his or her resignation and when should it be accepted or asked for. The answers seem to turn on the personal and political relationship between the minister and the prime minister. The principle is accepted, however, that where there is personal culpability on the part of a minister, in the form of private or public conduct regarded as unbecoming and unworthy of a minister of the Crown, the minister should resign.

The third responsibility is that of the ministry collectively to the House. If the confidence of the House is lost, it spells the end for the ministry unless the government is granted a dissolution and is sustained by the electorate.

CONFIDENCE FROM AN HISTORICAL PERSPECTIVE

The standing of a government in the House and the passage of its legislative program have come to be regarded as essential parts of responsible government. This was not always the case. In the nineteenth century political parties gained importance. This led to significant changes in the United Kingdom and in Canada as the parties, and particularly the leaders, appealed for votes in an enlarged and increasingly pluralistic electorate. The task of the House of Commons was reduced to voting on the legislation and estimates presented to it by the government.

The rarity of defeats of government measures in Great Britain (except in the minority situation in 1924) led rapidly to the development of a constitutional myth that every vote was a test of confidence. Any dissenting or cross-voting members on the government side were seen to be placing the government in jeopardy or risking dissolution of the House. In recent years, there has been more and more cross-party voting. In the seven-year period between April 1972 and April 1979, there were sixty-five defeats of government measures in the British House. This was not the end of responsible government. The government did not cease to govern. It was simply forced to modify or abandon some of its policies in deference to the House. Even with the large government majorities in recent years, there has not been a return to the inflexibility of the executive that marked earlier administrations. This kind of flexibility is not unlike what existed in early Canadian parliaments in the time of Sir John A. Macdonald when government measures were defeated a number of times without the government falling.

Recent British experience makes it clear that at present losing a vote, even on a financial measure, is not automatically a matter of non-confidence entailing either resignation of the government or a dissolution of the Commons. The government can decide how it will treat its loss. Whatever a government may say or imply in order to intimidate its own parliamentary supporters, a lost vote in itself does not involve resignation or dissolution.

The same phenomenon of lost votes that took place in Great Britain in the 1970s was also evident in Canada during that same period and, to a lesser extent, even earlier. At the start of the first session of the twenty-ninth parliament Prime Minister Trudeau said, 'Some things for us will be questions of confidence. Some things would mean the demise of the government . . . But I hasten to add that other questions, if they go against us, will not be interpreted by the government as a defeat of the government. We shall accept amendments.'

The minority government of Pierre Trudeau lost eight of eighty-one recorded votes between 1972 and 1974. Setting aside the vote of 8 May 1974, which brought down the Government, four of the lost votes were on government bills, two were on motions pertaining to parliamentary committees, and one was on a supply item, specifically on a supplementary estimate of $19,000 for Information Canada.

The minority governments of Lester Pearson lost three votes. Two were on appeals of a ruling made by the Speaker. The third came on 19 February 1968. A vote ended with the defeat on third reading of Bill C 193 respecting income tax. This vote was regarded as sufficiently serious to require the Government to introduce a motion to the effect that the House did not consider its vote of 19 February as a vote of non-confidence in the Government. The motion was passed, after debate, on 28 February.

It is clear from both British and Canadian experience that a government that has lost a vote in the House on a matter of confidence faces the choice of resigning or asking for dissolution. A government that has lost a vote on some other matter may remain in office and may choose to ask for a vote of confidence.

Since every vote in the House is not a matter of confidence, it is not true that a government that loses a vote in the House can simply have the House dissolved. As a rule, the Governor–General accepts the advice of the prime minister. In certain cases, however, the Governor-General is justified in refusing an immediate request for dissolution.

THE PRIVATE MEMBER AND THE CONFIDENCE CONVENTION

The important question is how far a government will go in tolerating votes lost as a result of freedom of action by its private members. How far can private members on the government side expect to deviate from party discipline without undermining confidence in the government? We believe that a government that wishes to give its private members a role in policy-making will let them know, first, what it can and cannot accept and, second, that unquestioned obedience to the ministerial line is not the only route to advancement in the party. Private members, public servants, and political advisers should be informed that the House is to be allowed to determine some matters, and that every detail of every measure will not be regarded as a matter of confidence.

The corollary to these statements must be that private members on the government side have certain rights and duties. How far can they fairly and reasonably go, even under a government willing to allow considerable freedom? In the normal exercise of their legislative functions, government members should be able, without fear of retribution, to amend or defeat clauses in bills; make amendments to bills implementing ways and means motions; reduce estimates as a mark of disapproval of either the administration or a particular programme; concur in committee reports critical of government activities and administration; and reject proposed legislation outright or pose amendments.

Precedent shows that responsible government does not break down and government does not become unworkable when the executive bows to the wishes of the House on a wide variety of matters in a wide variety of circumstances. It is useful by way of summary to place government defeats into three categories, noting that each one invites a different response from the government.

A government defeated on a vote of confidence is expected to resign or seek a dissolution. Three types of votes can be termed confidence votes. First, there are explicitly worded votes of confidence. These state expressly that the House has or has not confidence in the government. Next are motions made votes of confidence by a declaration of the government. The government may declare that if defeated on a particular motion before the House, even one that is not an explicitly worded vote of confidence, it will resign or seek a dissolution. Then there are implicit votes of confidence. Traditionally, certain matters have been deemed to involve confidence, even though not declared to be so by the prior statement of the government. Falling within this category is the granting of supply. Failure to grant supply is regarded as the established means by which the House can demonstrate its lack of confidence in the ministry. However, it should be noted that a single defeat on a specific estimate would not in itself constitute a vote of non-confidence. In fact, because of the multiplicity of votes on all the aspects of supply, this is largely a category that has fallen into disuse. One could argue that this type of defeat actually belongs in the category of defeats that are not votes of confidence.

The second category is lost votes on items central to government policy but not made matters of confidence prior to the vote. The government in this case can either seek an explicit vote of confidence from the House or resign or request a dissolution. If the government opted for resignation or asked for dissolution, this would make the lost vote one of confidence retrospectively. There should normally be few votes that fall into this category.

The last group is votes on items not at the heart of government policy; these are obviously the most numerous during any parliament. Although a lost vote on second reading of a major bill might fall within the second category mentioned above, a loss on one or more of the many divisions during the committee and report stages would usually fall within this third classification.

Our examination of the confidence convention leads us to conclude that a necessary step in conceding greater independence to individual members is for governments to relax their discipline over their supporters, at least to the extent of indicating in advance those measures and policies to which the confidence convention would apply. Any measure that a government regarded as essential to its overall program could be declared a confidence issue. Opposition parties would remain free to introduce non-confidence motions. Otherwise, it would be assumed that a lost vote on a government measure would not necessarily involve its resignation. Free votes have customarily been allowed on such matters of conscience as capital punishment, but our proposal extends and goes beyond that principle.

ATTITUDINAL CHANGE

Implementing this practice would call for a change of attitude on the part of governments. It would also call for a change of attitude on the part of opposition parties, which would cease to be able to extract the maximum political advantage from defeats of government measures. They also would need to reciprocate by relaxing discipline over their own supporters. But if neither governments nor opposition parties could be persuaded to change their attitudes, it would still be open to private members to take the initiative by changing theirs.

Once elected, MPs are legally and constitutionally entitled to act independently. In the House they can speak and vote as they like. If they choose to deviate from the line taken by their parties they are free to do so, provided they accept the political risks. Obviously, members frequently out of sympathy with party policy would probably come to the conclusion that they no longer belonged in the party. But it is not reasonable to expect that all members of a political party will agree invariably on every conceivable issue. Political parties in our country tend to be based on broad coalitions of opinion. There is agreement within parties on major policies and principles, but room for divergence of opinion on specific issues, matters of conscience, and matters of detail. Rigid discipline is hardly compatible with the philosophy of a democratic political party, and reasonable latitude consistent with loyalty to the party should be permitted the individual members of any party.

In conclusion, we offer several observations. Although they can have no legal effect in our system of government, they should serve as an indication of the direction in which this committee believes the House of Commons should develop.

1. A government should be careful before it declares or designates a vote as one of confidence. It should confine such declarations to measures central to its administration.
2. While a defeat on supply is a serious matter, elimination or reduction of an estimate can be accepted. If a government wishes, it can designate a succeeding vote as a test of confidence or move a direct vote of confidence.
3. Defeats on matters not essential to the government's programme do not require it to arrange a vote of confidence, whether directly or on some procedural or collateral motion.

4. Temporary loss of control of the business of the House does not call for any response from the government whether by resignation or by asking for a vote of confidence.
5. In a parliament with a government in command of a majority, the matter of confidence has really been settled by the electorate. Short of a reversal of allegiance or some cataclysmic political event, the question of confidence is really a *fait accompli*. The government and other parties should therefore have the wisdom to permit members to decide many matters in their own deliberative judgement. Over-use of party whips and of confidence motions devalues both these important institutions.

THE POSITIVE EFFECTS OF DISSENT

The expression of dissent can have positive effects for both the institution of parliament and its members. It may have a direct and sometimes observable impact on public policy. As a result of defeated measures, the threat of defeat, or simple dissent not entailing defeat, governments might modify or withdraw certain measures. This opens the way for the House to become more vital and significant in influencing policy than it has been for a long time and a more accurate reflection of Canadian public opinion.

Private members should take the lead in impressing this on the leadership of their respective parties. One member taking an independent stand might end up paying a heavy political price, but a sizeable body of members following the same line could not be ignored. Private members could exert their own pressures, even cross-party pressures, but this kind of initiative will require new procedures and new attitudes.

Ideally, we would like to see a change of attitude on all sides. If the greater flexibility we envisage can be achieved by mutual agreement, so much the better. Innovative action of this kind will call for political courage on the part of all concerned. Nevertheless, if the necessary changes of attitude come about, not only would the role of the private member become more meaningful, but parliamentary government itself would become effective. . . .

16

TOWARDS A BETTER DEMOCRACY: REPORT ON THE ELECTORAL SYSTEM

THE NEW ZEALAND ROYAL COMMISSION

4.2. After fluctuating in the nineteenth century, the size of the House was fixed in 1900 at eighty (including four Maori seats) and remained at this level until 1969. . . . The size of the House has since increased gradually following each five-yearly redistribution, by four (1969), three (1972), five (1978), and three (1984). It will be ninety-seven (including four Maori seats) at the next election. Of those who made submissions to us on this topic, some proposed a further increase but many preferred the present size or even a reduction. The Labour and New Zealand Parties favoured an increase to 121 and 125 respectively, while the National and Democratic Parties supported the present formula, which gradually increases the number of members.

FUNCTIONS OF PARLIAMENTARIANS

4.3. The number of MPs needed should be assessed in relation to the various individual and collective functions of MPs and the House of Representatives:

(a) to represent constituents;
(b) to represent the nation as a whole;

New Zealand Royal Commission, *Towards a Better Democracy*, from *Report on the Electoral System*, parliamentary paper H 3 (Wellington, New Zealand: The Queen's Printer for New Zealand, 1986). Reproduced with permission. The full text is available from the New Zealand Government Printing Office.

(c) to provide an effective Government; and
(d) to enact legislation and scrutinize the actions of the executive.

(*a*) *MPs as Representatives of their Constituents*

4.4. In their capacity as constituency representatives, MPs are expected to act as advocates of local interests. They are frequently approached by organizations such as local bodies, hospital and school boards, local industries and pressure groups, who seek support in their lobbying of central government or its agencies. If an organization covers more than one constituency, the MPs concerned may work together to co-ordinate their approach to government. Besides acting for local groups, MPs receive many requests for help from individual constituents. In some cases, the MP will need to do no more than refer the constituent to the appropriate person or body. In others, further action will be necessary, such as an inquiry to the local branch of a government department or a submission to the minister. The level of such 'citizens advice' work varies from member to member and constituency to consistuency. The demand for help with personal problems is generally greatest from those in lower socio–economic groups while the more affluent constituents are more ready to approach their MPs on behalf of interest groups.

4.5. New Zealand MPs give particular attention to this aspect of their work. Almost all MPs maintain homes in their constituencies and return to them regularly each weekend, usually travelling home some time on Friday and returning to Wellington on Tuesday morning. They often hold 'surgeries' or 'clinics' where their constituents may see them; they also attend a wide range of local functions, such as school fairs or bowling club openings, as a means of keeping in touch with their constituents. They have recently been given half-time secretaries in their electorates to help them with constituency work. The evidence of MPs' diaries made available to us indicates that MPs on average spend about a third of their time on constituency-related work when Parliament is in session and more during adjournments. New MPs, or those with a precarious hold on their seats, may spend more than half their time attending to their constituencies even when Parliament is in session.

4.6. MPs made it clear to us that they place great value on constituency work as a means both of keeping in touch with public opinion and of providing tangible benefits for particular groups and individuals. Some find it the most rewarding aspect of their work. Research shows that New Zealanders have a degree of personal acquaintance and contact with their MPs which is high by international standards. Moreover, the public appears to have a more positive attitude to MPs as local representatives than it does to them collectively as parliamentarians. Thus constituency work has a wider value in keeping MPs close to the people they represent and in cementing public support for the parliamentary system.

4.7. Cabinet ministers have a different routine from other MPs. They have houses provided for them in Wellington and their Mondays, which for other MPs are left free for constituency work, are taken up with cabinet meetings and departmental responsibilities. The pressure of their heavy workload means that ministers spend considerably less time on constituency business than other MPs. However, most ministers visit their constituencies regularly and attempt to keep in touch with individual constituents and local interests. The fact that they have superior secretarial and other support services and are particularly well known and well established in their constituencies helps to compensate for the relative lack of time they can give to constituency work.

4.8. The suggestion is sometimes made that New Zealand should consider adopting the Swedish and Norwegian practice of appointing substitute MPs (chosen from candidates who were unsuccessful in the election) to take over the constituency role of cabinet ministers. Such a practice has the advantage of allowing ministers to concentrate more single-mindedly on their portfolios while their constituents retain the services of a backbench MP. However, this would require a sharper distinction between the executive role of ministers and the parliamentary role of other MPs than is usual in the Westminster version of parliamentary government. Moreover, as we have said, constituency work is highly valued by all MPs including ministers, as a means of keeping in touch with public opinion. Giving up constituency duties is unlikely to be welcomed either by cabinet ministers themselves or by their constituents. We therefore do not recommend the introduction of this practice at this time. If, however, pressure on ministers continues to mount, the introduction of substitute MPs could be kept in mind as one possible solution to this problem.

4.9. The present number of MPs is, in our opinion, generally sufficient to fulfil the constituency function adequately. While a substantial increase in the number of MPs might improve the service to constituents, we do not consider that more MPs are needed for this purpose. . . .

(*b*) *Representing the Nation*

4.10. One of the collective functions of the House is to be representative of the nation in the sense of expressing and reflecting the various characteristics, values, and opinions in the community. In terms of their own characteristics of gender, age, and social background, New Zealand MPs are untypical and 'unrepresentative' of the community as a whole. The supporters of minor political parties are also under-represented. An enlarged House should provide some additional variety and diversity of opinion and occupational background in MPs. But we do not consider that size is a major factor in the unrepresentative nature of the present House. Some of the factors relate to societal influences which lie outside our terms of reference. In so far, however, as under-representation of women and ethnic minorities depends on political institutions, the nature of the electoral system and the method of candidate selection are the most significant factors. Systems of proportional representation in which parties offer lists of candidates are more likely to provide a balanced composition of the House than are systems with single-member electorates. While we continue to have a plurality system, a large House could possibly lead to more minority-party representation, but only in the unlikely case that support for such parties becomes geographically very much more concentrated than it has been to date. A larger House would not significantly reduce the likelihood of a relatively small lead in votes producing a larger lead in seats (or of a major party gaining fewer votes but more seats than the other). These problems are inherent in the plurality system and can be remedied only by reform of that system. Finally, we mention that an increase in the number of women and minority representatives in Parliament will make the need for an approved parliamentary timetable and better facilities all the greater. Over recent years steps have been taken in relation to both of these and we expect improvements to continue. . . .

(*c*) *Provision of an Effective Government*

4.11. The major function of the House as a whole is to provide a government which has the support of a majority of members and which is capable of fulfilling the wide range of functions which the electorate expects governments to perform. The constitutional role of the MPs who are ministers is to introduce policy and exercise control, individually and collectively, over the various government departments and agencies, thereby making them responsive to the wishes and interests of the electorate. In practice, however, as is well known, the size and complexity of the functions of central government make the task of ministerial direction and control extremely difficult. One critical factor is whether there are enough ministers to cover the wide range of government activities. Another is whether individual ministers, as the people's elected representatives, have the ability to run their departments or whether they will allow their departments to run them.

4.12. Reflecting the growth in State activity, the number of cabinet ministers has gradually increased over the century, from seven in 1900 to twenty in the last two governments. None the less, in spite of this increase, it is our view that the pressure of work on some ministers, especially senior ministers, is too high, and leaves them with insufficient time to concentrate on their major policy-making and executive functions. Many ministers carry a number of separate portfolios which divides their time and energies. Time is also spent in standing in for other ministers who are away. We think a good case can be made for a further increase in the total number of ministers, though without enlarging the cabinet itself which, at twenty may, if anything, be too large for effective deliberation. At present, some New Zealand Ministers are assisted by a few under-secretaries but the number and functions of under-secretaries fluctuate, and they do not have the status or clear executive responsibility which ministers have. Other Westminster systems, such as the United Kingdom and Australia, have a category of ministers who are not in the cabinet. We consider that replacing under-secretaries by a larger number of ministers who are not in the cabinet would help to relieve the burden on cabinet ministers. Such ministers could take over responsibility for some of the less important portfolios. They could supplement the cabinet ministers' supervision of their major departments and deputize for them in some of the myriad duties which deflect senior cabinet ministers from their main functions. Ministers who are not in the cabinet could also take over from cabinet ministers some of the time-consuming tasks connected with deputizing for other ministers.

4.13. Whatever the number of ministers, it is important that their individual ability should be as great as possible. Given the present size of the cabinet, the size of the House severely restricts the range of choice of which MPs are to be ministers. The majority parliamentary party must provide from its ranks a cabinet of about nineteen to twenty ministers and a number of under-secretaries as well as a speaker, a chairman of committees, and two whips. The size of the government caucus may be less than fifty (the lowest in recent years was forty-seven in 1981–4; the highest, fifty-six in 1984). As newly elected members are not normally considered for cabinet office, there is often little choice about who should be in the cabinet. Research indicates that three out of every four MPs who survive for more than one term and whose party wins office can expect to reach either ministerial office or some other senior post such as under-secretary, speaker, chairman of committees or whip. An enlarged House would provide a greater pool of talent from which the parties could drawn.

4.14. If Parliament increased in size and a smaller proportion of the caucus enjoyed ministerial office, the average ability of cabinet ministers could certainly be expected to increase to some extent. It should be remembered, however, that executive ability is not the only criterion for cabinet selection. There is also the need to provide a balanced cabinet, with ministers from the various regions of the country as well as women and Maori ministers. Ministerial office may also be a reward for long service or for loyalty to the party or its leader and there will always be some less able ministers preferred for such reasons. We see other factors, such as the attractiveness of a political career to able people, as also being important in improving the overall calibre of cabinet ministers. One of our reasons for advocating MMP [Mixed Member Proportional] is that a nationwide party list would allow the parties to include a wider range of candidates of proven ability. None the less, a larger governing caucus must provide a wider range of choice of ministers and must, at the very least, reduce the chances that mere length of service will virtually guarantee appointment as a minister. We therefore attach weight to the argument for increasing the House in order to enlarge the pool of potential ministerial talent. If the actual number of ministers is increased, there would be a greater need for an increase in the pool of talent from which they are chosen.

4.15. One other method of strengthening the executive ability of cabinets is to allow the appointment of ministers who have not been elected to Parliament. This is an established practice in a number of European democracies where ministers do not need to be MPs and in the United Kingdom, where nominated ministers may be brought in from the House of Lords. This is certainly a means of bringing people of proven executive and administrative ability into government. However, ministers who were appointed without being elected could be at a disadvantage in New Zealand. In our system, ministers, individually as well as collectively, are recognized as elected by, and responsible to, the electorate. They also have a strong involvement with their party and the development of its policies. As a result they have a status and authority which helps them to impose their parties' policies and views on government departments and the other public agencies and institutions with which they must deal. In the New Zealand context, we think it is debatable whether ministers who were not elected, however great their personal ability, would receive sufficient acceptance and support to be effective. Those European countries where this practice is readily accepted appear to make a sharper division between parliament and the executive than New Zealanders do and to have a more managerial approach to government (cf. para. 4.8). We note that the Constitution Bill, at present before the House, reaffirms the principle that ministers must be elected members of Parliament. We note also that the government uses a range of other means to engage the ability of specialists to help develop and implement policy. Though the Commission accepts the need to attract able people into government at all levels, we do not recommend the practice of appointing ministers who are not elected members of Parliament. Our inclination would be to contemplate such a practice only in the context of wider constitutional changes which lie outside our terms of reference.

(*d*) *Enacting Legislation and Scrutinizing the Executive*

4.16. The other main functions, or set of functions, of the House concerns its role as legislature. Though executive power and initiative are firmly in the hands of the cabinet, it must work through Parliament, seeking parliamentary authority for its legislation and funds and answering to Parliament for the administration of its policies. Parliament must therefore provide effective mechanisms whereby the executive is answerable to the electorate and subject to influence from the people it serves. There are three main arenas in which these processes of scrutiny and accountability are facilitated, in caucus, parliamentary select committees and the debating chamber.

4.17. *Caucus*. Ministers, both individually and collectively, are subject to many pressures from the community through working with their departments and with the great network of interest groups which surrounds the operation of government. Within the context of Parliament, however, the main pressure comes from daily competition with the opposition and the need for the majority party to maintain its political dominance. In this respect, ministers are part of their party's parliamentary team, the caucus. Through the caucus and contact with back-benchers, who are closer to the public and less caught up in departmental administration, the government is kept in touch with the electors and their concerns.

4.18. The small size of the caucus, it is often suggested, weakens this channel of influence. The members of cabinet, together with under-secretaries and the whips, now usually have a majority in caucus. Many government back-benchers are relatively inexperienced. They can all have reasonable expectations of ministerial office in due course and may therefore be unwilling to damage their career prospects by unpopular disagreements with the party leadership in caucus. For these reasons, it is claimed, cabinet ministers easily dominate their own caucus and government back-benchers have little influence. If there were more back-benchers, it is argued, they would not be so easily overridden. They would have more votes in caucus; some of them might prefer to forgo any prospect of a ministerial career and become, from choice, independent and outspoken back-benchers, a role more developed in other, larger parliaments and relatively rare in New Zealand.

4.19. Experience from other parliamentary democracies with larger governing parties, such as Australia and the United Kingdom, suggests that while this argument carries some weight, it needs to be treated with some caution. Parliaments in those countries certainly exhibit much more open divisions between ministers and back-benchers, but open opposition may be as much a symptom of impotence among back-benchers whose views are being ignored by their colleagues in the cabinet. The close personal relations between members of a New Zealand caucus, often cemented during years in opposition when there is significantly less difference in status or role between 'front-bencher' and 'back-bencher', mean that cabinet ministers usually have a very good understanding of what their caucus colleagues will tolerate. They will, therefore, often anticipate the possible reactions of caucus in such a way that the actual process of consultation may become a formality.

4.20. In general, we consider the intimacy of New Zealand caucuses helps rather than hinders the responsiveness of governments to the public. On the other hand, we recognize that intimacy may stifle discussion and the airing of alternative views. Some enlargement of the governing caucus would not unduly threaten the beneficial effects of intimacy, while it could provide greater encouragement for back-benchers to adopt a more independent role and thus increase their influence on party and public policy.

4.21. Another respect in which an increase in back-benchers could well help to strengthen the power of both the government and the opposition caucuses, is by enhancing the work of caucus committees. The system of caucus committees has developed rapidly over the last 2 decades as back-benchers have become increasingly interested in investigating policy alternatives. These committees are serviced by the party research units and allow back-benchers to examine aspects of policy from their own party's point of view. They can thus provide an additional political input to help counteract the official views of public servants and their departments. In this way, government back-benchers can help to check executive power, not so much by opposing their party colleagues in the cabinet as by helping them to impose a political, and therefore electorally accountable, slant on government policy. At the same time, opposition caucuses can develop alternative policies which are likely to appeal to the electorate and which will form the basis of their party's policy when it returns to power. On both sides, caucus committees can supplement and strengthen the system of select committees by making individual members more informed about particular areas of government.

4.22. *Parliamentary select committees.* The quality of legislation and the degree of public scrutiny of executive action is affected to a major extent by the performance of parliamentary select committees. We place considerable weight on the need to strengthen the select committee system as the best means, consistent with our constitutional tradition, of providing a parliamentary check on executive and administrative power. The increased activity of select committees over the last fifteen or so years is, in our view, the most significant recent development in the role of Parliament and provides the most powerful argument for an increase in its size. A generation ago, very few bills were referred for further consideration by a select committee. In the early 1960s the Public Expenditure Committee began to enhance Parliament's scrutiny of government spending. Standing orders now require all bills other than money bills to be considered by a select committee and public submissions are routinely heard. Moreover, the committees have recently been given authority not only to scrutinize legislation and consider estimates but also to conduct their own investigations into government administration. In order to develop specialization and expertise among committee members, each MP is now in general a member of only one committee instead of sitting on several as previously. At present, ministers do not sit on committees, a measure designed to encourage the committees' independence from the executive. The research and clerical support for select committees has also been increased. The committees are thus better able to gain access to government information and help inform both MPs and the interested public. Indeed it is becoming increasingly apparent that the possession of information is of crucial importance to the ministers and backbenchers of the governing party, the members of the opposition and the public. Power and information are closely linked and select committees can greatly enhance the flow of information both from and to government. They are becoming increasingly important organs of political scrutiny and public information, distanced to a certain extent from government, though the government caucus still retains a majority on each committee.

4.23. The size of the House has not, however, kept pace with these developments. Though significant improvements have been achieved, the committee system is still hampered by lack of members. In our view, an increase in the number of MPs is necessary before the committees can realise the full potential of their expanded role.

4.24. There are thirteen subject committees, each covering a major area or areas of government activity. . . . There are also several special purpose committees, for example, on regulations, standing orders, and electoral law. There are many fewer committees than portfolios, and some committees . . . deal with the activities of at least two major departments or government agencies. They are unable to cover their areas adequately. In particular, they have little or no time left, after examining legislation, for the important work of investigating administration. There is therefore a case for more subject committees.

4.25. The number of members on each of the thirteen subject committees is five, three from the government and two from the opposition. There is also a case, in our view, for increasing the size of at least some committees, from five to seven. Having seven members instead of five would encourage greater specialization among individual members and allow the committees to develop more continuity and collective experience. It would also lessen the disruption caused when individual members are unavoidably absent and their place taken by substitutes from the same side of the House.

4.26. There are problems, too, in giving representation to a third party on a five-person committee. As the government must maintain its majority, a third party must take one of the two opposition places, thus reducing the major opposition party to only one place . . . Any change to the electoral system which tends to increase the likelihood of minority party representation would increase the pressure to enlarge the size of select committees.

4.27. There is a particularly strong case for increasing the size of those committees which cover a number of important departments. The size of committees is, however, related to their number. Having more committees would lessen the need to have larger committees. Conversely, having larger committees may lessen the need to have more committees. In either case, however, there is a clear need for more MPs. . . .

4.28. We therefore consider that the full potential of the select committee system cannot be achieved without an increase in the number of MPs. At present, the committees are unable to develop the specialized expertise or to find the time necessary adequately to examine government legislation, scrutinize expenditure and investigate the administration of Government departments. Much has been achieved within the present system as it has evolved over the last decade or more. But if there were more MPs with collectively more time and specialized knowledge, a great deal more could be achieved.

4.29. *Parliamentary debates.* As far as debates are concerned, the average New Zealand MP is called on to speak in Parliament much more frequently and on a wider range of topics than his or her counterpart in most other parliamentary democracies. The quality of debate accordingly tends to suffer. Admittedly, the number of MPs is not the only factor affecting the standard of debate. It can be argued that the total time spent on debates is too long, leading to tedious and repetitious argument and reducing the time available for the important work of committees. Moreover, the traditions of the House encourage MPs to adopt a style of debate which concentrates on partisan attack and what often appears to the public as little more than petty point-scoring. Having more MPs would not necessarily make debates less partisan; it would, however, enable MPs to be better prepared and informed when they speak. An expanded role for select committees would provide opportunities for MPs to specialize more in particular areas of government policy and administration. Thus, when they came to speak in debate they would be able to draw on more specialist knowledge and experience. In this way, parliamentary debates would better be able to fulfil their functions of calling government to account and informing the public. At the same time, the public reputation of Parliament could be enhanced.

CONCLUSIONS

4.30. We support an increase in the number of MPs. Our principal reasons for making this recommendation are to make the system of parliamentary committees more effective, to enlarge the pool of ministerial talent and to allow for an increase in the number of ministers. We also consider that an enlarged House could provide more independence in caucus and improve the quality of parliamentary debate. We have reached this conclusion independently of our consideration of the electoral system in general, and we support an increase in the number of MPs whether or not the present plurality system remains. . . .

4.37. It is worth noting that if our House were increased to

120, or 140, it would still be small in comparison with Parliaments in similar countries.

While a number of countries listed in Table 15.1 have less favourable ratios of population to parliamentary seats, none have lower houses of smaller total size. This supports the conclusion that the New Zealand House may have enough MPs to service constituency work adequately, but would benefit from an increase in members to perform the collective parliamentary functions of the House as a whole, particularly provision of an effective government, enacting legislation and scrutinising the executive. The comparative difference in size becomes even more striking when it is noted that several of the countries listed in Table 15.1 have federal systems with an additional tier of state parliaments and state representatives and some have an upper house as an additional source of ministerial and parliamentary personnel. By international standards, then, we are committing fewer people and other resources to our central democratic institution, Parliament. This could be a source of satisfaction if Parliament were clearly fulfilling all its functions adequately. But when it has deficiencies which could be remedied by an increase in members the economy must be considered false.

TABLE 15.1. Sizes of some Democratic Parliaments in Relation to Population

	Number of seats in Lower House	Number of seats in Upper House	Estimated population (millions)	Population per Lower House seat	Overall population per seat
Australia[a]	148	76	15.5 (1984)	104,730	69,196
Canada[a]	282	104	24.1 (1984)	85,461	62,435
Denmark	179	0	5.1 (1984)	28,492	28,492
Finland	200	0	4.9 (1984)	24,500	24,500
West Germany[b]	496	41	59.4 (1984)	119,758	110,615
Republic of Ireland	166	60	3.5 (1984)	21,084	15,487
New Zealand	97	0	3.3 (1986)	34,021	34,021
Norway	157	0	4.2 (1985)	26,752	26,752
Sweden	349	0	8.3 (1984)	23,782	23,782
United Kingdom	650	1178[c]	58.1 (1984)	89,385	31,783

[a] Federation.
[b] Federation, excluding West Berlin.
[c] All those entitled to take their seats in the House of Lords, though many do not do so or do not take an active part in proceedings.

Source: *Europa Year-Book 1986* (London, 1986).

NOTES ON CONTRIBUTORS

Walter Bagehot (1826–77) was co-owner and editor of *The National Review* and, from 1861 until his death in 1877, editor of *The Economist*. His major work, *The English Constitution*, was published in 1867, reprinted with a new introduction in 1872.

Samuel H. Beer was formerly Eaton Professor of the Science of Government at Harvard University and served as President of the American Political Science Association in 1977. His publications include *Modern British Politics* (1965) and *Britain Against Itself* (1982).

Jean Blondel is Professor of Political Science at the European University Institute in Florence. From 1964 to 1984 he was Professor of Government at the University of Essex. His publications include *Voters, Parties and Leaders* (1963), *Introduction to Comparative Government* (1969), *Comparative Legislatures* (1973), and *The Organisation of Government* (1982).

Lord Bryce (1838–1922) was Regius Professor of Civil Law at Oxford University 1870–93 and was subsequently a Liberal MP and cabinet minister, serving as Chancellor of the Duchy of Lancaster, President of the Board of Trade, and Chief Secretary for Ireland. He was British Ambassador to the United States from 1907 to 1913. His publications include *The American Commonwealth* (1888), *Studies in History and Jurisprudence* (1901), and *Modern Democracies* (1921).

Bernard Crick is Professor Emeritus at Birkbeck College in the University of London. He was Professor of Political Theory and Institutions at the University of Sheffield from 1964 to 1971 and Professor of Politics and Sociology at Birkbeck College from 1971 to 1986. His publications include *The American Science of Politics* (1959), *In Defence of Politics* (1962), *The Reform of Parliament* (1964), *Socialism* (1987), and an acclaimed biography of George Orwell.

Anthony King has been Professor of Government at the University of Essex since 1969. His publications include *The British Prime Minister* (editor, 1969, 2nd edn. 1985), *Britain Says*

Yes (1977), *The New American Political System* (editor, 1978), and *Both Ends of the Avenue* (editor, 1983).

MICHAEL MEZEY is Professor of Political Science at DePaul University. He taught previously at the Universities of Hawaii and Virginia. He has published extensively in the field of comparative legislatures. His principal work, *Comparative Legislatures*, was published in 1979.

BARON DE MONTESQUIEU (1689–1755) was a lawyer, writer, and a member of both the French Academy and the Royal Society in Britain. He was President à Mortier 1716–26. His publications include *Persian Letters* (1721), *Dialogue de Sylla et D'Eucrate* (1745), *La Monarchie universelle* (1727), *Considerations sur la grandeur et la decadence des Romains* (1731) and *De l'esprit de Lois* (*The Spirit of the Laws*) (1748).

PHILIP NORTON is Professor of Government at the University of Hull. His publications include *Dissension in the House of Commons* (2 vols, 1975, 1980), *Conservative Dissidents* (1978), *The Commons in Perspective* (1981), *The Constitution in Flux* (1982), *The British Polity* (1984), and *Parliament in the 1980s* (editor, 1985).

ROBERT PACKENHAM is Professor of Political Science at Stanford University, having previously served there as Associate Professor (1971–81) and Assistant Professor (1965–71). His publications include *Liberal America and the Third World* (1973).

NELSON POLSBY is Professor of Political Science at the University of California, Berkeley. He was editor of the *American Political Science Review* from 1972 to 1977. His publications include *Congress and the Presidency* (1964), *Community Power and Political Theory* (2nd edn., 1980), *British Government and its Discontents* (with G. Smith, 1981), *Political Innovations in America* (1984), and *Presidential Elections* (with A. Wildavsky, 6th edn., 1984).

MALCOLM SHAW is Senior Lecturer in Anglo–American Comparative Studies at the University of Exeter. His publications include *Anglo–American Democracy* (1968), *The House of Commons: Services and Facilities* (with M. Rush, 1974), *Committees in Legislatures* (editor, with J. D. Lees, 1979), and *Roosevelt to Reagan: The Development of the Modern Presidency* (editor, 1987).

JOHN C. WAHLKE is Professor Emeritus at the University of Arizona, having previously served there as Professor of Political Science (1979–87). He was Professor of Political Science at the University of Iowa from 1972 to 1979, having previously taught at the State University of New York (at Stony Brook and Buffalo), Vanderbilt University, and Amherst College. He is a past President of the American Political Science Association. He has co-authored or edited several works, including *Legislative Behavior* (1959), *The Legislative System* (1962), and *Government and Politics: An Introduction to Political Science* (1966).

SELECT BIBLIOGRAPHY

THE main literature on legislatures is to be found in the footnotes, the significance of the works listed being identified in the various contributions to this volume.

Of books that treat legislatures in comparative perspective, the principal single-author works are:

BLONDEL, J., *Comparative Legislatures* (Englewood Cliffs, NJ: Prentice-Hall, 1973).

MEZEY, M., *Comparative Legislatures* (Durham NC: Duke University Press, 1979).

OLSON, D., *The Legislative Process: A Comparative Approach* (New York: Harper and Row, 1980).

WHEARE, K. C., *Legislatures* (1963; Oxford: Oxford University Press, 1968).

The principal edited volumes are:

FRANK, E. (ed.), *Lawmakers in a Changing World* (Englewood Cliffs, NJ: Prentice-Hall, 1966).

KIM, C. L., and BOYNTON, G. R., *Legislative Systems in Developing Countries* (Durham NC: Duke University Press, 1975).

KORNBERG, A. (ed.), *Legislatures in Comparative Perspective* (New York: McKay, 1973).

—— and MUSOLF, L. (edd.), *Legislatures in Developmental Perspective* (Durham NC: Duke University Press, 1970).

LOEWENBERG, G. (ed.), *Modern Parliaments: Change or Decline?* (Chi. Ill.: Aldine-Atherton, 1971).

—— PATTERSON, S. C., and JEWELL, M. E., *Handbook of Legislative Research* (Cambridge, Mass: Harvard University Press, 1985).

NELSON, D., and WHITE, S. (edd.), *Communist Legislatures in Comparative Perspective* (London: Macmillan, 1982).

PATTERSON, S. C., and WAHLKE, J. C. (edd.), *Comparative Legislative Behavior: Frontiers of Research* (New York: Wiley, 1972).

Useful comparative data are to be found in Blondel, *Comparative Legislatures* and, more contemporary, in the Inter-Parliamentary Union compilation, *Parliaments of the World* (2 vols., 2nd edn.; Aldershot: Gower, 1986).

The principal journal in the field is *Legislative Studies Quarterly*, which has been in existence since 1976, published by the Comparative

Legislative Research Center at the University of Iowa. Though the focus of most articles remains the legislatures of the United States (a reflection of supply rather than editorial demand), many valuable articles on other legislatures and legislatures in comparative perspective have been carried.

Much useful material (again, principally but by no means exclusively on US legislatures) is also to be found in the *Newsletter* of the Legislative Studies Section of the American Political Science Association. Founded in 1977 by a group of scholars led by Samuel C. Patterson, the Legislative Studies Section is now, in its own words, 'a large professional association linking the leading scholars and practitioners in the United States and other countries interested in legislative studies—national, cross-national, and local'. Its 1987 *Membership Directory and Research Register* listed in excess of six hundred members.

INDEX